THE
BIG
JUICE

Epic Tales of Big Wave Surfing

Edited by

JOHN LONG AND SAM GEORGE

FALCONGUIDES

GUILFORD, CONNECTICUT
HELENA, MONTANA

AN IMPRINT OF GLOBE PEQUOT PRESS

To buy books in quantity for corporate use
or incentives, call **(800) 962–0973**
or e-mail **premiums@GlobePequot.com.**

FALCONGUIDES®

FalconGuides is an imprint of Globe Pequot Press.

Falcon, FalconGuides, and Outfit Your Mind are registered trademarks of Morris Book Publishing, LLC.

Text design: Sheryl Kober
Layout artist: Sue Murray
Project editor: Gregory Hyman

Library of Congress Cataloging-in-Publication Data is available on file.

ISBN 978-0-7627-6993-3

Printed in the United States of America

10 9 8 7 6 5 4 3 2 1

CONTENTS

Preface by John Long v

Introduction by Sam George vii

Big Wave Timeline xxiii

Mavericks' Tombstone as told by Shane Dorian,
Mark Healey, and Dave Wassell 1

Surf Like Jay: The Life and Death of James Michael
Moriarty (1978–2001) by Ben Marcus 17

Road Agent: Greg Long's Life in Pursuit
by Brad Melekian 35

A Searching and Fearless Moral Inventory
by Kimball Taylor 53

Surviving December 1st, 1969 by Ted Gugelyk 67

Beyond the Blue as told by Greg Noll 87

Beal's Stash by Sam George 97

Tangled Up in Waimea as told by Maya Gabeira . . . 103

Hammer Down by Evan Slater 113

Spirit of the Foals by Leonard Doyle 129

Beneath the Waves by Chris Dixon 135

Reflections on Waimea by Brock Little 155

Dungeons Time by Rusty Long 163

Fisherman's Hunch: First Tracks at the Bosenquet
Bombora by Tony Harrington 173

Harsh Realm: Fifty Years on the North Shore
   by Sam George 183

Pat Curren Coffee Break by Mike Davis. 215

Dislocated: Mavericks and Me by Taylor Paul . . . 225

The Rush: A Profile of Garrett McNamara
   by Kimball Taylor 235

The 100-Foot Wave by Evan Slater 251

Aamion Goodwin's Circle Pacific by Daniel Duane. . . 259

The Eye of the Storm as told by Mike Parsons
   and Greg Long 273

High Noon at Bishop Rock by Chris Dixon 285

The Heart of the Matter as told by Vincent Lartizen . . 295

Sources 299

Acknowledgments 301

About the Editors 302

PREFACE BY JOHN LONG

What a blast working on this project with my friend Sam George. Our office was Rockreation, the local climbing gym in West LA. We'd "take a meeting" there every week or so, talk about the book for five minutes, and spend the rest of the time climbing and recounting to each other the most remote adventure stories, which we grew up on and continue to read incessantly. We both are prodigious talkers and could never get a word in edgewise. But we climbed a lot of plastic. I'm not sure how this book ever got done, considering all the other projects we had going concurrently. For most of this past year, *The Big Juice* stretched before me like a gracious bridge over the gray ditch of my other assignments. *The Big Juice* was never work, rather a passion.

Per the stories, we've tried to stay close to first-person accounts with people who were physically there, embedded "in the pit," so the writing is rooted in the iconic moments or taken from direct contact with the key players. But there is much more to the big wave milieu than just monster surf and survival stories. So we've sprinkled in some arcana and anecdotes that evoke the mood and atmosphere of the big wave continuum, including the equipment—as sacred as an Indian's wampum—a few personalities for the ages, and the spirit and vibe of the whole shebang. Many are enchanted by the big juice but not the two-wave hold-downs. For those, we offer this volume.

Yet, even here we run the risk of misrepresenting the basic allure and betting against the mystery of the sea. Big wave surfing has become increasingly popular in the last decade, but it's nothing new, and something lasts, an enchanted slipstream you can feel reaching through these stories and through the fissures of time. To the bold and the restless, the ocean has called forever. Few have said it better than Algernon Charles Swinburne:

I will go back to the great sweet mother,
Mother and lover of men, the sea.
I will go down to her, I and none other,
Close with her, kiss her and mix her with me;
Cling to her, strive with her, hold her fast;
O fair white mother, in days long past
Born without sister, born without brother,
Set free my soul as thy soul is free.

A massive Jaws left—like trying to outrun chain lightning. Sebastian Steudner (above) and Yuri Soledade (below)
PHOTO © ERIKAEDER.COM

INTRODUCTION BY SAM GEORGE

Shane Dorian sat high on a hill overlooking the harbor at Half Moon Bay, California. It was a late afternoon in February, the end of an unseasonably warm day along the northern California coast. Scattered around the inner harbor, behind the protective arm of the Princeton Jetties, both the commercial fishing fleet and the private yachts nestled against the quay, snug and satisfied.

But not Shane Dorian.

Sitting on the back deck of a friend's hillside home, Shane gazed out on the far side of the black stone jetty to wild, open ocean, out past the jagged black sea stacks, toward the lineup of the surf break known as "Mavericks." It was hard to imagine that within a few hours on this calm, glassy afternoon, this same lineup, so benign and indefinable from this vantage, would transform itself into a battlefield, churning under the assault of a titanic north-northwest swell and breaking waves in the 50- to 60-foot range, monster waves, some twelve hours out yet but descending relentlessly on the bay, predators from the deep.

Dorian knows what's coming, just as he knows what's required of him when the waves come marching in. So he sits there, scraping wax onto the deck of the brand-new 9'8" big wave gun laid across his lap, trying not to look at the Mavericks' lineup, trying not to think about the first time he surfed the place—the very last time he surfed the place—when he came within a half-breath of drowning.

Dorian recounts his epic story in full on page 1. But sitting there just then, counting down the minutes to the winter's first danger swell, Shane was speaking about anything but that episode, so I did most all the talking. I'd known Shane since he was a fourteen-year-old grommet competing in his first professional

Shane Dorian's mind-bending Teahupoo barrel, 2009
PHOTO © ROBERT BROWN

event, and even then, as now, his steely aplomb was evident; it was hard not to envy him for it.

Shane enjoys one of surfing's most enviable careers, transitioning from hot up-and-comer to top-ranked pro to fabulously sponsored free-surfer to big wave hellman with hardly a ripple in his gunslinger's cool. The outrageous wave in Tahiti that won Dorian the 2008 Billabong XXL Ride of the Year award epitomizes surfing's right stuff. When, after recovering through a series of near-disasters on a 30-foot Teahupoo widowmaker, he was blown out of the humongous barrel upside down—totally cool and seemingly in control even when wiping out.

I've had my own surfing career, a path that sometimes crossed Shane's in various oceans. But watching him quietly preparing for the next day's adventures, I told Shane that if I regretted anything about my surfer's life, it was the big waves I hadn't ridden and that as someone sitting on the shoulder of big wave surfing, both literally and figuratively, I wished I had on occasion pushed myself into the heavy water alongside the Shane Dorians of the world.

"No, you don't, Sam," he said, looking out again toward Mavericks like an infantryman on the eve of battle. "You enjoy your surfing. You always have. This . . ."

Shane looked down at the board on his lap, regarding its curves, pointed nose, and stiletto tail—it really did look like a weapon. "This is an obsession. And I'm really not sure how healthy it is in the long run."

If anyone has earned the right to make that statement, it's Dorian. And yet he's hardly the first.

Big wave surfing has always represented the obsessive nature of top-end adventure sports, though of the millions who surf worldwide, only a handful ever ride big waves, at relatively few spots across the globe, and only then on relatively rare occasions. Compared with the legions of surfers whose commitment requires daily surf regardless of conditions, work and school schedules, or relationship status, big wave riding is a tiny aspect of the surfing experience. Yet, it looms huge in the surfing world's collective imagination, establishing the distal end of the scale of what we, as surfers, believe is possible, a benchmark against which, despite our relative comfort "on the shoulder of the big wave," we constantly measure ourselves. And it absolutely dominates the civilian (read: the general nonsurfing public) perception of the sport. What casual observer knows the current pro circuit ratings, let alone that on a 2-foot wave some Santa Cruz surfer finally pulled off the sport's first successful kick-flip? No, when it comes to representing the height of surfing action, it's always been big waves.

"The higher the sea and larger the waves, the better the sport," wrote William Ellis, a clear-eyed Calvinist missionary who, upon his visit to the Hawaiian Islands in the late 1820s, was impressed by the water skills of local surfers.

"Sometimes they chose a place where the deep water reaches the beach, but generally prefer a part where the rocks are 10 or 20 feet under water and extend to a distance from shore, as the surf breaks more violently over these."

Even the ancient Polynesians gravitated toward big waves, no doubt intoning their surf chants as a modern deep-water hunter would check his surf-forecasting website.

Ku' mai, ku mai, ka nalu
Mai Kahiki mai
Alo poi pu ku mai ka po huehue
Hu kaipo o loa.

(Arise, ye great surfs from Kahiki
The powerful curling waves,
Arise with pohue hue
Well up, long ranging surf.)

There is even evidence of history's first big wave surfer. Researching a pair of antique Hawaiian *koa* wood surfboards abandoned at Honolulu's Bishop Museum in the early 1930s, surfing innovator Tom Blake discovered that they belonged to Chief Abner Paki, who once ruled over a fiefdom in Makaha, a wave-swept shore on the west side of the island of Oahu. Blake, adding to a number of firsts that included designing a lightweight hollow board, putting a fin on a surfboard, and inventing the waterproof camera housing, penned *Hawaiian Surfboard* in 1935, the first serious examination of the sport, in which he described Paki and his passion:

"It is said that Paki would not go out surf-riding unless it was too stormy for anyone else to go out," wrote Blake. "His reputation of going out only in big surf is a natural thing when a man gets beyond his youth. Today it takes big waves to get the old-timers out on their boards."

It wasn't too long after Blake's book came out that a new wave of surfers began getting out there when it was too stormy for all others, and the history of Hawaiian big wave riding has been well and often chronicled: the development of the narrow-tailed hot curl in the 1940s, the first serious "bigger wave" board, and the modern exploration of ancient blue-water breaks like Makaha Point Surf by Island pioneers Wally Froiseth, John Kelly, and George Downing, to mention a few, and later the first crew of California adventurers like Pete Peterson, Whitey Harrison, Wally Hoffman, and Buzzy Trent. (For a detailed account of the discovery of Oahu's North Shore and its subsequent status as big wave surfing's mecca, see "Harsh Realm" on page 183.) A question largely unanswered, however, is why it took surfers so long to look beyond Hawaii in their search for big waves. It was as if the scale of the waves being ridden in the Islands during the late 1950s and early 1960s was so outrageous, the prospect so daunting, that perhaps the surfing world was silently grateful that huge surf existed nowhere else. Consider this narration from the most influential surf film of all time, in which filmmaker Bruce Brown, justifying 1965's *Endless Summer* eureka moment of discovering 3- to 4-foot Cape St. Francis peelers, emphatically stated:

"No one goes looking for a really big wave. If you found one you'd never ride it—it would be much too dangerous."

This from a film that introduced the surfing and nonsurfing worlds to the enchanting concept of Planet Surf, albeit with small waves everywhere but Hawaii.

Tiny board on a giant wave.
Dan Moore taking his 2005
Billabong XXL Global Big Wave
award-winning ride at Peahi.
PHOTO © ROBERT BROWN

For almost half a century the surf world's general perception limited big wave riding to an 8-mile stretch along the northern shore of Oahu, even when surfers saw swells rising elsewhere with their own eyes. A 1972 issue of *Surfer* magazine, for example, featured the first photos of giant Mexican beachbreak at Petacalco, one particularly fearsome shot running with the caption "15 to 18 and it ain't Hawaii," the editor's disbelief impossible to hide. Fourteen years would pass before the big wave paradigm shifted forever.

In 1986 *Surfing* magazine ran a cover story featuring two-time world champion Tom Curren, along with future big wave hero Mike Parsons, riding a massive winter peak on Isla Todos Santos, a remote and barren islet off the coast of Baja California. Known as "Killers," this thick, powerful right-hander had previously been ridden only during moderate summer and autumn swells, and never mind the big winter days like this one. Working with then-fledgling surf forecaster Sean Collins, the *Surfing* team anticipated double-overhead surf during one particularly strong, long-interval, northwest swell. But when the Ensenada fishing *pangas* delivered the surfers and photographers into Killers' lineup, even the world champ knew at once he was seriously undergunned. The photos that ran—including the Curren cover shot—detonated like a bomb, blasting away the idea that "20 foot" could mean only Hawaii.

"We couldn't believe our eyes," said hellman Mike Parsons, whose longtime association with the break later earned him the moniker "Todos Parsons." "Waves as big as Sunset Beach right here in our own back yard. But we had to call it '18 feet.' We just couldn't say '20,' not here on the West Coast."

Whatever you called them, the winter waves at Killers were huge, and over the next few seasons it was discovered that those big, big days occurred more frequently than at most of the time-honored Hawaiian breaks. Todos Santos became the first new, truly legitimate big wave arena outside of the North Shore, and, as if

Fearless Mark Healey, backside in the peak at Waimea Bay
PHOTO © JEREMIAH KLEIN

suddenly realizing that their world was not flat, surfers all over the globe began considering the possibilities.

Of course, nobody then knew that a quiet, intense young goofy foot from Half Moon Bay, California, was riding four-story waves, *all by himself*, and had been since 1975. Jeff Clark tried for years to convince his friends that the ferocious peak jacking up off the Pillar Point headland was a world-class big wave, and for over fifteen years, Mavericks' waves were giant redwood trees falling in the forest that only Clark could hear. That finally changed in 1992, when Clark finally talked Santa Cruz big wave stars Tom Powers, Dave and Richard Schmidt, and Vince Collier into making the short drive up the coast to his private, cold-water Waimea. *Surfer* magazine's cover story soon followed. The concept introduced six years

Caught inside—a dilemma with consequences at Isla Todos Santos, Mexico
PHOTO © ROBERT BROWN

earlier at Killers on Todos Santos now gained widespread credence: This wasn't just Planet Surf, it was Planet Big Surf.

During that same year, a third, epoch-bending big wave innovation occurred: the advent of tow-in surfing. On the seminal first day in '92 when Laird Hamilton, Derrick Doerner, and Buzzy Kerbox took Kerbox's inflatable Zodiac out into a huge swell at Backyard Sunset Beach and towed each other into 20-foot swells at the end of a ski rope, the big wave world's axis shifted. By the next winter Laird and crew had swapped out the cumbersome Zodiac for a jet ski and moved their operation to nearby Maui, where they drafted the jet assist to campaign a colossal peak called "Peahi," whipping each other into what previously was considered the "unridden realm." During each successive Peahi swell (known to most *haoles* as "Jaws") and each remarkable ride, surfing's arcane wave scale was recalibrated once and for all. Not so many years before, Mike Parsons simply could not say the words "twenty foot." Now 40-, 50-, and even 60-foot waves were being ridden. And not just ridden, but ripped apart as on their tiny, foot-strapped sleds tow-surfers proved they didn't need big surfboards to ride big waves, only to catch them. Freed from the need to paddle barehanded, this new full-throttle generation of big wave riders applied small-wave, short-board maneuvers to jumbo surf, resulting in the great-est quantum leap in performance the surfing world had ever seen.

This movement was epitomized in a single ride. Up until 2002, towing in was generally reserved for massive, expansive, deep-water breaks like Jaws and Mavericks, waves traditionally consid-ered too big to paddle into by hand. That summer, however, Laird Hamilton shipped his skis and tow boards across the Pacific to Tahiti, chasing a powerful southern swell to the coral reef pass known as "Teahupoo" (pronounced *te-a-hu-po-oh*). This violently abrupt, cylindrical left tube had already gained a reputation as one of the heaviest waves in any ocean; nobody yet dared tow-ing this shallow-water meat-grinder. Just as nobody—not even Hamilton himself—was prepared for what happened when, during a supersized set, Laird dropped the rope and whipped into a wave so thick, so hollow, and so treacherous as to be impossible to ride. But ride Laird did, spontaneously improvising technique as he shot through the seething vortex, powering through one unbelievable section after the next. It literally was like nothing any surfer had ever seen, which explains why after successfully negotiating this horizontal hurricane, Hamilton burst into tears. And when the first image of what later became known as the "Millennium Wave" appeared on the cover of *Surfer* magazine, it was accompanied by three simple words: "Oh my God!"

This one wave did more to change the game of big wave riding than anything in the past forty years. Before, danger-wave perfor-mance was reserved for either hollow-wave tubes or megasurf. By merging these two genres, Laird's Tahitian titan redefined *rideable*. Almost before the ink dried on the *Surfer* cover, motivated surfers set their sights on those scary cloud break waves and gnashing "slabs" that had previously been no-man's-land. More importantly, they now had the vehicle to explore this terrain, the jet ski providing unprecedented mobility and access to a brand-new world of big waves.

Scouring the globe for the spawn of massive oceanic low-pressure systems, bold watermen scoured the coastlines of Australia, Tasmania, South Africa, South America, Ireland, France—even international waters—and it seemed that everywhere they looked there were epic new big waves in waiting. Imagine if the mountaineering world had only now discovered the Himalayas. In terms of surfing history, nothing has so characterized the first dozen years of the new century as the proliferation of global big wave riding—and on a sliding scale that goes only up. This includes a trend within the trend, as many of the sport's top heavy-water masters have dropped the tow rope and returned to tackling 50- and 60-foot waves "by fair means," with nothing but bare hands, brawn, and balls (with all due respect to the rising swell of talented female big wave riders), paddling themselves over the edge on their long big wave guns.

This elemental challenge of man against the sea defines the essence of big wave riding and has since Chief Abner Paki stroked out past his peers to take on alone his island's "long-ranging surf." Generated by tremendous low-pressure systems, huge groundswells sweep across trackless seas, growing in power and mass as they silently roll toward waiting reefs, islands, and continents. When these swells meet the shore the result ranks with the most massive energy exchanges on Earth. Throughout the ages storm swells have swept away armadas, destroyed cities, taken back measure-less tracts over which man had for centuries claimed dominion. If, as the great writer of the sea Herman Melville maintained, the sea is a mirror in which all men see themselves, then those both watching and riding 30-foot swells are bound to feel insignificant. The question becomes: How can they do that?

To deliberately place oneself in a maelstrom seems reckless, yet big wave riders rush to the raging lineup as if to a tryst. Danger is not entirely subjective, however, and statistics insist that big wave riding is actually quite safe. In modern surf history only three experienced big wave surfers have died in action: big wave star Mark Foo, who drowned at Mavericks in 1994, Todd Chesser, a fearless young pro who died in huge outer-reef surf in Hawaii in 1997, and Sion Milosky, an experienced charger from Oahu who in March 2011 became Mavericks' second drowning victim. Three deaths in over fifty years of giant waves, heavy closeout sets, and gnarly wipeouts are an almost insignificant figure compared with the staggering losses in other high-risk adventure sports like high-altitude and alpine-style mountaineering, free-solo rock climbing, BASE jumping, and extreme skiing. But what big wave riding lacks in staggering body counts it more than makes up for in terror.

The Everest mountaineer or solo climber squares off with the *high lonesome,* while the BASE jumper or extreme skier battles gravity. Extremely high risk—yes. But the mountain does not move, and in many cases the route can be studied, rehearsed, and tackled in stages. For the big wave rider, the medium is a monster not merely moving but pursuing: the hunter becomes the hunted, the snarl-ing, roaring waves are imbued with a deliberate intent to do harm. Big wave jargon tells the story clearly. Surfers get "caught inside" for a brutal "wipeout," the surfboard "tombstoning" at the surface

South African Grant "Twiggy" Baker center-punches Mavericks, in Northern California.

in the "impact zone" while the rider thrashes far below, trapped in a horrifying "two-wave hold-down." For climbers or skiers, infrequently swept off their feet by an avalanche, the fear tells them they just might perish. But from the very first moment surfers are driven underwater by a breaking wave, they begin to die. Suddenly and violently plunged three atmospheres deep, then four, then five, breath smashed out of the lungs by the impact, they're driven as by a giant's fist, slammed down into the darkness. Equilibrium is stripped away; the pressure builds in their ears, behind their eyes as a red-hot coal fans to flame inside their chest, and they'd scream if they could, "Not yet! Not yet!" Tumbled, buffeted, ragdolling through a breathless whirlwind, no control of arms or legs, nothing but a brain and a pair of lungs. Every second feels like a minute now, their body betraying their mind, suddenly demanding what it once took for granted, threatening to take control if not appeased, prying open the clenched jaw to let the sea flow in; the roar of the wave exploding overhead, the howling of the storm, whispering into their ear, "The clock is ticking . . . count the seconds . . . maybe this time . . ."

Maybe this time they won't come up. Like Mark Foo didn't. Like Todd Chesser didn't. Like Sion Milosky didn't, even though he was surfing a crowded day at Mavericks wearing a flotation vest and a surfboard leash. Caught in the chaos beneath a monster wave, cut off from life-sustaining oxygen, Sion must've heard that voice, except at one point, right before that last, desperate moment, it was probably his own, wondering, "Will I be next?" Helpless to do anything but hug to his burning chest the belief that he would eventually come up . . . any second now.

It is not the danger, but rather this terror that keeps the vast majority of surfers from riding big waves. The big wave surfer moves toward these moments of lifelessness, accepts them, in some cases becomes comfortable with them. Big wave riders willingly risk each little death for the intense sensation of living found at the bottom of each elevator drop, in every cavernous tube, in every no-exit hold-down.

Just ask Shane Dorian. At thirty-eight no longer a brash young Turk. Bountiful income, solid stock portfolio, beautiful home, lovely wife, two bright and loving kids . . . and here he sits on a hill above Mavericks with his gun slung across his lap, looking out across Half Moon Bay's harbor toward the flat blue plane, considering the wave that almost took it all away forever, and the tightrope strung between satisfaction and desire.

"I'm not sure if this kind of obsession is healthy in the long run," he tells me. "And I just don't mean physically."

Shane rubs a few more ounces of wax onto the board, his eyes still fixed on the unbroken horizon.

"But I'm out there," he says.

James Hollmer-Cross exploring the
offshore wilds of Tasmania

BIG WAVE TIMELINE

1935

Tom Blake, doing research in Honolulu's Bishop Museum, discovers that the last remaining redwood olo surfboard in existence belonged to Chief Abner Paki, reportedly a nineteenth-century big wave rider from Makaha.

1936

Honolulu surfers Fran Heath, Wally Froiseth, and John Kelly collaborate to produce the first surfboard designed specifically for bigger waves. They call their narrow-tailed, deep-V creation the "hot curl."

1937

The Waikiki "hot curl" crew begins riding winter surf at Makaha, establishing the right reef/point break on Oahu's West Side as the epicenter of big wave riding development.

1937

Northern California's "Steamer Lane," a booming right reef/point in Santa Cruz, is first surfed.

1943

Trapped outside by a rapidly building swell at Sunset Beach on Oahu's North Shore, surfers Woody Brown and Dickie Cross attempt to paddle 6 miles down the coast to the ordinarily calm waters of Waimea Bay. Caught by a huge set that closes out the bay, Brown washes to shore naked. Cross is never seen again.

1951

George Downing, a surfing prodigy from Waikiki, shapes the first modern big wave board, a 10-foot balsawood pintail complete with

Pete Cabrinha on one of the biggest waves ever ridden—70-plus at Jaws—good for a 2004 Billabong XXL Global Big Wave Awards check and a Guinness Book world record
PHOTO © ERIKAEDER.COM/BILLABONGXXL.COM

raked fin. Thus armed, Downing establishes himself as the sport's premier big wave rider.

1952

A front-page Associated Press photo of Woody Brown, George Downing, and Buzzy Trent sliding across a 15-foot Makaha wall lands on America's doorstep, triggering an almost immediate migration of intrepid California surfers to Hawaii.

1955

Surfers Downing and Froiseth and California transplants including Flippy Hoffman, Buzzy Trent, Peter Cole, Rick Grigg, and Greg Noll begin regularly riding the big waves on Oahu's North Shore.

1956

Waimea Bay is successfully ridden for the first time in modern times. Its summit team included Greg Noll, Mike Stang, Mickey Munoz, Bob Bermel, Bing Copeland, and Pat Curren.

1961

The hollow left-breaking North Shore tube later known as the "Banzai Pipeline" is first board-surfed by Californian Phil Edwards.

1962

Greg Noll and Mike Stang ride an 18- to 20-foot winter day at Palos Verdes's Lunada Bay, a hint at the potential of West Coast big wave riding that would not gain traction for another twenty-five years.

1963

Noll and Stang again make North Shore history by riding the seldom-breaking, deep-water cloud break known as "Third Reef Pipeline."

1964

American International Pictures releases *Ride the Wild Surf,* a full-length Hollywood feature set in Hawaii's big wave surfing scene. California hot-dogger Miki Dora doubles for star Fabian, Greg Noll for his nemesis "Eskimo Dobbs."

1965

The Duke Kahanamoku Invitational, the sport's first big wave competition, is held at Sunset Beach. It's won by sixteen-year-old Jeff Hakman.

1967

A massive winter swell hits Waimea Bay, creating what were then considered the biggest waves ever surfed. Filmed by a score of surf filmmakers, this day seals Waimea's reputation as surfing's ultimate challenge.

1969

The biggest North Pacific swell ever recorded (even to this day) rocks the coasts of California and Hawaii. Santa Barbara's Rincon is ridden at 20 feet. In Hawaii Greg Noll, alone in the lineup at Makaha Point Surf, drops into surfing immortality when he takes off and survives on the biggest wave thus far attempted, an estimated 55-foot closeout.

1972

Surfer magazine runs a travel article featuring Craig Peterson photos of huge, 15- to 18-foot tubes breaking along the coast of mainland Mexico. Although the break is left unidentified (it's later revealed to be called "Petacalco"), it inspires a few hardy West and East Coast surfers to begin ordering 9-foot guns.

1974

The Smirnoff Pro-Am, then the most prestigious competitive event on the North Shore, goes off in giant Waimea Bay surf. In the biggest waves ever seen for a contest, Hawaii's Reno Abellira just barely edges out Jeff Hakman for the $5,000 first-place check.

1975

Sixteen-year-old Jeff Clark, a surfer from Half Moon Bay, California, begins regularly riding a break outside the town's harbor jetty. Named after a fishing captain's dog, the spot is called "Mavericks."

1977

North Shore standout James "Booby" Jones methodically attempts to ride the massive tube at Waimea Bay. His first completed ride, caught by photographer Dan Merkel, would be a feat that would not be repeated for another thirteen years.

1978

Big wave ace and pioneering North Shore lifeguard Eddie Aikau dies while attempting to rescue fellow crew members of the Polynesian voyaging canoe *Hokulea,* which foundered off the coast of Molokai. Neither Aikau's body nor his board was ever recovered.

1983

With the sport's focus shifting to exotic travel and the burgeoning pro tour, big wave riding takes a back seat. *Surfer* magazine addresses this issue with a major cover story entitled "Whatever Happened to Big Wave Riding?" The sport would find out soon enough.

1984

The Billabong Pro, ordinarily held at Sunset Beach, is moved to maxed-out Waimea Bay during a supersized swell. While a number of top-ranked pros refuse to even paddle out, the event is won by four-time world champion Mark Richards of Hawaii, ironically better known for his development of the small-wave, twin-fin design.

1984

The wave known as "Dungeons," a four- to five-story peak located off South Africa's Cape of Good Hope, is surfed for the first time.

1985

The Quiksilver in Memory of Eddie Aikau Memorial contest is held at Waimea Bay for the first time. Perhaps appropriately it's won by Clyde Aikau riding one of this deceased older brother's surfboards.

1986

Surfing magazine runs its cover story entitled "Big Time" featuring California stars Tom Curren, Dave Parmenter, and Mike Parsons riding 18- to 20-foot peaks at Baja's Isla Todos Santos. Surfers the world over begin looking beyond Hawaii.

1990

The "Eddie," as it's more commonly known, is held again at Waimea Bay but this time in epic, 40- to 50-foot conditions with smooth offshore winds and eventually is won by Keone Downing, son of the legendary George Downing. Big wave performance takes a quantum leap, led most noticeably by young Haleiwa local Brock Little, who, though falling both times, successfully exits a humongous Waimea tube and takes off on one of the biggest waves ever attempted.

1991

Eschewing the Eddie at Waimea, along with all of its invitees, surfers Buzzy Kerbox, Laird Hamilton, and Darrick Doerner motor out to Backyard Sunset in Kerbox's inflatable Zodiac, pulling each other into 20-foot waves at the end of a tow rope. Tow surfing is born.

1992

Hamilton and crew trade the Zodiac for PWCs and begin riding Peahi on Maui. The 60-foot wave mark is broken.

1992

Surfer magazine's cover story "Cold Sweat" reveals the Waimea-sized waves of Mavericks—and the fact that until Jeff Clark lured a crew of Santa Cruz big wave riders up the coast, he had been riding it alone for fifteen years.

1994

Hawaiian big wave star Mark Foo drowns while surfing Mavericks for the first time. His death draws more mainstream attention to big wave riding than anything in the previous one hundred years.

1995

One year to the day after the death of Mark Foo, California surfer Donnie Solomon drowns while surfing a big day at Waimea Bay.

Big waves aren't always tall: Set waves at Tahiti's Teahupoo are measured by sheer mass and madness. Mark Healy, handling it all

PHOTO © JEREMY KLEIN

1997

Playing hooky from his stunt work on the Columbia Tri-Star big wave feature *In God's Hands,* popular North Shore surfer Todd Chesser drowns while surfing an outer reef break. More big wave riders died during this three-year period than in the previous half-century.

1998

The Reef Brazil Big Wave Championship is held at Isla Todos Santos, won by Brazil's Carlos Burle. The bigger paycheck, however, went to California's Taylor Knox, who, as judged in the newly conceived K-2 Big Wave Challenge, rode the biggest wave of the year, taking home a nifty fifty grand for a nasty 52-footer.

1999

During the biggest, cleanest swell in decades, tow-in teams take to the North Shore's outer reefs where big wave stalwart Ken Bradshaw pulls into a wave at Outside Log Cabins estimated to be just over 70 feet.

2000

Wedge local and surf impresario Bill Sharp, creator of the K-2 Challenge, introduces the Billabong XXL, a season-long event that rewards the biggest wave of the year with a dollar a foot. The 2000–01 award goes to Mike Parsons for his 60-foot giant caught at Cortes Bank, 100 miles off the coast of San Diego.

2000

On August 17 Laird Hamilton tows into what is now referred to as the "Millennium Wave," an impossibly thick, unthinkably heavy tube at Tahiti's Teahupoo, completely redefining the concept of rideable.

2001

Photos begin emerging from the antipodal island of Tasmania depicting Aussie surfers riding a giant, triple-up, surreal-looking danger wave breaking off a headland called "Shipstern Bluff." Dubbed a "slab," Shipsterns continues to redefine what is considered rideable. The worldwide hunt for slabs is on.

2002

Located off the eighteenth hole of Carmel's famed Pebble Beach Golf Course, the break known as "Ghost Tree" is towed into at size by Santa Cruzers Peter Mel, Adam Replogle, and Shane Desmond. The rocky ledge break is considered as much a stunt as a wave.

Mike Parsons's 2000 Billabong XXL Global Big Wave award–winning ride during the first-ever tow-in assault at Cortes Bank
PHOTO © AARON CHANG/BILLABONGXXL.COM

2003

French surfers Sebastian St. Jean and Fred Basse post video of themselves riding Belharra, a huge, heretofore-unseen peak breaking a half-mile off the Basque coast. One wave easily tops 60 feet but doesn't win the Billabong XXL because the rider was deemed to have taken off too far out on the shoulder. It does, however, make the point: Atlantic surf gets huge.

2005

A giant, 50-plus-foot day at Monterey's Ghost Tree cements the West Coast as one of the world's top big wave riding destinations.

2005

A women's division is added to the Billabong XXL Awards. It is won by Santa Cruz's Jamiliah Starr, a regular in heavy lineups from Waimea Bay to Puerto Escondido.

2008

Mike Parsons returns to Cortes Bank, where during a terrific winter storm swell he tows into a wave that tops out at over 70 feet. He wins the XXL Biggest Wave Award for the second time.

2008

Goofy footers Keala Kennelly and Maya Gabeira tow into giant Teahupoo and score a pair of outrageous tubes.

2009

Shane Dorian and Mark Healey, two of the best big wave riders in any ocean, take off together on a massive Waimea Bay cloeseout set, announcing to the surfing world that bare-handed "paddle-in" is definitely back.

2009

Greg Long, cementing his reputation as perhaps the best all-around big wave rider in the world, wins the Eddie, just edging out then-nine-time world champion Kelly Slater. Held in epic conditions, the contest is an all-day big wave highlight reel.

2011

Shane Dorian, Danilo Couto, and Ian Walsh paddle surf big Peahi, riding some of the biggest waves ever caught by hand.

2011

During a big wave competition held at Mullaghmore, Ireland, surfers are faced with grinding 40-foot tubes. One particularly awesome barrel earns Benjamin Sanchis from France the first-place trophy and a 2011 Billabong XXL Ride of the Year award nomination.

2011

North Shore local charger Sion Milosky dies while surfing Mavericks. After dominating one of his first trans-Pacific sessions at the fearsome NorCal break, Milosky goes down on a monster set and is never seen alive again. His body is discovered floating almost a half-mile away from the lineup, reigniting controversy about a recent ban of PWCs at Mavericks, even for safety and lifeguard use.

Two common variations of the
elevator drop at Mavericks
PHOTO © ROBERT BROWN

MAVERICKS' TOMBSTONE

as told by Shane Dorian, Mark Healey, and Dave Wassell

The day before, Shane Dorian was on top of the world. At the urging of friends the Hawaiian big wave star and 2008 Billabong XXL Ride of the Year award winner had flown over from the Islands to northern California, chasing a huge swell to Mavericks. There, on his very first day out at the fearsome break, Dorian put on a display of paddle-in big wave surfing that many longtime observers were calling the greatest first session ever seen—and maybe the best ever. So it was with plenty of confidence that Dorian paddled out the following day, with the swell even bigger, eager to build his Mavericks resume. And came within a single breath of losing his life.

Shane Dorian: Soon as I learned a monster swell was heading for Mavericks I flew up to San Francisco and drove south and joined the crew at Half Moon Bay. The first day was all-time, and this was day 2, and a group of us were set to go out on Rob Brown's boat. Greg Long was organizing, and he kept texting me: *No good—too low. Well, it's high tide right now, and we're gonna wait a little while. Oh, the swell got smaller.* I figured, let's eat breakfast and go out there later. It's not that good, right?

So we ate, got our stuff together, and eventually piled onto Rob's boat and powered out to the lineup. And it's totally huge and epic. I pulled on my wetsuit, jumped in the water, and caught a bomb right off the bat. I felt pretty confident and started talking with the guys in the lineup. It was super crowded. Couple guys had been out since early morning, and they said maybe once an hour, a huge set rolled through. But nobody had tried to snag one. Yet. I asked, *Where's it breaking?* and they said, *The giant ones are breaking a ways off the outside boil, maybe 80 yards farther out.*

1

It was one of those magic days when everything comes together, and I quickly scored big. But after an hour I still hadn't seen one of those giant waves, and now I wanted one. So I paddled farther out and waited for a bomb. I'm not out there long, and this [wave] started piling up way out, one of the biggest I'd ever seen in the ocean. Everyone inside started paddling out like maniacs because it's a huge set, getting bigger.

My first instinct was, *I can't paddle onto this. Too big. This is a tow-in wave. Period.* But then I'm thinking, *Well, I'm out here, so I'll try and get into a good position. When it rolls through, I can decide if I'm going or not.* I got lined up perfectly and a couple strokes, and the wave almost caught *me*. I'm on my feet, no problem, totally confident. I'd already caught ten or so solid waves, and I hadn't fallen, so I'm like, *Sweet. This is gonna be one of the biggest waves I've ever caught.* And another part of me is going, *This is a monster. I can't believe I'm catching this wave.*

Mark Healey: Shane had been going nuts, pulling it off all day long. Now he was way out there, and here comes a wave that probably stretched 5 miles in either direction, as far as we could see, like a mountain range on rollers. It's a huge wave. A giant wave, with more water in the swell than we could imagine. I'm thinking, *Oh my God. Shane's in the spot. He's gonna go. He's definitely gonna go.*

Then he's up and charging, and I'm yelling, *Holy crap! That's the biggest wave anybody's ever paddled into.* He starts shooting down the face, but he flattens out weird, barely handling the speed wobbles through sloppy, knee-high chops. I'm surprised he's still up. Then just ahead a couple big chop bumps are shoved up together, and I'm like, *Nobody makes that. It's ass over teakettle for Shane Dorian.*

SD: I get a third of the way down the face, and I'm flying. Then I'm way down, toward the end of the drop, and there's a couple big lumps. But it doesn't look so bad from my angle. *So what,* I tell myself. *There's a lump or two. That's Mavs. I got it.* I brace and bash over, going crazy fast—not normally a problem, but I'm on a 10-foot long gun that's 3½ inches thick, and it handles like a canoe. So smacking these ledges feels like hitting speed bumps in a Cadillac at 40 miles per. My board goes, *va-voom, va-voom.* Somehow I'm still up. Then I nail the next one, and I'm saying, *I got this. I got it. Uh, I'm not sure if I got it.* Then it was all slow motion, like the worst movie in the world. And in my head I'm saying, *This is bad.*

I hit the water and skipped. I tried to catch a breath but instead got plowed under and sucked up the face. It felt like it took an hour to rise up to the top of the wave. I had to get a good breath or I was finished, because I was taking the ride for sure. So I stroked hard to the surface and for a split second punched out the back of the wave, hovering at the top of the lip. I pulled down a breath right as I got sucked over. Then I shot down the falls and got absolutely annihilated. Just annihilated.

Without a floatation vest I got drilled deep and bounced off the bottom, and the wave kept shoving me along forever. I tried to relax and go with it because there's no way to fight a wave that size. Finally the pressure eased, and I started up for the light, and I got pounded once more, beat right back down to the bottom and started tumbling over the shallows. Then off a shelf, and I plunged down into deep parts, freezing cold and almost black. I kept tumbling along hole to hole, and I'm thinking, *All right. Anytime now you can let me up.*

As it happened, I went over the falls on the edge of the outside bowl. So the moment I pitched off, the concentrated force of the wave launched me onto the reefs. The power out at Mavericks happens in surges. The wave hits a reef, doubles up and barrels, then stalls for a second until it impacts the next reef, where it jacks and barrels again, then lurches onto another reef, and so on. I got to know all those reefs.

So I'm dealing, trying to stay relaxed until the spin cycle finally starts dissipating and it's time to use my energy and get to the top, no matter what. I start kicking like crazy, pulling for the surface. Finally it's right there. It has to be. But it's all white, all foam and bubbles, but still I'm thinking, *I'm okay. It's only 4 or 5 feet to surface. Maybe less. But I need a breath* right this second.

By now I was making involuntary gurgling sounds, the throat spasms deep free divers had warned me about. They said these happened shortly before you black out. I didn't have much time. I needed air bad, and I'm straining for the surface, and my arms reach out through the spume, and that's when I heard, and felt, the next wave break. *Ba-boom.*

MH: We watched Shane get whooped all the way through. Actually, we could see only the tip of his board, tombstoning along on the surface, because he's way down there at the end of his taut leash, getting keelhauled over the bottom. The next wave doubled up to pretty much the same size as the first bomb, and the tip of Shane's board disappeared for a while until this next wave was almost on him. This was bad.

Frank Quirarte was out patrolling on his ski, buzzing around in circles trying to find Shane. But we're talking about many acres of water here, and Frank was the only water safety guy out there. So he had only one shot between waves before he had to blast out past the shoulder to calmer water and then go all the way back around for another try. Meanwhile we're all up on top of the boat, bobbing out there off the edge of the reef and the impact zone, looking across at Shane's board tombstoning through avalanches of foam. Then everything settled for a moment, and Shane's board straightens and points straight up from the water because he's fighting his way up his leash to the surface. Sure he was. But he never got there, and the third wave breaks right on his board. You had to be there to appreciate how

Dorian's thrée degrees of
separation on the wave that
almost killed him
PHOTOS © ROBERT BROWN

The dreaded "tombstone," meaning Dorian's board has surfaced (pulled taut against his leash), but he hasn't

much water was in that third wave. I'm just going, *This isn't good. This isn't good. This isn't good . . .*

SD: The next wave absolutely pounded me, and I instantly went from, *I need a breath right now* to *I'm dead.* Like, really, my hopes fell right off a cliff. There I was, swimming up, almost to the surface, and then I'm drilled right back down to the bottom where I just came from. And I had no air. None. At all. I honestly thought my chances of surviving this situation were really low.

And I started panicking, straight up panicking. Then I saw flashes of my son's face looking at me, and I was thinking, *What the hell am I doing at the bottom of the ocean in San Francisco? I could be at home right now, on a soft longboard, surfing Pine Trees with my son. This is so stupid. Why am I down here?* It sounds dramatic, but I knew—*This is how it happens. Right here.* This is what Todd Chesser went through, totally out of breath, pinned on the bottom and getting pounded by a huge wave. This is what my friend Donny Solomon went through. This is truly what big wave guys experience right before they drown. It's a shitty feeling.

I struggled like hell. I was on the cusp of blacking out, and weird things started happening. I kept struggling, and finally the turbulence spun me up to the surface, and I got a breath. There were spots everywhere, and I couldn't tread water, and I couldn't swim. I had zero energy. I was zapped.

MH: We didn't see if Shane popped back up after that last macker, and I was hoping to God his leash didn't break. We were searching for the nose of his board, tombstoning around. It was scary. I have a certain level of detachment sometimes, when stuff like that happens, and I knew this is what it looks like when people drown in big waves. And it was happening right then and right there. We were definitely worried, yelling at guys to go try and find Shane. Luckily, Frank was close, and he swooped in and got him.

Dorian, seriously shaken but still breathing, on the way back to the boat
PHOTO © ROBERT BROWN

SD: After the fourth wave washed over me, Frank and one of the photographers sped up on the jet ski, and I could barely crawl onto the sled I was so wasted. Frank got me over to the boats. I instantly had this pounding migraine headache, and I could barely move my arms. I had no batteries left. Zero. I wanted to get the hell out of the water and out of the ocean. The thing was trying to kill me. I needed to get out of there. Get away. I was desperate.

Dave Wassell: Once we hoisted Shane up onto the boat I kicked into lifeguard mode and gave him a quick assessment to see how serious it is. Obviously, Shane's physically worked and emotion-ally shaken—broken, really. I looked in his eyes. He mumbled something about hitting things on the bottom, so I checked for lacerations, contusions, anything. I tried to get a fix on his pupils, but he starts vomiting something squeezed out of his liver. It's green and fluorescent. Food doesn't look like that, let me tell you.

He still couldn't really talk. His lips were blue, his eyelids were blue. He looked like a Smurf. That's oxygen deprivation for you. He kept yanking at his wetsuit, trying to pull it off, and spewing this jade shit all over. And mumbling, making no sense. I'm, like, *Hey, look at me real quick, Shane. I need you to answer me.* I'm asking very simple questions, and he's still not responding. He's only puking that day-glo crap and literally shaking apart.

SD: When I crawled up onto the boat, Dave was right there. He's been a lifeguard forever, super capable and experienced, and he was looking at my pupils and asking all these questions, and I was like, *Give me a ride to the beach, anywhere, just get me out of here.* Physically I was alive. I was safe. But it was close, and it was bad. I had that insane headache and didn't want to eat. I didn't want to talk to anybody. I didn't want to be around anybody. I wanted to clear out and go sleep for like two days because mentally, I was totally thrashed.

MH: Anyone who's been through something heavy knows it's like a fighter pilot after a close call. What do you say? *Hey, that was intense, but good job. You didn't kick the bucket.* And he's like, *See how my lips are blue? No shit, I almost died. Now beat it; you're bugging me.*

All that *blah blah blah* is so annoying. You leave the guy alone and chill until he rattles his way back to the living. You can be there for him, but he's gotta come back on his own. And it might not be pretty. Like that lime green stuff he kept hurling. *Dude.*

DW: People on the boat didn't know how to approach the situation— what to think, what to say, what to do. Shane was a wreck, was still in that wave, tumbling through this huge gamut of emotions. We're both in the back of the boat, and after ten minutes, he says, *My son! I'm so selfish.* But all broken and jumbled, little broken tidbits from a broken man.

When he was getting dragged along the ocean floor, he apparently saw his son's face, with his hair blowing in the wind. He actually had that vision.

It was tough to hear and see this guy I respected and looked up to reduced to a quivering mess like this.

But a lot of guys who surf the big stuff have groped through these experiences. It's personal, you know, so I did my quick assessment and left him to deal with it alone. But he was disturbed right then, literally disturbed, so over the next forty-five minutes I kept checking in on him, and all he said was, *I gotta get outta here. Just get me outta here. Get me off this boat!* So we got him a ride in.

I called Shane that night, and he said, *I can't believe I did that. That was the stupidest thing. It was selfish. It was immature, and I'm never doing this again. I'm over it.* That's a bold statement there. I was like, *You did exactly what you were supposed to do: Show up and blow up. That's what Shane Dorian is all about.* And now one of the great hellmen is going to up and quit? I was blown away.

SD: The next day I flew back home and didn't mention anything to my wife except that I'd surfed Mavericks, and it was good. She's not usually worried when I leave, but later she's like, *Everyone's calling me telling me you almost died and stuff. What's up with this?* And I'm saying, *You know people are dramatic like that, blowing things out of proportion.* But when she kept getting phone calls from guys who were there or in the water, and she heard the same basic account from them all, she knew who was lying, and she definitely got scared. I tried playing it down, but I still wasn't right, and she knew it.

I had a concussion from hitting the water and being out of breath, or whatever. Physically, emotionally, mentally, I was rattled, totally, to the core. It was all fun and games when I was catching those mackers and everything was going well and confidence was high. It never crossed my mind that the game could get fatal—until it did, and there wasn't a thing I could do about it.

I live and breathe big wave surfing. I train all year long and try my hardest to stay in top physical condition, try and eat right, do all the things I need to be the best I can be. But if a wave comes along and wants to drown me, it's going to drown me. I thought again about my close friend, Todd Chesser, who was in such great physical condition, so experienced, so mentally strong in big waves. And in 1997, on an outside reef near Alligator Rock on the North Shore of Oahu, a wave wanted to kill him, and it killed him. Now I knew what that meant. *A realization at depth,* I think they call it.

I needed a break. At first I was like, *I don't know if I'm gonna do this anymore. Maybe leave it to some younger guy that doesn't have kids.* But then a couple weeks went by, then a month, and I'm thinking, *I'm gonna surf Mavericks next year for sure. But I'm getting a custom floatation vest made because if I'm in the right place*—well, just thinking about it I get excited and caught up in the moment because I know one thing for sure: *When that big wave comes, I'm not gonna not go. I'm going.*

Shane Dorian, fully recovered from his close call at Mavericks and back in the saddle at Peahi—logging this 2010 Billabong XXL Global Big Wave award–winning ride

SPECIFICALLY DESIGNED FOR BIG SURF

The showpiece of ancient Hawaiian surfing was the royal *olo* (surfboard), the *wiliwili* wood colossus used exclusively by the ruling *alii* class. Specs for the *olo* were almost cartoonish: 20 feet long by 2 feet wide, 200 pounds, and domed along both the deck and bottom so that the center was nearly 8 inches thick.

During the mid-1920s, Tom Blake, America's first surfing champion, visited Hawaii and restored a pair of weather-beaten *olos* that for years had hung on an exterior wall at Honolulu's Bishop Museum. Blake was the first surfer of his generation to take a real interest in ancient surf history and lore, but part of his response to the *olos* was a simple wide-eyed awe, like a rural schoolboy seeing his first skyscraper. A few years later, Blake and Hawaiian surf icon Duke Kahanamoku each made themselves 16-foot *olo* replicas, more than half again longer and heavier than the average board of the time. Duke's *olo* weighed a full 130 pounds. Both surfers reported that the boards worked especially well in large waves. "During our last big surf, which only comes three or four times a year," Blake wrote in 1935, "the Duke did some of the most beautiful riding I have ever seen on his new longboard."

While just a handful of examples survived into the twentieth century, the *olo* is nonetheless viewed as the showpiece of ancient Hawaiian surfing. Replicas stand in museums and are sold to collectors for tens of thousands of dollars. Yet, the *olo* has about it a kind of grand absurdity, like a stretch limousine or a floor-dragging ceremonial robe. There are no eyewitness accounts of *olo* surfing, but it seems likely that the boards were used solely for riding unbroken waves.

"It is a good board for a wave that swells and rushes shoreward," nineteenth-century Hawaiian scholar John Papa Ii said of the *olo*, "but not for a wave that rises up high and curls over."

Huge, heavy, and finless, the *olo* would have been nearly impossible to guide or steer—less a surfboard than a small canoe, which was also used by the Hawaiians to ride waves but with the operational advantage of a paddle. The *kapu* laws preventing commoners from using the *olo* may have been a matter of public safety, given that a loose *olo* would blast through the wave zone like a log pitching through rapids.

Another theory is that the *olo* was specifically designed for big surf. Large waves move faster through the ocean and are much harder to catch than small waves, and the *olo* had a great paddling advantage over other types of boards. Even more so in big surf, however, it seems likely that the idea would have been to steer clear of breaking waves. Many Hawaiian surf spots have a deep-water channel adjacent to the break, allowing the surfer to paddle out without running into any broken waves. Some of these breaks, too, have a broad shoaling area beyond the surf zone, where open ocean swells first begin to tilt. This may well have been the intended field of play for the colossal *olo*, *he ʻe nalu* of the kings.

—From *The History of Surfing*,
by Matt Warshaw

Backside at Mavericks can be an advantage—Tyler
Smith can't see what's chasing him.

SURF LIKE JAY: THE LIFE AND DEATH OF JAMES MICHAEL MORIARTY (1978–2001)

by Ben Marcus

While the young Santa Cruz surfer was best known for a single spectacular wipeout, by the time of his tragic death in 2001 Jay Moriarty had earned a reputation as a great all-around waterman and, even better yet, as a great all-around human being. Longtime surf journalist Ben Marcus grew up in the original Surf City and was the obvious choice to pen what amounted to a paean to lost youth and potential unfulfilled.

HE HASN'T DIED AT ALL
Name: Sonny Rains
Date: 06-18-01 20:18

I didn't know Jay. I'm stuck 150 miles inland of the southern North Carolina coast. But Jay Moriarty has touched my life. And he has touched my girlfriend's life. She doesn't even surf. I don't fully understand it, but everyone recognizes Jay's importance. The newscaster on the local news channel, whom I guarantee has never ever heard of even Kelly Slater before, was visibly moved when reporting Jay's death. Even the fact that this story was reported was amazing to me. I will not forget Jay Moriarty and not just when I'm surfing either. I won't forget him when I'm having a bad day. I won't forget him when I don't feel motivated at work. I won't forget him when I'm too tired to practice my music and follow my passion. I will learn to smile like Jay Moriarty. And if his life touches so many, then surely he hasn't died at all.

With love,
Sonny Rains

Jay Moriarty was close to that rarest of things: a pure talent and a pure soul. Jay was a made guy, a stoked guy, a reverse of the Cheshire Cat. Here was a Santa Cruz guy without an attitude, a guy who had it, was glad he had it, knew what to do with it, and wouldn't dream of letting it rust. His grace and humility were our blessing, and his smile sustained us. Successful in his teens, going full steam in his early twenties and still on his way up, Jay was always looking around the corner for the next big thing. Then the ocean took his breath away and left the rest of us gasping.

The drowning of Jay Moriarty in the Maldives on Friday, June 15, 2001, shocked the world. People who knew him and people who didn't were stricken in ways hard to understand. Newspapers and TV news, from California to Tasmania, covered the story. But the real measure of Jay's effect was found on *Aggroville*, the chat forum on MavSurfer.com.

The first post, from Bodhi, at 8:46 p.m. on June 15, was timid: *Is True that jay passed away?* Chat forums are notorious for malicious *So-and-So Died at Teahupoo!* rumors. But this one was true, and when word got out, *Aggroville*—typically a snide, mean-spirited dungeon—was soon awash in more than three hundred posts, all about Jay, from family, friends, bros, and strangers, all respectfully sharing their thoughts and feelings in honor of Jay. It wasn't so much his passing as his person that restored some dignity to what one detractor called the "Jerry Springer Show of the surfing world."

There were short and long tributes from people who knew him and from people who knew of him, from people he had taught, and from people from whom he had learned. There were posts from Santa Cruz, England, South Africa, and beyond, and if you read them all, the words that kept popping up most often were "smile," "stoked," "tragic," and "why?"

In the weeks following Jay's death there were two video benefits in Santa Cruz, a memorial paddle-out at Santa Cruz attended by several thousand, and more private memorials throughout northern

California and around the world. Thousands of people paid tribute to Jay in many different ways, but you need look no farther than *Aggroville* for proof of the effect Jay's life had on people.

WHAT WAS AND WHAT SHALL NEVER BE
Name: a wig
Date: 06-19-01 11:14

As sad as it is . . . imagine how moriarty would have been out at mavs when he reached his prime. Untouchable.

Jay Moriarty moved to Santa Cruz as a boy and immediately fell in love with the ocean, as many have done and will continue to do. When his parents divorced, Jay and his mother moved to Santa Cruz. Jay's father Doug was an airborne Ranger. He and Jay did some jumps together, and they surfed at Trestles when Jay went down to southern California. Jay lived near the end of 36th Avenue, but home was just down the street, at Pleasure Point.

"When I started I didn't have a wetsuit. I just had shorts and a T-shirt," Jay said in a 2000 interview with swell.com. "And I had a 7-foot Haut from like the '70s. It was a little pintail, like a 3-inch-thick '70s board. It was cool. Single fin. I was unequipped and clueless, but I didn't give a shit. It was just so much fun. I learned to surf at Insides and then moved up to the Point."

Felix Alfaro remembers twelve-year-old Jay as "a chubby kid who was always out at 38th Avenue and all around the Point. He was a good surfer but not a real standout, but he was just a pleasure to be in the water with. He always paddled out with a smile and kept that smile on the whole time. That is what I remember about Jay Moriarty. He was good but not exceptional. But, man, he sure got a lot better."

Danilo Couto, grab-rail backside at Jaws
PHOTO © ERIKAEDER.COM

Jay just wanted to get better. He was self-motivated but wasn't afraid to soak up advice or criticism from anyone. The friendship and mentorship between Jay and Rick "Frosty" Hesson were well-covered in a piece entitled "The Apprenticeship of Jay Moriarty" by Jason Smith in *Surfer's Journal*. A few days after the news of Jay reached Frosty at home, he felt like he had "lost a son."

"He just wanted guidance," said Hesson. "What he approached me about was becoming a better surfer. I worked with him a little bit and gave him some things to do. There was as much mental preparation and writing as there was physical, and it had as much to do with developing a human being as a surfer. It's the same philosophy I use to raise my children, but Jay took it to an extreme. He was the only person to complete the program in its entirety, and he did one incredible job."

Self-motivated and directed by Frosty Hesson, Richard Schmidt, and others, Jay took tentative steps at Mavericks in April of 1994, and then in one giant leap he introduced himself to the world by paddling into a bomb at mega-Mavericks on December 19, 1994. Jay's youthful gusto overpowered his horse sense. He scratched onto the first wave that came his way on an offshore, high-tide morning, launching him into what at that time was the most spectacular wipeout in the history of surfing. The Bob Barbour photo made the cover of *Surfer,* and it made Jay. If he did nothing else in his surfing life, he had stroked into that Homeric wipeout and lived to laugh about it, and for that he was a sixteen-year-old legend. World champion Kelly Slater sent Jay a fax: "Keep charging."

Jay's plunge introduced to the surfing community a stoked guy with a goofy smile pasted onto a rock-hard melon, a young guy on a longboard who didn't give a shit, part of the '90s movement concerned with riding what *felt* right—and hang the fashion. Jay was a longboarder who also charged giant waves, took ridiculous lumps, and came up howling.

"I bounced off the bottom out there. I don't think anyone has done that before, huh?"

Jay arrived with a bang, then settled into a quiet groove, working, going to school to study fire science, traveling, competing, but staying focused on Mavericks, surfing it whenever he could and preparing for it the rest of the time. Over the following years, there were occasional shots of Jay surfing Mavericks in magazines and videos but nothing that overcame the first impression of his historic wipeout.

Many northern California surfers watched Jay grow from a chubby grom to one of the men at Mavericks, and a lot of these surfers helped Jay along the way, including Mavericks pioneer Jeff Clark.

Not much happens at Mavericks that Jeff Clark doesn't see, and Clark watched Jay go from *banzai* grom to Clark's own tow partner. He has his thoughts on why Jay didn't get the attention that others did or that he deserved.

"A lot of guys surf extreme waves, but if it looks easy it must be easy, right? Or maybe the person who makes it look easy has a different understanding of the elements. That's where Jay was. People remember his full-charge wipeout at sixteen, but he made very few mistakes out there. He rode a lot of really big waves, steep and deep."

During the winter of 2000–2001, Moriarty was split between paddle-in and tow-in surfing, coming into the power game a little later than others and working on his tow partnership with Clark. On December 22, Moriarty got some of the biggest bombs ever ridden at Mavs, using his size and weight to surf them with the same authority as Peter Mel. Jay was one of the stars of all the raw tow video from that historic day, but Clark says that videos and photos and magazines don't come close to telling the whole story.

Late in the evening of the 19th, when it was almost dark and the boats and cameras were safe at home, Jeff Clark towed Jay into a giant wave behind the outside bowl, and a few witnesses watched Jay get the barrel that everyone has been hunting for a decade. "I saw it," said Colin Brown, "and became a grudging admirer of the God Scooters. Jay got whipped in so far behind the bowl on a giant wave that I instinctively began paddling toward the impact zone to retrieve the wreckage. There was just no way. I was shocked when Jay came flying out the end, and guys in the channel said he pulled into a monster barrel. You had to be there to see and feel the power. That was an awesome wave. Jay was at the top of both paddling and towing after last winter, and he had nowhere to go but up."

OUR OCEAN TEACHER
Name: The Spears Family
Date: 06-18-01 11:57

We are all deeply shocked by the news in this little part of England. We live near Croyde Beach where Jay and the O'Neill Academy came to introduce grommets to our wonderful sport. Both Connor and Kathleen were taught by Jay the basics of surfboard control, and both were looking forward so much to meeting him again this weekend. Our thoughts are with Jay's family and friends. We will never forget him.

Ester, Barbara, Connor & Kathleen

Jay Moriarty's tragic drowning in the Maldive Islands had facets of the deep-sea diving accident that took Jose Angel, combined with the Mavericks wipeout that drowned Mark Foo. Like Angel,

Jay Moriarty was free-diving and pushing himself, if not for deep-water penetration like Angel, then for maximum time underwater as part of a big wave training regimen. And like the situation at Mavericks with Foo, in the Maldives there was a breakdown in the buddy system—as important in diving as in surfing—that might have saved Jay's life.

Friday, June 15 was Jay's last day in the Maldives. He had been there for a week, one of around 150 surfers, photographers, judges, and models from around the world who flew all the way to South Asia to compete in the five-star WQS O'Neill Deep Blue Open event. Jay was there to surf and train and do fashion shoots but not compete. The contest ran Monday to Thursday, with Chris Ward winning the final in the last few seconds. By Friday, most of the competitors had left, leaving Jay and less than a dozen other surfers on Lohifushi Island. Jay would turn twenty-three on Saturday, and he was looking forward to meeting his wife Kim in England for a late party and then beginning a five-week tour of Europe as the head instructor for the O'Neill Surf Academy. Moriarty had worked for the academy for five years, teaching fifty new kids a day for five weeks, from Europe to Italy. This was his first year leading the team, taking the position from Richard Schmidt, who had taken it from Robert "Wingnut" Weaver, all big wave surfing royalty.

Friday was a lazy day. A morning boat expedition, by the dozen or so stragglers on Lohifushi, was turned back by a dropping swell and increasing winds. Muslim custom dictates a 1:30 lunch on Fridays. With a little time on his hands, Jay told Brazilian ASP judge Renato Hickel that he was going free-diving, to work on his breathing, at the end of a 150-meter pier that connects the island with the reef.

"I told him to be careful and take it easy," Hickel said. "There had been a little drinking the night before, and a day or two earlier I had seen Jay come in from diving in convulsions and nearly throwing up, he had pushed himself so hard."

Frosty Hesson had talked to Jay before he left for the Maldives, and Hesson knew Jay wasn't pleased with his conditioning following an ankle injury at Mavs.

"Jay didn't like to get out of shape, and he worked hard as soon as he got the cast off and his ankle was ready. He was riding bikes pretty hard, and I knew he was a little concerned about the Surf Academy in Europe because it would interfere with his training. Jay knew how important it was to stay in top condition for Mavericks, and he knew it was a year-around commitment. He was determined to work hard at it over the summer any way he could."

At around 11:30, Cory Lopez went down to the pier to feed bread to the fish, another local custom. Cory saw Jay's backpack with swimfins and some bread sticking out of the pockets, but he didn't think much of it and went to lunch. Jay didn't make the lunch, which was unusual, Hickel said, "because he liked to eat a lot." Some thought Jay had gone over to Club Med on the next island. Others thought he was sleeping.

Dinner was at 7:30, and everyone was there but Jay, which led to a search of the island and Jay's room, where he was probably sleeping. When his room appeared untouched, Lopez and Hickel began asking around. There were five Spanish surfers staying on Lohifushi. Hickel speaks fluent Spanish, and he recounted what the Spaniards told him.

"We asked the Spanish guys, 'Have you seen Jay?' and they said, 'We don't know him.' Then they understood that Jay was the bald-headed guy they had seen free-diving at the end of the pier earlier in the day around noon. The Spanish guys were snorkeling around the end of the pier and saw a guy pulling himself down a buoy rope to the bottom in about 50 feet of water. Viktor the photographer knew about diving, and he was impressed by Jay, who was sitting on the bottom in a kind of lotus position, holding his breath. A few times they heard Jay's watch go off under water, which meant he was timing himself. They saw Jay come up the rope, take big, deep breaths at the surface, and go back down. Viktor was the last one in the water and the last to see Jay. The other Spanish guys wanted to go to lunch and told Viktor to get out of the water. They didn't want to disturb Jay, and as they were leaving they heard his watch again. That was the last anyone had seen of Jay Moriarty."

The island went to red alert. A group went to the pier and found Jay's backpack with the swimfins and bread exactly as Cory had seen it almost eight hours before. Tim Godfrey, an Australian staff diver and dive base manager at Tari Resort, was one of two divers alerted to start a search for Jay.

"After someone told me Jay had been free-diving at the end of the jetty and went missing around lunchtime, I immediately became concerned as the currents at that time would have been flowing strongly out of the atoll," said Godfrey. "Just over a year ago a scuba diver disappeared without trace near the same location—the currents are strong and often swept divers out into the Indian Ocean, sometimes for good. I asked if Jay was wearing a weight belt and fins and got a 'no.'

"Even though it was nighttime and Jay had been missing for ten hours by now, there was a slim chance he could still be alive, drifting outside the atoll. He could have been hyperventilating at the surface before his free dives, to prolong his bottom time, and this would have increased the risk of shallow-water blackout on ascent. If this happened, he could have possibly regained consciousness at the surface and drifted off in the current. This was our only hope.

"Someone said Jay had been free-diving near the rope on the house reef. I hurried off to the dive school, where I joined a group of divers preparing for a rescue dive. Someone was already organizing search boats. My dive buddy and I immediately descended the reef slope and followed the rope toward the flat, sandy bottom at 24 meters. In the faint beam of the underwater light, I saw Jay's body lying on the bottom a short distance away from the reef. It was apparent he died while diving at depth and not on ascent, as his body remained near the bottom of the rope. He most probably died of hypoxia, caused by low oxygen in the blood, in his last seconds when his oxygen reserves would have been severely depleted. He may have become disoriented and unsure of which way was up or down and been overcome by the desire to breathe. More probably, he prolonged his dive so much that he blacked out instantly. The condition in which I found him seems to confirm this as his body remained rock hard and cemented in his final pose. Being at more than three atmospheres of pressure, with little body fat, his airspaces compressed and possibly with his lungs full of water, Jay's body was negatively buoyant and very heavy, hence the reason it didn't drift away in the strong current.

"When I first saw his shadowy outline, it was like an apparition, as if a gladiator statue had toppled over. He was lying face-down in the sand with his head tilted to one side and his mask and snorkel firmly in place. His legs were spread apart, as if balancing to do pushups, his arms bent at the elbows and tucked under his body. His fists were clenched and fingers closed tight, like he was bracing himself for an onslaught. He was wearing only his O'Neill board shorts, a watch, and a ring on his wedding finger. His back muscles rippled in the torchlight. That dying image was one of strength and determination, not confusion and panic, as one might have expected."

Over the weekend and into the week of June 17, many people were concerned about Kim Moriarty, the twenty-three-year-old Pleasure Point surfer who was looking forward to a summer trip to Europe when she received the news that her husband had drowned. It is a tribute to the Santa Cruz surfing community that Kim didn't have to bear the tragedy without support. Once the surfers of Santa Cruz and Mavericks had recovered from the shock, they organized a series of benefits and memorials, designed to remember their friend and provide some emotional and financial security for his wife and family. On Saturday night, Jeff and Katharine Clark had a benefit showing of Eric Nelson and Curt Myers's Mavericks video *Whipped*, which they screened at the new Mavericks Surf Shop in Princeton Harbor.

"Eric and Curt put together a beautiful video memorial to Jay in just a couple of hours," said Katharine. "I still cry when I think about it."

On Wednesday night, June 20, Nelson and Myers showed *Whipped* at the Rio Theater in Santa Cruz, with all ticket sales and raffle proceeds going to Kim Moriarty. Katharine Clark was at the door, and she was overwhelmed.

"We had scheduled two shows but ended up selling those two out and adding on a third show for a couple hundred people. We sold about a thousand tickets but raised more than $9,000. People were handing me hundreds and saying, 'Keep the change.'"

Whipped showed many of the highlights from the winter of 2000–2001 at Mavericks, including Jay Moriarty pulling impossibly high-lined carves on December 22. *Whipped* ended with a shot of Jay charging some giant bombs, as the crowd went berserk in memoriam. It was eerie coincidence that *Whipped* ended with a shot of Jay checking out his board on the beach and walking away, and then there was a memorial, with footage of Jay surfing, inter-cut with an interview he recorded in Tahiti in 1998.

"Jay talked about how we're only here for a short time and be kind to everyone," said Clark. "Embrace the positive and let the negative go through you. It was stirring, and you couldn't help buckling from the raw emotion. I was three and a half years old when JFK died, and the emotion in the Rio was as strong for Jay as it was for the president. Everyone was feeling the loss of a magical human being."

On Friday night, Frank Quirarte got the same response when he hosted a benefit premiere for *Return of the Drag-In* at the Capitola Theater. Quirarte's benefit showing also raised thousands of dollars for Kim Moriarty. Frank held on to Kim's shoulders as she choked out a speech and thanked everyone for remembering Jay and helping her through a hard time.

Jay's body was returned to Santa Cruz on Friday the 22nd, and there were thousands of friends and fans there to say goodbye. At Pleasure Point on Tuesday, June 28, almost two thousand surfers and ocean-lovers paddled out into the kelp, and Jay's ashes were released into the ocean that had given him so much life.

Name: Lurker
Date: 06-18-01 23:17

I am coining a new phrase that will help me deal with the stress of surfing in crowds and aggroness in general. Live like Jay. Today I was driving, and I started to get road rage, but then I started to think about Jay's life and his aloha nature. I started to not care that we were going too slow. I know it will help when I'm out surfing and get mad. Live like Jay! You can't go wrong. *A hui hou,* Jay!

When Jay so famously torpedoed over the falls at Mavericks, it was my pleasure to interview what was left. Jay was a Pleasure Point guy, and it was good to see a Pleasure Point guy go beyond Sewer Peak legend and accomplish something on the world stage. Truth is, that now-famous Bob Barbour photo of Jay taking a plunge for the ages knocked another Jay image off the cover.

The photo in question, taken from the water, showed a nuggety sixteen-year-old Jay dropping in steep and deep in a power stance, with the hook of the lip throwing over his head. Crouched in the middle of all that power, glaring out past the terrible shoulder, the position of his arms and the circular lip made him look like the character in a Mickey Mouse watch. That was Jay Michael Moriarty, always looking around the corner for the next big thing. And finding it, too.

I knew only of his courage. He was loved and respected. There are only good things to say about Jay. He was happy. We ask ourselves, Why so young? So many more things to do and time to share. Yet, maybe he learned what he needed here. Maybe he was saved from the burdens of living. We mourn out of our own selfish desire to be with our loved ones who have gone. But if we knew that they were in a better place and at peace, wouldn't we celebrate their fortune? Heroes linger, and Jay's deeds will be spoken of around campfires for many generations to come. Our time and place of departure are a great mystery. We know only that it will come, and it is written: When I go, please have a party for me. Jay would want his passing celebrated. It's one of the unspoken rules of his kind. Goodbye, Jay, a man of the sea. There you will always be. Keep an eye on us.

Your brother,
Laird Hamilton

DIFFICULT AND DANGEROUS MANEUVERS

As far back as the eighteenth century, some of the earliest accounts of the Polynesian pastime drew attention to the Hawaiian Islanders' penchant for heavy water—i.e., big ass surf. Consider the following passage from The Three Voyages of Captain Cook Round the World, *which could just as easily be describing a contemporary session at Waimea Bay. Seventy-five years ago, Tom Blake, surfing's first serious historian, provided even more detail of an early epic session in his seminal book* Hawaiian Surfboard, *illustrating that, despite not knowing what actually causes big waves, there have always been surfers daring enough to ride them.*

The surf, which breaks on the coast round the bay extends to the distance of about 150 yards from the shore, within which space the surges of the sea, accumulating from the shallowness of the water, are dashed against the beach with prodigious violence. Whenever, from stormy weather or any extraordinary swell at sea, the impetuosity of the surf is increased to its utmost height, they chose that time for this amusement, which is performed in the following manner: Twenty or thirty of the natives, each taking a long narrow board rounded at the ends, set out together from the shore. The first wave they meet they plunge under, and suffering it to roll over them, rise again beyond it and make the best of their way by swimming out into the sea. The second wave is encountered in the same manner with the first; the great difficulty consisting in seizing the proper moment of diving under it, which if missed, the person is caught by the surf and driven back again with great violence; and all his dexterity is then required to prevent himself from being dashed against the rocks. As soon as they have gained, by these repeated efforts, the smooth water beyond the surf they lay themselves at length on their board and prepare for their return. As the surf consists of a number of waves, of which the third is remarked to always be much larger than the others, and to flow higher on the shore, the rest breaking in the intermediate space, their first object is to place themselves on the summit of the largest surge, by which they are driven along with amazing rapidity toward the shore. If by mistake they should place themselves on one of the smaller waves, which breaks before they reach the land, or should not be able to keep their plank in a proper direction on the top of the swell, they are left exposed to the fury of the next and, to avoid it, are obliged again to dive and regain the place from which they set out. Those who succeed in their object of reaching the shore have still the greatest danger to encounter. The coast being guarded by a chain of rocks, with, here and there, a small opening between them, they are obliged to steer their board through one of these or, in case of failure, to quit it before they reach the rocks and plunging under the wave make the best of their way back again. This is reckoned very disgraceful and is also attended with the loss of the board, which I have often seen, with great terror, dashed to pieces at the moment the islander quitted it. The boldness and address with which we saw them perform these difficult and dangerous maneuvers was altogether astonishing and is scarcely to be credited.

—Captain James Cook, *The Three Voyages of Captain Cook Round the World*

A Billabong XXL Global Big Wave Awards candidate at Mavericks, Greg Long puts his trust in the laws of gravity

PHOTO © FRANK QUIRARTE/BILLABONGXXL.COM

ROAD AGENT:
GREG LONG'S LIFE IN PURSUIT

by Brad Melekian

*The template for a successful pro surfer's career generally looks
like this: early amateur success, first photos in the surf magazines, first sponsorship deal, subsequent promotional surf trip/
magazine travel feature, a season or two on the qualifying pro
tour, more photos, new, more lucrative sponsors, a jump to the
world championship tour, more surf trips, more endorsement ads,
success on the tour for a few years, eventual retirement, and
finally a magazine profile chronicling the sweet ride. But surfers
like Greg Long, the most successful professional big wave surfer
in the world today, took a different path to the top: a totally new
type of ride, examined by talented surf journalist Brad Melekian.*

It was February of last year. The swell he had been waiting for
his entire life had lit up the California coast the day before, but
it did so at night, leaving him on land and predictably outraged.
The next day was sunny and warm, and Greg Long and I sat in the
uncrowded enclosed patio of a plastic-tables-and-chairs Mexican
restaurant in San Clemente, where he trembled with frustration.

"We would have caught the biggest waves ever ridden at Todos
Santos," he lamented between pulls off a lunchtime beer, "if the
timing had been just a little bit different."

Greg was downright gracious with his "we." I just sat, and
watched, and listened. He drummed the table nervously and
looked out the window of the restaurant before launching into the
facts, without prompting, as I knew he would. "When Brad Gerlach
caught his 68-footer out there two years ago, the buoy was reading 17 feet, and the swell direction was 270 degrees. Yesterday the

Long, fully insulated and focused
on the business at hand
PHOTO © ROBERT BROWN

buoy peaked at 20.9 feet, and the swell direction was 270 degrees. You do the math."

I had already done the math, which was exactly why, were it not my job to get a sense of Greg Long's disturbing commitment to big wave surfing, I wouldn't have even considered being anywhere near Todos that day. For one thing, a storm was battering the entire West Coast with 20-knot south winds and rain projected for the next two days. So foul was the weather and so rough the ocean that the harbormaster at Ensenada closed down the harbor and wouldn't allow boats out to Todos. "Not to worry," Greg said, "we'll lift up the chain blocking access to the water, slide the skis under, and get out that way."

For another thing, the swell was supposed to hit late in the afternoon on a Sunday, peak at night, and be gone by first light, which meant that there was little to no chance that we were even going to see the big waves if they arrived, and if they were rideable, in the storm. I mentioned this on the phone to Greg.

"Well, here's the thing," he said. "I could surf Uppers—maybe go down to Blacks—but if I did that I'd go crazy. I'd much rather go down to Todos and see that it's no good. At least then I tried."

So it ran for the past two months. A glossy mainstream men's magazine tapped me to shape a shotgun-riding profile on Greg Long, and I was thusly thrust into the puzzling and hard-driving orbit of a no-bullshit twenty-five-year-old focused on discovering and taming the world's tallest waves at the exclusion of anything else.

The Todos Santos mission, for example, was hands down the most energy I'd ever put into not going somewhere. Greg and I spoke on the phone a dozen times in a matter of hours the day before the swell was to hit, followed by another dozen times over the next twelve hours. We spoke so many times, amid the updates on swell direction, wind speed, and buoy readings ("Buoys are massive up north!" Greg texted between phone calls), that his name spontaneously appeared in the "Favorites" list on my cell, a feature I didn't know the phone had. Meanwhile, while we were speaking at eleven at night, it was pouring rain and howling onshore wind. Not to worry. We spoke again at 4:30, when it was still raining, still windy, and Greg was still raring to go.

Over the last month, with every hint of swell Greg would call with possibilities: to make the ten-hour drive from his San Clemente home to Mavericks, where we'd sleep in his van and be up at dawn; to motor 105 miles out to sea to Cortes Bank, where 100-foot waves could conceivably be ridden, maybe; to steam out to a handful of island breaks that Greg said he might be able to take me to but that I could never write about; to investigate a heavy-water slab that he said a bodyboarder in Huntington Beach once told him about but that he wasn't sure was really even a wave; or to wake up hours before first light to drive to fetid Ensenada and sneak jet skis out to Todos Santos for a swell that sounded like it would never be anything at all.

One Friday afternoon, Greg was in his van driving to Mavericks when he stopped on the side of the 101, took out his laptop, and called me. He told me that he was headed to Mavericks but that there was a change of plans and that now we had a boat booked for Cortes and that we'd leave in the morning. "Okay," I said and started to get ready. He called fifteen minutes later. "We're going out to Shark Park." Fifteen minutes later: "Mavericks." An hour later: "Todos." An hour after that: "Mavericks" after all, and lucky for him, he was already halfway there, "but it probably wouldn't be that good, so don't bother coming."

Such is the hurry-up-and-wait, tightrope-walking life of the modern big wave rider, and so went the entire big wave season, until the only swell that showed full promise decided to appear at night. Greg went to Todos Santos that day, regardless. I stayed back. He and Mike Parsons had a paddle-in session and then stayed at a harbor motel in northern Baja, where Greg presumably lay in bed and listened to giant waves crash in the distance, the waves he had been waiting for his whole life breaking in lonely explosions, Greg trembling with fury.

The next day he and I surfed the tail end of that swell at a crowded beachbreak near his house. There is almost nowhere in the world that he would like to surf less.

Greg Long grew up in Orange County in the 1990s and became a professional surfer, which makes you wonder. He is neither insufferable nor obnoxious. He has absolutely zero sense of entitlement. And he's uncannily focused on what he wants and pursues it with dogged enthusiasm regardless of his circumstances.

What Greg wants, very simply, is to surf big waves, the biggest in the world, in fact. Twelve months out of the year if he can. And, hopefully, if things go well, he'll push himself into situations that cause others to rethink the limitations of big wave surfing.

But in a big wave world sometimes co-opted by opportunists looking to extend their sagging surf careers, Greg isn't interested in the trophy-hunting element that seems to have overtaken the sport. Instead, he pursues his surfing thoughtfully, with purpose, and in the tradition of previous generations.

It's in this sense that Greg is as much of a purist as one is going to find in the modern big wave scene—as adept on a gun as he is on a ski and willing to put in an uncanny amount of time and energy to score waves regardless of the financial rewards or in-print accolades.

This, to be sure, is refreshing in modern surfing but particularly in big wave surfing, where self-promotion has taken deeper root than in any other arm of the modern scene. Much of Greg's outlook can be traced back to his upbringing. He was raised in the surf industry's backyard in Orange County, yes, but he was as much a part of that world as he was removed from it. He was brought up in the state park employee housing alcove, steps from the sand in San Clemente. It's a small cluster of houses that's easy to miss, and when you're inside the tiny, wooded neighborhood, it's hard to believe that Interstate 5 is there at all, let alone a tenth of a mile from your back while you're focused on the sound of sea directly in front of you.

For Greg and his older brother, Rusty, it was the proximity to the ocean and the people who understood it, rather than the proximity to Lower Trestles and the people who ripped there, that seems to have had the most reverberating impact through the years.

Their father was a celebrated lifeguard captain and local surfer (he recently retired and skipped town after thirty-plus years of service), and he passed down his knowledge to his boys through the years.

Greg's first taste of big wave surfing came as a teenager with a trip to Todos Santos, and it immediately threw him into the conflict by which the rest of his life has been shaped—follow the well-worn path of professional surfing or do what you want and ride big waves.

"I was sixteen when I went out to Todos and caught my first really big wave," he remembers. "And after that, that's all I wanted to do. I remember one contest in Newport that I went to rather than going down to Todos with my friends. They came back and said it was the biggest in who knows how long, and I was in tears. I was up at the contest in tears—literally crying—when I got the voice message. I was just devastated."

Still, Greg eventually became the dark-horse winner of the NSSA nationals at the age of eighteen when that title still carried a lot of weight. It's a feat that's hard to reconcile with Long the big wave surfer today, but even after he's eschewed jersey-surfing, Greg still relishes this as one of the proudest moments of his surfing career.

"I'll always count that as one of the things I'm most proud of," he says. "There wasn't a person on the beach who thought that I could win that thing, and I worked hard, and I did it." But that taste of contest victory seemed to have been enough. After high school, when most of his friends set off on the formulaic route laid out for them by the ASP, Greg decided to make his own path.

The shifting lineup of Cortes Bank necessitates
a jet assist. Greg Long, bleeding off the speed

PHOTO © ROBERT BROWN

Along with Rusty, the two made names for themselves in two ways—as big wave surfers and as peripatetic searchers willing to poke around for weeks and months in search of a wave to themselves. They succeeded in both regards. On the big wave front, early accomplishments included a slew of scores, perhaps most notably a stealth Cortes mission with Gerlach and Parsons that established the Longs to anybody who hadn't been paying attention. And, as searchers, Greg and Rusty seemed to have an uncanny knack for disappearing for days and then coming back to town clutching photos of themselves in the treacherous barrels of heaving waves that nobody had seen before but that were supposedly right under our noses.

But it was always just that: the Longs, the Long brothers. It seemed impossible to talk about Greg without talking about Rusty. Magazines ran profiles on both brothers together. Companies sponsored and marketed them together. Until recently, when Greg set off with fierce determination to ride the biggest waves in the world, come what may. He drove his van to Mavericks every weekend and slept in it, and he motored off on his jet ski at any sign of a major swell. Rusty, meanwhile, had devoted himself to travel. He continued to prove his worth as one of the world's hardest-charging barrel riders, but he spent time building a house on a plot of land he bought in Mexico. He took up organic gardening. He fully immersed himself in the slow pace of travel. There's no discord, Greg says, just two brothers pursuing divergent interests.

For his part, 2008's big wave season (which Greg turned into a twelve-month-out-of-the-year affair) was a coming-out party for Greg, an announcement of his solo tour, and a vindication.

The defining moment of that year, no doubt, came in January 2008, when Greg, along with Grant "Twiggy" Baker, Parsons, and Gerlach, braved a bracing storm and 15-foot seas to head out to Cortes Bank and surf the biggest waves anybody had ever seen. Getting to that moment was vintage Greg Long.

Twiggy was in San Francisco, hanging out after a Mavericks session, when Greg told him to get to SoCal in a hurry. Baker

Long, earning yet another Billabong XXL Global Big Wave Awards nomination, charges off the bottom of a 65-footer at Dungeons, Capetown, South Africa.
PHOTO © AL MACKINNON/BILLABONGXXL.COM

couldn't reconcile Greg's enthusiasm with the fact that throughout northern California power lines were down and the forecast called for only more storm. He came anyway.

Greg and Parsons saw something they liked in a forecast that called for one fierce storm to die with another one directly on its back. It looked like there might be a small, slight window of time that they could surf between the two storms. One hundred five miles out to sea. Alone.

Today Long recalls thinking that there was only a 30 percent chance that he'd surf that day, but the risk paid off. "I'll remember that day until I die," he says. "I'll tell that story to my grandkids, even if it wasn't the smartest thing I've ever done. If you wrote it in a column—safe versus unsafe—there was nothing really telling you to go out there. If one of us had wiped out at that top peak and had to take a couple waves on the head—I

At Mavericks in 2008, Long hefts the winner's check, which he later splits with his fellow finalists.

don't know if you'd find us. The whole inside of the reef that day was Armageddon if you fell."

A week after the score at Cortes, Long drove his oversized van up to Mavericks and won the Mavericks surf contest, checking another accomplishment off his list.

And yet, while he was as intrinsically satisfied as he can remember being in his surf career, he was beginning to worry. He wasn't making any money, and he couldn't get a sponsor. He and Rusty had gotten dumped from the OP surf team along with the rest of OP's athletes when that company was sold in late 2006. For a year and a half, Long, who had cemented himself as one of the top three big wave surfers in the world—at the height of the big wave surfing boom, no less—had as his only sponsor a sandal company.

And it wasn't for lack of trying. Greg had taken meetings with every major surf brand during that time—many of them two and three times—and had still found it all but impossible to get a deal. On this point, though, Greg was pragmatic: "Kelly Slater, Mick Fanning, Andy and Bruce Irons—they're the surfers that are selling boardshorts. I like my trunks high and tight so they don't get caught, not below the knee. Nobody's going to look at me and go, 'Wow, Greg Long wears those shorts. I want a pair.'"

Greg thought about going back to school, getting a job. But he fended it off. He spent all of his savings, and when he was about to make a rash decision, the Mavericks contest money (about nine grand, which could have been thirty had Greg not suggested splitting it with the other contestants at the start of the final heat) bought him some more time.

"I know I could've signed a couple of different deals throughout the year but far below what I would have felt comfortable letting them use my image for. I'm a pretty proud individual, and I wouldn't have felt right selling myself short."

His solution? Keep surfing, keep doing what he loved, and let the money work itself out. And it did. In June 2008, Greg finally broke through, signing a deal with Billabong that has made him a very happy big wave surfer. Not that he was around to enjoy it. He was off to South Africa to spend the winter surfing Dungeons and other breaks on the African coast, where he scored yet again some of the biggest waves anybody had seen down there.

Which brings us to this moment. What's next for Greg Long is fairly obvious: His life, for the foreseeable future, will be dictated by swell models and the search for big waves at the cost of almost anything else. And he'll continue to be a refreshing dose of pure stoke in an increasingly misbegotten big wave world.

"This is my absolute passion in life," he says. "Surfing big waves. And it's my personal goal to be on every big swell at the best place at the best possible time. The way I rationalize it is simple—I mean, what else am I going to do?"

Dylan Fish but hardly out of water
at Thundercloud Reef, Fiji
PHOTO © ERIKAEDER.COM

ALMOST TOO BIG TO COMPREHEND

California. September 1939. A hurricane originating off the coast of Panama broke away from the standard northwest storm track and became the only tropical storm to ever make land in California, heading straight into Long Beach. The day it made landfall, forecasters had predicted clouds but no heavy weather, and the storm went completely unnoticed until it brushed past San Diego—killing thirty-nine people in a deluge of rain, wind, and waves. Surfers had a heads-up, as a rising swell moved out in front of the storm.

A few hours before the rain hit, PVSC (Palos Verde Surf Club) member LeRoy Grannis drove to Malibu with some friends and later recalled that the surf was well overhead, rising, and much louder than usual, thanks to a vaultlike atmospheric stillness. The waves came up steadily. By noon, only a half-dozen surfers were left in the water, and they were streaking the entire length of the point on double-overhead set waves, all the way to the end of Malibu Pier. Then a gale-force southerly wind hit and chopped the waves to bits. Grannis and a friend were the last two surfers in the water; when the other surfer lost his board, the two men draped themselves over Grannis's plank just outside the lineup, paddled in as best they could during a lull, and allowed themselves to be churned to the beach by the next set of waves.

Another swell arrived on Thanksgiving Day, out of the west, and big enough that a Santa Barbara surfer at one point counted thirteen distinct and simultaneously breaking lines of whitewater lined up in rows. A New Year's Eve swell was just as big, maybe bigger.

LeRoy Grannis sat this last one out. At twilight on January 31, 1940, LeRoy walked to the end of the pier in Hermosa Beach, just north of Palos Verdes, leaned against the vibrating guardrail, and watched astounded as a school of dolphins torpe-doed through the interior of a huge incoming swell. As the wave fringed, the dolphins all broke the surface at once, arced through the cold air, then disappeared back into the water ahead of the whitewater explosion.

This was how the sport was actually proportioned. The surfer wasn't anywhere near the center of the action. In fact, he stood at the feathered edge of something too big to see—almost too big to comprehend.

—From *The History of Surfing,* by Matt Warshaw

Ian Walsh and the late Sion Milosky
all caught up in the lip at Peahi

PHOTO © ERIKAEDER.COM

A SEARCHING AND FEARLESS MORAL INVENTORY

by Kimball Taylor

Anybody who had witnessed Darryl "Flea" Virostko riding Mavericks in the biggest, gnarliest conditions could see that he was a wild man in the water; one look at the leopard-spot dyed hair and Santa Cruz homeboy tats gave you an idea of how wild he was on land. Over the year prior to the events of this story, Virostko averaged a half-gallon of vodka a day. This massive consumption was made possible by the "sparks": smoking crystal methamphetamine four or five times daily, sometimes more. But until ace surf journalist Kimball Taylor broke pro surfing's long-standing code of silence with this unflinching Surfer *magazine profile, the world had no idea just how wild—and ultimately how self-destructive—Flea's ride has been.*

Thirty-seven-year-old big wave champion Darryl "Flea" Virostko and I stood on a cliff above the gray North Pacific. The wind howled.

The surf spot we'd come to check folded in upon itself far below. Flea unburied his golf bag from the bed of his Toyota Tundra. Barely two years old, the pickup belched white smoke, bled steering fluid, and ran unevenly on seven of its eight cylinders. The right-hand door and mirror were mangled from when Flea was driving wasted and side-swiped a tree. "Tow Fag" was etched on the windshield by Morro Bay groms unaware they slandered the current poster boy for the Eddie, the world's most prestigious paddle-in contest.

The truck's interior was brimming with remnants of his former three-bedroom house. No longer able to make his mortgage, he'd lost big by selling during a recession and paying back taxes but still stood to pocket a fraction of his principal. Waiting on that check was tough duty. Flea, his girlfriend, and their two dogs had spent time living out of the truck. They'd recently found a cabin in the hills above Santa Cruz, but they might be hiking in and out of there. Letters tossed on the floorboard of the Tundra threatened repossession.

We took turns driving balls into the wind. Flea knew the surf would be crap, yet activities were essential—hiking in the woods, building a dam in a creek bed, smashing golf balls into the sea— anything to occupy his mind. There was surfing, too, but these days he might catch a wave or two, whereas in years past his sessions could stretch through night and day.

Three-time consecutive winner of the Mavericks big wave event, Flea was closing in on four months' sobriety in a twelve-step program. Hovering somewhere between steps 4 ("a searching and fearless moral inventory") and 5 ("admitting . . . to another human being the exact nature of our wrongs"), Flea somehow remained buoyant. There were the darker moments, of course, and the just plain being-Flea moments—like rolling down the windows to blare "Eastside fags" and getting in the face of a Steamer Lane surfer who'd been dropped in on by one of Flea's buddies and had the gall to raise his arms in protest. Despite "slips" of such public posturing, the candor with which he now framed his life was courageous to the point of endearing.

This was a mission. Rambling upcoast from Santa Cruz, Flea was determined to assemble his story and drop straight in on his fifth step—to get it all out and come clean. He'd been high for the last big chunk of his life, so the details and the sequence were fuzzy, but not the painful bottom line.

"My contracts were up," he said. "The recession hit. And I was, basically . . . a drug addict."

Over the past year he'd averaged a half-gallon of vodka a day. First thing every morning, if he'd slept at all, was to grab a

Gatorade, pour out half and top it off with vodka. His "little sipper" accompanied all his surf checks. This massive consumption was made possible by the "sparks": smoking crystal methamphetamine four or five times daily, sometimes more. On the morning of the '07–'08 Mavericks event, Flea hadn't slept a wink. Surfing high was nothing new, nor did it boost his game. He fell out in the first round.

During the paddle-out for this year's Mavericks opening ceremony, when asked by Jeff Clark to say something to celebrate the event, Flea said, "My name is Flea, and I'm an alcoholic." His battle with methamphetamine—a substance that's plagued an entire generation of Santa Cruz surfers—has remained the gorilla in the room for most of the past decade.

"It got dark up here. Dark, dark, dark. . . . It got grim," said former WCT competitor Adam Replogle. "The partying started in high school and continued on, until that *substance* hit."

That January afternoon, Flea and I visited another white rock cliff just down the coast, nicknamed "90 Degrees" because the track descending to the beach is vertical for over 100 feet. At the bottom of the goat trail is a mangle of steel, the only remains of a pier that serviced the nearby cement factory. Last year Flea was partying on the beach with other friends. In the early evening, while climbing the cliff trail with his dog, about two-thirds of the way up, in response to a friend yelling down from up top, Flea gazed upward, grew dizzy and blacked out.

Witnesses say his body completed a full backflip before striking dirt and stone. He eventually found himself sprawled on the metal leftover from the pier—60 feet below. His arm was shattered and his face cut up, blood streaming down in dark ribbons. Once he came to, he went to scale the cliff once more, but friends stopped him and called for a medevac. Flea recuperated in a nearby hospital for four days. "I was dead," he said. "I mean, I should have been."

When we visited the white cliff overlook on our upcoast tour, he pointed down at the ledge far below. I descended, expecting him to follow, but Flea Virostko wouldn't budge.

"So you're not coming down?" I asked.

"No way. I haven't been down since."

The cliff is impressively steep. It's difficult to imagine a human being surviving such a ragdoll fall to the gathering of steel below. I considered this drop in terms of Mavericks at its biggest. Perhaps Flea hadn't bailed from such altitude while paddle-in surfing, but he must have pitched from even greater heights while towing in. He soberly remembered the perils of his storied Mavericks career: "I know that every time I paddle out at Mavs, I'm going to get worked bad at least once. It's just part of the program. There are guys who won't face that fact, but they're fooling themselves."

Now recovering from his own addictions, Peter Mel recalled that when high on meth and surfing maxed-out Mavericks, he could take two-wave hold-downs, pop up, and never think through the baptism of death he'd just endured. Sober, he said, those hold-downs "sit with you. They haunt you."

I looked up to Flea's head peaking over the cliff's edge and hollered, "You ever fallen from a wave at this height?"

"Yeah," he said, "I've probably bailed from this far at least."

Amazingly, Flea's fall was not his "rock bottom" moment. After the hospital stay he spent a couple of weeks "only drinking." Then he was back on the "program," a word that can mean a serious athletic regimen or a spell swilling hard liquor and binging on the meth pipe. In the cases of some of the world's most elite big wave surfers, the term meant both.

Despite the fallout from surfing massive waves while feeding addictions equally huge, "rock bottom" remains a fleeting experience. Seeking a contrast, I considered Flea's fleeting years of glory. Santa Cruz surfers are often late bloomers in the cash game. At twenty, after a disenchanting attempt to relocate to the North

Shore, Flea secured his first paying endorsement deal as an aerial phenom. This was the early '90s, and the agreement paid $200 a month, a stipend he supplemented with work as an apprentice plumber. That same year, Vince Collier, a local charger who'd made inroads into professional surfing, began introducing young Santa Cruz rippers to the scene 58 miles north at Mavericks. Flea's performance surfing then merged with a rare fearlessness for the bigger realm, the optimum combination. "He wasn't afraid," said Hawaiian big wave vet Brock Little. "And he was super talented."

Collier can only be praised for introducing the best young surfers from Santa Cruz to the next big deal in surfing. Yet, Collier partied as hard as he surfed, which served as another kind of introduction for the area's youth. "There were two polar influences growing up in Santa Cruz," said Replogle. "Richard Schmidt, clean and sober. And then there was Vince Collier." Flea famously tells the story of his first go out at Mavs as a twenty-year-old, and the half tab of acid that he'd dropped an hour before. As the acid kicked in, Collier drove him up to Mavericks and ushered him into the lineup. In the early days, such a story only magnified Flea's reputation as a badass.

Peter Mel, who rose alongside Flea in the most important generation of big wave chargers since Pat Curren and Greg Noll, pointed to Flea's paddling ability as a prime factor in his success. Whatever the ingredients—boldness, rare athleticism, or paddling skill—Flea sufficiently harnessed his talents to dominate in a lineup of committed surfers pushing the boundaries of big wave paddle surfing. He won the inaugural Mavericks event in 1999 (earning 98 of 100 points on a single ride) and backed it up with another victory in 2000, and when the contest failed to run a few years due to small surf, Flea returned in '04 to beat world champion Kelly Slater in the final for a third consecutive win. By comparison, no surfer has won the Eddie even twice. Financially and emotionally, Flea considered this the height of his career. Until late last year, these

Flea Virostko outrunning the
avalanche at Mavericks
PHOTO © ROBERT BROWN

legendary performances buoyed his market value, and he pulled down ten to twelve grand a month in endorsement pay.

Eighteen years and a harrowing hellman career beyond his first session at Mavericks, much of that success seemed to have vanished through a glass pipe. After his hospital stay and return to drugs, Flea's broken arm failed to heal, and the arm went gimpy—a debilitating injury for a surfer known for his paddling prowess. By fall of '08, friends and family gathered for a surprise intervention. It wasn't the first one, but this time it stuck.

"What was Flea's bottom moment?" asked Mel. "Walking into a room and seeing all of those faces, that's what it was. Everyone's bottom occurs when you realize you're not just killing yourself, that you're affecting the people who love you—because the people who love you are the last ones to leave."

The night before committing to rehab, Flea smoked speed and drank through the wee hours. He emptied the tobacco from a pack of cigarettes, combined it with weed, and repacked the cigarettes to smuggle in. On arrival, he blew a .28 on the Breathalyzer, a sometimes-fatal blood alcohol count. Even though his girlfriend accompanied him, inside the facility Flea announced his presence with, "Where are all the bitches?" The staff pounced, quickly discovering the weed cigarettes. And because of his hammered state, they pushed a little red detox pill on him, chemically landing the high-flyer to the ground.

By January, more than one hundred days sober, filling out physically and surfing again, Flea appeared to be growing younger. He busied himself rebuilding a life, a big part of which was work on an ambitious new plan that just might set things right.

"Still," he said, "I wish I would have felt like this ten years ago. I think there would have been a lot more success than there was."

The meth epidemic gained a hold on Santa Cruz County around 2002, and by 2005 more than half of the local sheriff's arrests were meth-related. A 2007 *Santa Cruz Sentinel* piece estimated that the epidemic still hadn't peaked. Housewives, people with day jobs, and teenagers were caught up in it. Although members of Santa Cruz's big wave community fit a sheriff's study of dominant users—male, Caucasian, over twenty-five—as professional athletes at least midway through their careers (supported by contracts largely dependent on their public images), the decision to begin using made no sense.

"Bottom line, doing drugs was just fun and acceptable among my friends," Flea said.

"You add what we were doing [surfing big waves] on top of that, and we were high—lit up like marlins on a double shot," said Mel, two years sober at the start of the year.

Flea and Mel had shared nearly everything—from doing solitary go-outs at Mavs in which they traded bombs, spun under lips, and pushed the sport further in singular rides to chasing the raucous surf party into addiction. More than once they ended up surfing giant waves while high. "Fuckin' crazy," Mel admitted, his face in his hands.

"We were a peer group. We all pushed each other in whatever we did," he said. "We spent a lot of time together, surfed every session together, called each other every morning. Who got the best barrel? Did the biggest air? Who's partying the hardest? We were pushing each other, but we weren't helping each other. We partied, and it seemed innocent at the time. But it got out of hand, and then some drugs came out that took a hold of us. The drugs that brought me to my knees are the same drugs that brought Flea to his knees. It just took him a little longer to figure it out."

The addiction, in fact, would end up fracturing the peer group. While still using, Mel said that he began to hear voices. He became paranoid. He thought that his home was under surveillance, that "they" were listening to him. Mel eventually acted on his psychosis by cutting the cable lines to his house, which, in his mind, sealed the listeners out. "It [meth] basically made me crazy. I was crazy—losing it," he said. This was a low moment but not the bottom. Mel last used with Flea. He remembered staying up tossing around the idea that he would actually move in with Flea and that they would come clean together. In hindsight, it was just another attempt at hatching a plan to keep using.

"I knew in my heart that that wasn't going to work."

Mel finally realized that his immediate family was "not going to take any more of it." He outed himself to his extended family and thereby began a path toward recovery. "My love for my family is what turned me around and brought me back. That and the twelve-step program." Yet, there were high costs.

"The drug doesn't leave you," said Mel. "You have to keep working on it. I had to disconnect myself from all the things that led me down that road. I had to stop seeing my other family [his close friends]. When I first started getting clean, that was the hardest thing I had to do." Other than supporting Flea at a recent meeting, Mel hadn't really communicated with him in two years.

One of the things that allowed them to keep using, Mel believed, is that drug use is not talked about in the surf world—and this unwillingness to address the issue eventually hurts the grommets. "The kids know. Nat Young and those kids know. Maybe the parents don't, but the kids are talking. But no one [in the media] wants to touch it."

Flea's sponsorship pretty much dried up early last year, so he hasn't much to lose there. Quiksilver continued to sponsor Mel. Socially and financially, it was not an easy decision to talk. And yet a major part of the twelve steps is providing service to the community, helping those who need it, and offering the "experience, strength, and hope" that only recovering addicts can. That and a very tough form of honesty.

Mel admitted, "I'm embarrassed by the things I did. I'm so embarrassed I don't even want to talk about it. There's a quote. But what's the cure? To communicate about it. And that's what Flea is doing."

If a surfer is injured at Jaws,
there are only two ways out:
by air or by sea.

Without forewarning, Flea drove me to another spot on our coastal tour. Wedged into a wooded canyon that leads to a private beach and the same towering white cliffs, there lay a ranch owned by family friends. Flea's esteem for the place was obvious. He knew where to find a fossilized tree buried in a creek, a kind of stone comprised of oil that would actually burn, an abandoned tree house nearly invisible from the ranch. There was a good break on the south end of the beach. On the north end he pointed to ancient shells gathered in bands of the cliff face. Flea didn't mention that the ranch was for sale nor the grander possibilities he saw in it as he detailed its qualities. I wouldn't learn until later that instead of an expected return to the well-paid ranks of surfing, Flea's ambition was a pie-in-the-sky idea he saw himself developing here at the ranch.

The entire impetus for coming clean—and for this article, in fact—was a plan for community service Flea had been in the midst of creating with wetsuit manufacturer Jack O'Neill and Santa Cruz big wave pioneer Richard Schmidt. The working name was "Fleahab." It proposed to serve surfers and athletically minded addicts through a twelve-step program while restoring the body and connecting with nature—"Using the ocean as a healer," as Schmidt put it. This idea contrasted sharply to Flea's experience of rehab, which lacked physical activity. Further, though, Flea envisioned a special program capable of connecting with the ethos of "Surf City."

The three would-be founders met early this year at O'Neill's home overlooking Pleasure Point. At eighty-six years old, O'Neill's awareness of drug culture and its aftermath is long and personal. He'd experienced the '60s counterculture through his children as well as many of the surfers he met since opening his shop in 1959. "The surfers, especially in the beginning, were always adventurous guys—and they tried everything, too. Some of them got stuck, you wouldn't see them anymore," O'Neill said, later adding, "It's extremely disturbing when your kids get involved."

As well as a longer view of history, O'Neill offered his financial power and business acumen to the planned rehab. Schmidt offered his organizational expertise in running camps as well as his more recent experience with interventions. Flea offered life's experience, counseling, and name. "There's a big, big need for this," O'Neill said, "and I think Flea can really do something. You've got to have been there in order to impress these guys and gain a following."

Mel, however, openly worried that Flea was taking a lot on his shoulders for someone just a few months sober. "I'm two years sober," Mel said, "and I struggle every day. Sometimes it's more than enough work trying to save yourself." He did add, however, that accountability, responsibility to others, and service to the community might just be the things to serve in Flea's recovery.

After our tour of the coast, life grew a bit tougher for Flea. He learned that back taxes on his house would virtually clean him out. And a hoped-for sponsorship deal failed to materialize. Still, sponsorship or not, Flea was invited to the Mavericks event and the Eddie, and he knew he would be present and clearheaded when they ran. His dream of creating a rehab moved slowly, but the ranch was still a possibility. He said that recent hardships wouldn't drive him to use again but that "It's hard to suck up sometimes. Getting clean and all that shit is good, but it gets harder as I go. There's wreckage."

And yet Flea has taken hold-downs before, sucked it up, and paddled back out.

Billabong XXL Global Big Wave Awards nominee
Shane Dorian at Peahi, on what many are calling
the biggest wave ever paddled into.
PHOTO © BATEL SHIMI/BILLABONGXXL.COM

SURVIVING DECEMBER 1ST, 1969

by Ted Gugelyk

Of all the legendary big swells in surfing history, nothing stands above what has come to be known as "the Swell of '69." Generated by the largest storm system ever recorded in the northwest Pacific Ocean—at one point the humongous low-pressure system covered most of the North Pacific Basin—massive waves hit the Hawaiian Islands on December 1, with the brunt of the swell focusing on the North Shore of Oahu. For all its size, not much surfing was done during the episode—too stormy, too big, too out of control—but that didn't mean that this swell of swells didn't impact surfers' lives. In fact, surf mythology has it that the wave Greg Noll rode at Makaha that day was so big that, not long afterward, he quit surfing forever. He'd found the summit of surfing's possibilities. More than forty years later, the September 2010 issue of The Surfer's Path *featured a detailed account of the swell from fellow North Shore veteran Ted Gugelyk, one of those caught up in the maelstrom, the power of which stands the test of time.*

Sunset Beach, North Shore of Oahu, Hawaii, USA

November 30, 1969, Sunday. We had perfect, small, glassy North Shore waves. Not bigger than 4 feet. Pupukea was breaking in front of Fred Van Dyke's house. Lots of fellows were out, all of them my friends. But no surfing for me. The next day, Monday, December 1, 1969, was my Important Day.

I was nervous about it, so I spent that weekend preparing hard. My first official seminar, a discussion for public health professionals and academics at the University of Hawaii's School of Public Health, where I had a part-time position as a researcher, working on my PhD in sociology. My topic was *leprosy stigma and prejudice*. The question I was working on was, *"Why did patients afflicted with leprosy all around the world avoid treatment and very often confine themselves to the former leprosy 'colonies' like Kalaupapa on Molokai?"* There Hawaiian leprosy patients lived in isolation, in a self-imposed prison. Leprosy patients all over the world did the same thing. Why?

So . . . no time to think about surfing.

There was a slight onshore wind, and I was in a sweat. Through the wall of intense concentration I was aware that a high surf warning had been issued. Nothing new about that. They said very big surf was coming. How big, they couldn't predict. In those days, ships at sea fed information to the Hawaiian Weather Bureau, and satellite images were in their infancy. No TV reception yet on the North Shore either. Big surf coming. That's all we knew.

Our home, on Ke Iki Road at Sunset Beach, was located northeast of Sharks Cove and the Sunset Beach fire station, halfway between Waimea Bay and Sunset. The house was adjacent to a lava peninsula jutting out 400 yards straight into the Pacific Ocean. Off that lava peninsula there was an extreme drop-off into deep blue water, 30 feet down, then deeper.

East of the peninsula the sandy beach fell off quickly into deep water.

The area was notorious for a horrendous and deadly shorebreak. No surfing there. That shorebreak was worse than the one at Waimea Bay. When the surf was up, it offered top-to-bottom explosions onto shallow sand and lava. Each year unwary tourists and Vietnam-bound soldiers from Schofield Barracks died there, bodies never found.

That beachbreak was a beast, an ugly, voracious maw of a wave, and living next door to it was like living next to some wild beast, avoided at all costs. When the beast was awake, we heard the roar. Our little cottage shook, windows rattling.

Life in that house was good. One could say I had it all. I was thirty-one years old, I had a professional future in academia, two lovely little daughters and a gorgeous Hawaiian-Chinese wife, and a house on the North Shore, a stone's throw from the Pacific Ocean. What more could a young man ask for?

Big Monday

1:00 a.m. Monday, December 1. Startled awake by the beast lashing out in our direction. Waves were rolling over the lava peninsula, hitting our seawall and rattling the house. We were just 20 feet above sea level, and that seawall was the only thing between us and the ocean.

But big waves were nothing new. They happened all the time. Twenty-foot waves breaking top to bottom onto 3 feet of water just outside the house? That was my nighttime signal—Waimea would be breaking, for sure Sunset Beach. I tried to sleep but couldn't.

My family was already up when sunrise exposed an ominous scene: a gray mist of sea spray, a fog so thick you couldn't see 200 yards. How big were the waves? No telling. We could only hear the roar all around us. The air was thick with saltwater, to me a familiar odor that led to apprehension, something I always felt before surfing big Waimea.

5:30 a.m. Hot black coffee. I packed my papers, kissed my wife and young daughters goodbye, and off I went in my VW Bug, headed for Honolulu and my Important Day. Leaving the house, I thought my wife looked worried. Scared. She was Hawaiian, and she had a profound respect for the sea and nature. But I was a surfer. That earth-trembling roar just meant there was a challenge for me out at sea that day—albeit one I couldn't rise to on this the first day of my professional life. But today some lucky guys would get great waves. Movies! Photography! A moment of fame. Memories for a lifetime. But not me.

Waimea Bay—Heading to work in Honolulu, I took the old Kamehameha Highway toward Haleiwa. As I came to Waimea my windshield wipers were on, the spray was thick and wet, obscuring my view. Five or six surfers stood on the east cliff surveying the scene. Nothing unusual there. But it was right then that the morning seemed to turn surreal. In the mist I couldn't make out who the people were. Strangers? In those days, we knew everyone who surfed the North Shore. These fellows wore hooded sweatshirts, hoods up over their heads. They looked like gray monks in the dawn gloom, members of some mysterious society—the society of surfers pondering whether they should chance it and paddle into the maelstrom. I had no doubt what they saw. But would they paddle out? And who were they, anyway?

I wondered in passing, but my mind was absorbed with research data, my presentation, the people I needed to impress, and how best to impress them.

I don't remember driving past Haleiwa or into Honolulu or onto the Manoa campus at the University of Hawaii. I remember my desk in the School of Public Health and then late in the afternoon, one hour before my seminar, a surprise phone call from my wife. She had fear in her voice. "Waves are coming under our house," she told me. The whitewater had washed our lawn furniture down to the bottom of the property; she was worried she wouldn't be able to get the girls out of the house; the neighbors had left, and the fire department was driving up and down the highway, loudspeakers blaring, telling people to get to high ground.

"People are evacuating," she said. "Come home."

Again, my memory goes blank. I must have cancelled the seminar. My secretary later told me I did. I know I grabbed my notes, my picture slides, and camera and raced for the parking lot.

5:30 p.m. Afternoon traffic. Even in 1969 Honolulu traffic was bad. Oahu is a small island, and at the time 700,000 people lived there. Bumper to bumper from Honolulu all the way up to Wahiawa, up to the pineapple plains above Honolulu leading north, back to the North Shore. I drove like a maniac.

Fighting traffic, in my mind I heard over and over again the fear in my wife's voice and my little daughters crying in the background. This was serious. Why did I even leave the house this morning? What was I thinking? How big was that surf? I knew. It was too big. A nightmare. I punched the steering wheel.

Then I remembered those hooded people standing in the mist at Waimea. Perhaps they somehow signaled this dreaded event—like ominous spirits, a menacing omen I hadn't heeded. Nor had I listened to my own common sense.

By 1969 I had been living in Hawaii for twelve years and surfing Waimea since 1958. I knew the place. I knew it wasn't to be trifled with or underestimated. The sea is a living thing with many personalities. It can turn angry, violent, and when it does we must keep our distance, use our heads, and let it have its way. Which meant I should have stayed home and looked after my family on that day. But I was absorbed with my professional ambitions and ignored the warnings.

Driving north, dizzy with anxiety, I felt guilty and furious at myself.

Haleiwa. I couldn't see the town coming down from Wahiawa. Usually there's a beautiful view of Haleiwa Bay, all the way from Kaena Point, the westernmost point of the North Shore, and east almost up to Laniakea. But not today. That salt fog was a heavy blanket, and it was turning dark. Night was coming.

As I reached the bottom of the hill before Haleiwa I could smell it. Nasty. The smell of saltwater mingled with earth and overflowing septic tanks. Saltwater, human excrement, and a whiff of gasoline.

Road blocks. The police stopped me. I showed them my ID and explained that my family was at home waiting for me. The policeman shook his head and said, "You can go, but you're risking your life." He waved me on.

I couldn't see the highway clearly. Whitewater had spilled over the Haleiwa boat harbor, and sand and coral covered the roadway.

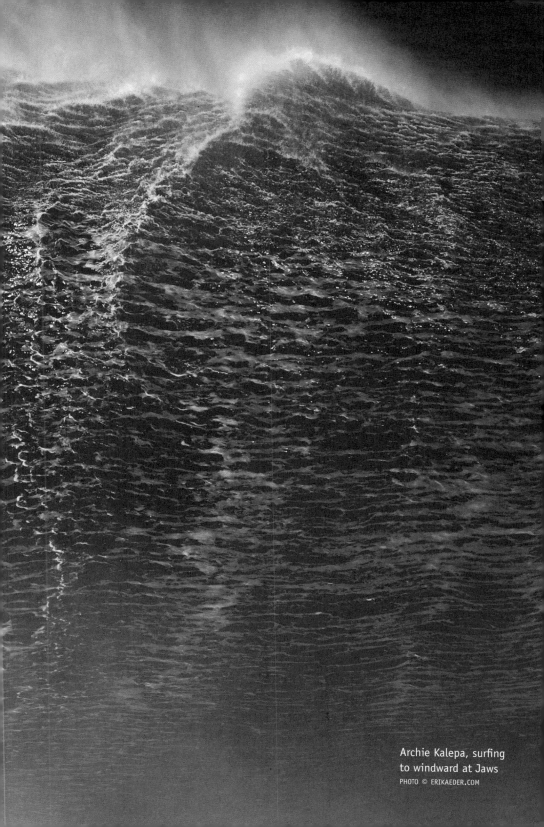

Archie Kalepa, surfing
to windward at Jaws
PHOTO © ERIKAEDER.COM

I made it to the Haleiwa bridge and slowly rolled over the waves. Whitewater was breaking into the Haleiwa River, soaking the bridge, the road top splashed with sand. Amazing. How big were these waves? I'd never seen anything like that before.

There were no other cars on the road, only me. Past the bridge, fire trucks were parking uphill from the highway, their signal lights flashing red and yellow. A fireman stopped me and asked where I was going. I explained and he said, "I don't think you can make it around Waimea Bay, and Laniakea is under water, so good luck."

It was getting dark. I felt fear. I realized this was a life-and-death situation. I must hurry. Drive faster.

My VW Bug skidded through pools and around rocks all the way up to Laniakea. Nobody else was driving in the cloudy darkness of night. I pushed that little car as fast as I could, spinning the tiny wheels as I headed to Waimea. Once past Laniakea the land ran to Waimea Point. Somehow I made it, but in my rearview mirror I saw whitewater as high as the car rolling in behind me. Luck was with me, but what about my wife and daughters?

Waimea Bay. At the top of the hill looking down into the bay, firemen stopped me and said, "No way you can get around the bay. It's too big, brother, the road's closed. There *is* no road."

"But my family. I have to get to them," I explained.

"Where are they?"

I told them, and someone said, "My god. They should have left this morning."

"I'm going!" I shouted. And no one stopped me. It was my life.

Again, I was lucky. The VW skidded, slipped and slid through sand, rocks, and water. I could only guess where the road was. Luckily the highway markers were still standing, and the light poles were standing and lit. My headlights on, windshield wipers going full blast, I drove through the spray to the bottom of Waimea Bay. Again, somehow, I made it through during a lull in the surf and on toward Waimea Catholic Church. Above the bay I noticed for the first time that the roar of the waves was deafening.

I raced for home. Past the fire station. Again police and firemen tried to stop me, but I drove through them like a man possessed, up to Ke Iki Road, made a left turn, and drove to the lava peninsula upon which stood our home. Amazingly, the lights were on.

But I could hear my wife screaming hysterically, almost like an animal sound—trapped, with nowhere to go. I could hear her, but I couldn't see her. My children were also crying for me, and all these noises were almost smothered by the roar of the surf. It was breaking over our seawall and then rolling under our home and down to the driveway. All around me there was salt spray and a dirty brown mist, a thick fog, and I found myself struggling against hip-deep water up toward our house. As I did, my Volkswagen Bug began to float away toward the Kamehameha Highway, toward the mountains.

Finally I struggled up to the house and found my family clinging to one another, a kind of disbelief and horror in their eyes. We were alone. Everyone else had evacuated long ago, and it was almost too late to escape—just us, stuck in the dark of night, without a car, and the ever-rising waves.

Then my mind went blank again. All I remember was walking to the ocean side of our home. There was no lawn, just sand and coral. The spotlights were on and turned toward the ocean, illuminating our Hawaiian foliage. There were palm trees 15 feet high planted beside our seawall. And thick *naupaka*, *milo* trees, and bamboo 15 to 20 feet tall. And heavy, strong *lauhala* (*pandanus*). I had planted these as wave breaks to protect our home from high surf. What a naïve thought. Those beautiful plants could never protect us from what was still to come that night.

For some inexplicable reason I didn't immediately rush my family to high ground. Another mistake. Maybe I was in shock. What I did next was to get some plywood and start nailing it against our sliding glass windows facing the sea. While I was hammering I heard a roar louder than all the rest, and what I saw will always remain with me. I saw something impossible.

The roar sounded like a jet taking off, and with it came a wall of whitewater at least 15 feet above my palm trees. It came so suddenly, so forcefully. I do not remember exactly what happened next. An explosive crash, breaking glass, and I went blank. I was swept off the ocean-side veranda, away from our house. I found myself down by our driveway, 100 feet away from the home. I remember struggling through hip-deep whitewater, forcing myself against it, uphill back to the house. Our yard had turned into a shorebreak.

My wife was screaming. She and my daughters had been swept through the plate-glass doors on the mountain side of the home. My youngest daughter lay beneath the home's broken wooden-frame wall and under a plate-glass window. I could see blood gushing from my wife's arms and legs. My little daughter. I pulled on the wood, trying to lift part of a wall off and get her out from under the broken glass window frame, certain that another wave would come and hit us soon.

We got her free. Her tiny head was covered with blood. Her eyes stared big and wide at us, and she was completely silent. Shock.

Somehow we got ourselves to the Sunset Beach fire station at Sharks Cove. I'll never know quite how. They had set up an emergency center and were tending to other injured people. They immediately started treating our wounds, my daughters and wife first. We were all cut up by glass, deep cuts. All the while, there was the roar of the sea at Sharks Cove.

Suddenly the firemen told us to evacuate the fire station. They feared the waves would destroy it, and they needed to get us all to higher ground. Immediately.

I don't remember how my wife and daughters were evacuated to Wahiaha Hospital. Helicopter? I doubt it. But I found myself not wanting to leave. I told them to go, but I would stay behind. Why? I can't remember.

I limped to the Sunset Beach Elementary School a quarter of a mile away, the whitewater coming across Kamehameha Highway often reaching up to my knees. The school was perhaps a quarter of a mile inland from the beach, on the Pupukea Pali side of Kamehameha Highway. It was a small wood-frame building. Other people had already gathered there, evacuees, too scared to move. Remarkably, the electricity was still on, and the telephones still worked. I called my wife's mother to tell her what was happening, but the phone went dead.

It was dark. From the beach perhaps a quarter of a mile away I could hear the sound of wood breaking and trees snapping as the surf plowed over homes. Cars were washing up to Kam Highway, some upside down. Police cars and a fire truck were parked beside the elementary school, radios blaring, emergency lights flashing. Then another tremendous roar, and a giant wave, bigger than the rest, exploded on the shore, and perhaps 7 feet of whitewater rushed across the Kam Highway.

It lifted the elementary school off its foundation, and we began floating backward toward the Pupukea Pali. Panic set in. Police and firemen abandoned their vehicles and yelled, "Everyone, up to the Pali, up to the Pali!"

Panicking, too, they seemed sure that the surf was about to inundate all the lands of the North Shore and that the only escape was to get to the escarpment, maybe three-quarters of a mile from the beach—and do what? Climb it? But nothing like this had ever happened before, and who could tell what would happen next?

I'll never forget the sight of brave policemen and firemen running in the dark, away from their vehicles toward the mountains, toward the Pali. Us, no. We stayed in the school and prayed for the best. There were perhaps twelve of us. No one spoke, and now it was pitch black. No lights, only the flashing lights from the emergency vehicles that lay abandoned and now partly underwater. One police car was overturned. All around us were the sounds of terrible roaring surf and splintering wood and crashing walls. The sounds of disaster. And death.

It lasted through the night, but so did we. The elementary school became a floating boat. Up and down, bobbing. Whitewater came in, hit the small wooden building, and then it floated, did circles, then settled down again when the water receded. This happened over and over again throughout that night. How big were those waves pounding the shoreline? We were perhaps 70 feet above sea level, and still we weren't safe. There seemed to be no escape.

Dawn. The waves had receded. The sound of breaking wood and glass became intermittent, then stopped. The policemen and firemen returned to their smashed vehicles. And here again I draw a blank. How did I reunite with my wife and children in Honolulu? I don't remember. And why did I choose to stay and not get out with them? I don't know.

I thank God we survived. Other people didn't. Seven or eight people were killed, though it is a miracle it wasn't more. We survived. We had our lives. All our physical possessions were lost, but most of them could be replaced—though not my lecture notes, study notes, my library of books, my IBM typewriter, my cameras, slides, et al. Years of study and research—gone. Irreplaceable.

A few days later in Honolulu, reunited with my family at my mother-in-law's home, I received my scoldings. She and my wife had a right to be angry. Why did we live there? I had been warned. Hawaiians never lived that close to the sea. Before World War II and after, *haoles* moved in, planted trees, built homes, brought in dirt fill, sand was trapped, a wide beach created, but all artificial. Now the sea took it back. "Only a crazy person, *lolo*, would live there," my wife's mother scolded. She was right.

Years ago the Oahu Railway once took sugarcane around the island, even around Kaena Point, and carried passengers, too. One can still see remnants of those train tracks on the North Shore. My mother-in-law rode that train before the war and saw what was there. It was all lava on the seaside, and indeed, after the high surf, which washed the sand away, we discovered thousands of Hawaiian petroglyphs carved into the lava on the beach. This is how the seaside looked a long time ago. All lava and no homes. The petroglyphs are still there. I'm sure folks who live on the North Shore today see them occasionally after huge swells, but there are many more under the sand—a hidden historical record of the Hawaiian fishermen and farmers who also once called the North Shore home—though their houses, of course, were up toward the Pali.

I took one year off. Leave of absence. I spent the next year rebuilding our home. Mr. Honda, the farmer across the road, loaned me his front loader, and I went up and down Kam Highway gathering up sand to bring back to our land. But there was no land left. Only deep holes down to lava. The sea had washed everything away. I received a Red Cross loan to reconstruct my property—and rebuild my life. Disaster assistance. But I found myself in heavy debt. No flood insurance in those days. And that was the end of my PhD program.

It took me five months to fill those holes where our house once stood. I had suffered a concussion and other minor injuries, but I worked through them. I replaced the *milo, naupaka*, coconut trees, and most of the Hawaiian plants. And it took me another five months to rebuild the house. But the place never looked the same. Not as green. And it was tainted in my mind with bad memories.

The concussion? Perhaps that is why I let my family go and I stayed behind. I have no other explanation for my actions.

Many of our neighbors' homes were also destroyed. They never came back to live there again. They sold them and forgot about North Shore living.

Fred Van Dyke, Jose Angel, and Peter Cole lived east of me. Beach homes also. Their homes suffered minor damage. The Log Cabins, Pupukea, and Kami Land Reef forced the huge surf to break offshore before hitting their land. We had no such reef, thus the horrendous exposure to giant waves.

Then, again I was lucky. The next year after rebuilding the home, I was offered the position of dean of students at Maui Community College, a job I took with much gratitude. We started a new life on Maui. Our Maui home was 3,000 feet above sea level. And that dean position was a stepping-stone to other jobs, international work with the East West Center. I sold the North Shore property with no regret. We just felt lucky to be alive.

On Maui, my students coaxed me into surfing Honolulu Bay in 1970–1971. No one out but us. But I never again surfed big waves, nor did I wish to. I couldn't forget what I saw and experienced that night. December 1, 1969.

2009: Northeast Thailand

Now it is forty years later, and I am retired. After I moved to Maui and became dean of students, my wife and I divorced, and I raised my daughters as a single dad for many years after. My eldest daughter became a teacher. She married a Punahou School athlete, and they have four children. My youngest daughter became a corporate attorney in Honolulu and is now executive director of the Waikiki Community Center. At least I was a good dad, and my children did well as adults. But none of my daughters surfs. Wonder why?

Over ten years ago I married a Thai woman, and we live in northeast Thailand in an area called "Isan" in Ubon Rachathani city. It is a university town. We live on two acres of rural property, high above the Moon River (Mei Nam Mun), which flows into the Mekong River, not far from us. Here I fish, paddle my kayak, grow fruits and vegetables, and swim long distance in Olympic swimming pools. I stay in condition; I am still a waterman, in a way.

I thought I was finished with those appalling surf memories, but I am not. They refreshed themselves here in Thailand. The Phuket or Boxing Day tsunami. No, I wasn't in it, but my friends were.

David Sanaman was from Hanalei, Kauai, and after retiring he built a beautiful beach home in Khao Lak, northeast of Phuket—right where the tsunami did the most damage.

My wife, my eight-year-old step-daughter, and I were invited to David's house party on December 26, 2004. By dumb luck, we didn't make it; 5,321 people were killed in Thailand by the tsunami, among them everyone who attended David's Christmas party.

Four days afterward my wife and I went to Phuket to help look for David's body. What I saw made December 1, 1969, at Sunset Beach look like a rehearsal for greater dreadfulness. There is no stopping the sea. Where once stood resorts, we saw canyons 20 feet deep, holes down into bedrock. Earth and sand and cement buildings swept away and holes down to the Earth's bone layer. But that is another story.

Today I surf Google Earth and look at the homes on the North Shore of Oahu. As my senior surfer-attorney friend Wesley Lau says, "The *haoles* have rebuilt million-dollar homes along the beach, and the ocean is just biding its time to reclaim the shore."

I'm sure there are technical oceanographic explanations for why that surf was so big that night, and there are many explanations about the Boxing Day tsunami. But I know enough about what happened on the North Shore that day and night, just from experiencing it. It was a once-in-a-generation big wave episode, and it will happen again.

The surf still stays with me in my memory—surfing with my friends as a young man. But I know how the sea can turn, and as a senior man I now live a more agrarian rural life and look at my old surfing pictures of Waimea Bay and think, "How did you do that? Why were you crazy enough to do that? And to live there?" But then think I'm glad that I did. It was great fun and in a way a rite of passage to some kind of understanding about the nature of things—how precious life is and how fleeting. And how wonderful.

SCARED SHITLESS

Makaha, prewar. Wave-riding in Hawaii during the late 1930s was still done almost exclusively at Waikiki, where the surf was generally biggest from May to September. Everyone on the beach had a vague understanding that the waves on the north and west sides of the island came up during fall and winter and that they were often bigger, *much* bigger, than anything that hit the southwest-facing reefs at Waikiki. Yet, this was an abstract thought, the way a skier might wonder about snow conditions in the Himalayas. Before the hot curl, surfboards were all but nonfunctional in waves bigger than 6 feet; a surfer paddling boldly into the Castle Break lineup on a summer's afternoon with a 12-foot swell pumping through had every right to think he'd just placed himself at the very back of beyond.

Returning to shore, of course, the surfer was almost tradition-bound to play up the experience. Jack London, after all, had described the Waikiki surf zone as a place filled with "white battalions of the infinite army of the sea." Tom Blake often told the story about Duke Kahanamoku launching into a Castle Break wave that measured "30 feet high," with surface rills hitting the bottom of Duke's board like the "patter of a machine gun." Two or three generations later, Hawaiian surfers, to look cool, would reduce their wave height estimations to such a ridiculous degree that a 15-footer could be offhandedly pegged down to 6 feet. In the 1930s, though, wave measurement was still very much in its golden era of exaggeration.

John Kelly and Wally Froiseth got an early lesson in big wave relativity in late 1937, when they loaded up Kelly's Model T and drove west into the dry coastal outback near Waianae Town. This was an overnight lobster-hunting expedition, so their new hot curl boards were left behind. After parking next to a long, broad crescent of sugar-white sand, they walked north to a rocky intertidal zone, carefully laid a pair of lobster nets, returned to the car, and eventually set out their bedrolls and fell asleep on the beach to the gentle murmur of flat surf.

At 3 a.m. Kelly woke to a kettledrum roar of a new swell, and even in the black-gray duotone of night, he could tell the waves were huge—bigger, thicker, faster, and longer than anything they'd ever ridden in Waikiki. "We went home later that day," Kelly recalled, "and told everybody about what we'd seen, and they all just scoffed. But next time we took our boards, and we had Makaha to ourselves for two or three years."

Oahu's West Side is hemmed in by the towering Waianae Range, and for centuries it had been a badlands. Tribes here, having remained independent when the rest of the islanders unified, were known as Hawaii's best fighters—*Makaha* translates to "fierce"—and missionaries sent to the area were mostly ignored. The Waianae-based community that developed around a nearby sugar plantation was tight-knit and occasionally generous to outsiders but also ghettoized and crime-ridden.

The landscape was dazzling and harsh. Jutting lava-black hillsides gave way to canopied valleys spilling into the island's clearest, bluest ocean water. Less rainfall meant less muddy run-off. This was the last stretch of coast on Oahu to have paved roads. Kelly and Froiseth drove on a graded dirt track from Barber's Point north during their early visits to Makaha, and they were occasionally turned back by an unpassable gully washout.

Makaha's enormous wave field hasn't changed over the decades. With a moderate swell running, three distinct take-off areas are in play, each one good for a playful if somewhat meandering right-slide that terminates, just a few feet off the beach, in a spectacular backwash-generated shorebreak. For spectators, this last feature has become a Makaha favorite: A spent wave rolls up the sandy berm, doubles back, and plows head-on into the next wave. Surfers and boards caught at the moment of impact are often launched like tiddlywinks, 10 feet into the air.

The hot curl surfers enjoyed riding on these kinds of small and midsize days. But in years to come, what they really hoped to find after the long drive from Honolulu—what each succeeding generation of big wave surfers has hoped to find—is something called "Makaha Point Surf": long 10-foot-or-bigger right-breaking waves that start at the top of the point and thunder into the bay for 100 yards or more with no loss in size. In the middle of the bay, where the wave should obligingly spill into a deep-water channel and die, it instead funnels into an end section called the "Bowl," where it fans out like a cobra's head, not only gaining height—10 or more vertical feet in some cases—but also bending in on itself.

The takeoff and middle sections of a Makaha Point Surf wave are twice as powerful as anything found in Waikiki, and the power doubles again at this last stage. Furthermore, as Kelly, Froiseth, and the rest of the hot curlers quickly learned, the speed and steepness of a Point Surf wave mean that it has to be taken as an all-or-nothing proposal. Nine times out of ten, the surfer who manages to race across the Point and deliver himself to the Bowl section fails to negotiate the last 50 yards to the channel; he either sizes things up and ejects voluntarily (by doing a cannonball move off the back of the board or by dropping prone and sledding for the beach) or continues full speed into the Bowl to be overhauled by a dropping cataract of whitewater.

Waianae natives likely rode Makaha in the centuries before Cook's arrival, but nobody knows for sure. The break's only premodern surfer of record is Kuho'oheihei "Abner" Paki, the partially Westernized high chief father of Hawaii's revered Queen Liliuokalani, who rode Makaha during the mid-nineteenth century on a 14-foot, 150-pound *olo* monstrosity.

When Kelly and Froiseth began riding Makaha, they did so believing they were the first. They eased into it. Full-size Point Surf was too much for the early hot curl prototypes, but the Empty Lot Boys were confident in their new equipment and pumped to the gills with immortal teenage swagger. They understood that new big surf techniques were theirs to invent; three or four years later, they were confidently paddling into waves bigger than anything they'd ever seen in Waikiki.

Other Waikiki surfers were curious enough about Makaha to venture out and give it a try, but just a few made it a regular thing. "We'd lose guys in two ways," Froiseth recalled. "We'd drive out there, bragging the whole way about the surf, and it would be totally flat. And they'd say 'Ah, you guys are bullshitting,' and there was nothing to do then but turn around and drive back. The other thing that happened was, the surf would be so goddamned big they'd just sit on the beach, scared shitless, and not go out at all. Same thing. They couldn't wait to get back to Waikiki."

—From *The History of Surfing,* by Matt Warshaw

Shaun Dollar's glory drop on the "wave of the day" at Mavericks. Dramatically played out in Billabong XXL Monster Paddle contests, such efforts underscore a renaissance in paddle-in adventuring.

PHOTO © FRED POMPERMAYER/BILLABONGXXL.COM

BEYOND THE BLUE

as told by Greg Noll

It's one of surfing's greatest tales and one that big wave legend Greg Noll has told often enough: the epic day during the Swell of '69 when Noll, out alone in gigantic Makaha Point Surf, took off on what until only recently was considered the biggest wave ever ridden. But in the many magazines, books, and movies that have chronicled this epoch-ending event, the story almost always stops with Noll catching "the Wave," seldom examining the ride itself and, for the man who rode it, its life-altering consequences.

Once I made the decision to go for *"the Wave,"* I just put my head down and paddled. When I surfed big waves, I had the ability to dump all the side chatter and just go. People have always asked, *"Why'd you paddle for that wave when you knew you were never going to make it?"* But I always believed when you paddle for a big wave, if you start wondering, *Am I gonna make it? Am I gonna do this? Am I in the right spot? Am I blah, blah, blah?* that you tend to hesitate, to stall out and get caught in the top of the wave. And then you're done. So the moment I decided to go, I turned everything off, put my head down, and just went for it.

On these epic waves, once you commit you forget about everything else. You put the nose of the board down, and if the fucking thing's breaking 2 miles in front of you, that's immaterial. You focus everything on catching the wave and getting down the thing. And if you're lucky enough to get down it, to pull your bottom turn and to make it, that's okay. And if you don't, that's okay, too. Except this wave was different.

I can only speak for myself, but that bomb at Makaha was the biggest wave I ever caught, at least 10 feet bigger than anything

Tahitian tube-master Raimana Van Bastolaer emerging
from the spit at Teahupoo on yet another Billabong
XXL Monster Tube ride for the ages.
PHOTO © BEN THOUARD/BILLABONGXXL.COM

I'd ever ridden at Waimea Bay or anywhere else. And it scared the shit out of me. You should understand that Makaha's a whole different ball game—it's like no other big wave out there. Waves like Waimea and Mavericks and Jaws are all concentrated peaks that jump up out of nowhere and grab you. But at Makaha—I'm talking giant Makaha Point Surf—you have to sit there like a goddamned deer in the headlights and watch these monsters come charging down the coast and around Kaena Point. It's intimidating, you know?

Everybody else had already gone in, so I'm sitting out there alone, watching this huge set breaking from Yokohama, all the way down the line. They were like—well, you could easily have stacked two sixteen-wheeler tractor-trailers inside each barrel as they were dropping sections 3 blocks long. And as each wave broke, the concussion made the water droplets dance on the deck of my board. That's power right there.

I'd never, never been in a situation like that. It wasn't like the normal big surf emotion, where I'd go, *Goddamn, this is huge!* then grit my teeth and paddle on through. It was more a mixture of fear and anguish: the fear that I might let this opportunity pass me by because I was a chicken shit. So as the set rolls closer I just put my head down and paddled into what I thought was the channel. And I remember thinking, *Do I really wanna do this shit? Do I really want to find out what's on the other side of the cliff, especially if it means not being able to get back?* And the answer wasn't heroic. It was probably nothing more than picturing myself as some old shit in a wheelchair, lashing the ground with my cane and saying, "*You chicken shit, motherfucker. Why didn't you go for it?*" I wouldn't be able to live with that, so when the set hit the point, I shut everything else off and started paddling. *Hard.*

I got into the wave pretty early, but then the bottom dropped out, and I could see the Bowl lining up all the way to goddamned Waianae. I remember thinking, *Just don't pearl!* That would mean cartwheeling onto my ass and not penetrating the face. Really, my only hope was to get to the bottom on my feet and then look for a place to punch a hole and penetrate. Which is what I did: I got to the bottom and dove off the rail, trying to get as deep as I could while the thing detonated above me. And for a second it was so quiet, I thought I had it made. But this wave was so much thicker, had so much more mass than anything I'd ever experienced, that when the lip finally folded and exploded, I just got pummeled. It swept me along like a leaf. And this wasn't Waimea, where you get drilled hard but bounce down and then ricochet up again. This wave just kept rolling and rolling with me tumbling around inside—I must've been underwater for 100 yards or more when I started to worry a little bit.

When we first started surfing big waves, we'd come busting to the surface after what we thought was a bad wipeout—like when we'd almost be out of breath—and think, *Oh God, I almost drowned.* But the waves kept coming, and we kept riding and getting all this experience, so maybe a year later, say, we'd get held down so long we were seeing stars, and we'd finally burst up to the light and say, *"Christ, I almost drowned."* Then a couple more years and a couple thousand more big waves, and we got washed out past regular stars and started seeing red stars. And we'd say, *"Jesus Christ, I almost drowned."* And this last time we were right.

Of course, we were experiencing the progressive stages of oxygen deprivation and learning to deal with heavier and heavier wipeouts and in the process getting better at surviving hypoxia. Toward the end of my big wave career, if I got held down long enough I could anticipate the different stages. I could almost see what was coming and deal with it. Like, *Okay, here's the thrashing-around stage.* And *Here come the stars,* and then *Hello, red stars.* But under that wave at Makaha, I shot right past the red stars and actually saw blue. Dark blue stars. And I remember thinking, *Uh-oh, I don't want to know what's behind blue.* Because I got a

How deep is too deep? Dan Moore looks for the "doggy door" at Jaws.

Fiji's Cloudbreak has only recently been ridden on the really giant days. Ian Walsh, breaking new ground glimpse, and all I saw was darkness. And luckily it was right at that point that I struggled back up into daylight, back into reality.

Problem was I was still getting the shit beat out of me by the rest of this giant set. I got washed all the way down past Klausmeyers to the east end of the beach at Makaha. I tell you, I barely made it through the thing. Buffalo [Keaulana] was following me in the lifeguard Jeep, as far as he could drive. I could see him off to my left, but there was nothing I could do because the current and the shorepound were ripping sideways so bad I could hardly swim against them. Finally, I staggered out onto the sand about 20 yards from the start of the lava rocks. Had I not gotten out there I'd have been totally screwed. The next sandy beach is 3 miles down the coast, and I never could have made it. Then Buff comes up and stuffs a beer in my hand and says, *"Good ting you make 'em, brudduh, cuz no way I was comin' in afta you."*

So it was a hairball deal start to finish. And you know, that morning, when I went in the water, I thought, *Boy, I'm gonna be surfing until my arms fall off. This is the only life for me!* But that night, after the mist slowly settled, everything in my life settled down as well. I woke up the next day and felt like I could finally go surfing for fun and enjoy my family and eventually go fishing. The monkey was off my back so far as proving anything. I'd ridden a wave at least 10 feet bigger than anything I'd ever ridden before. And I realized I didn't want to know what was way, way out there, beyond the blue. So that's where I left off.

Although the view from inside a giant tube can appear sublime when frozen by the camera's shutter, it's really a wild, violent moment.
PHOTO © RUBEN PEÑA

BEAL'S STASH

by Sam George

It was one of the greatest days in surf history, rendered into the stuff of legends by the fact that its ultimate moment—the giant Makaha Point wave ridden by Greg Noll during the epic winter of 1969—wasn't captured on film. Over thirty years later, however, a chance discovery provided a glimpse of one of the more subtly dramatic moments to occur on that fateful big day.

If you've ever been to Makaha Beach, that classic slice of sea and sand nestled against the Waianae Range on the west side of Oahu, you've probably found yourself wondering about that house. The stylishly designed, opulent home that, when viewed from almost anywhere on Makaha Beach—from the main lifeguard tower down to the bathhouse—sticks out over the point, its concrete pylons anchored in the flat lava reef, the back deck jutting out almost over the water. The one with the flagpole, Old Glory as reliable as a windsock. The house that always makes you wonder, "What's it doing there?" having outlasted so many of the funky Quonset huts that once typically comprised the neighborhood. The house that countless photographers have settled into the foreground of a thousand exposures, utilizing its deck and flagpole for scale when shooting Makaha Point Surf, a perspective that has the Point's thundering walls appearing to rear up and swallow the place whole.

"The Rich People's House," or so it's been described by generations of *keikis* like Anna Trent, daughter of Buzzy, who during the 1960s spent her childhood playing in the vast tide pool below its deck. A very unnatural tide pool, it turns out, deliberately dynamited into existence by its builder to provide a safe swimming area for the neighborhood kids.

Anyhow, a couple years ago I was at Makaha, competing in Buffalo's annual Big Board contest. There on the beach, between tandem and canoe surfing heats, I struck up a conversation with a group of spectators I first thought was a tourist family who'd missed the turnoff to the Ko'Olina resort back past Nanakuli. They certainly looked like tourists: no tan creases or splayed feet and a little too neat in their beach garb. Southern U.S. accent, probably Texan. But after a few moments of chat, I picked up on something running beneath their "out-of-towner" appearance, an easy rapport with the milieu rarely seen in tourists, who normally gawk and fidget on Hawaiian beaches. In a few more minutes it became obvious why. The father's name was Stuart Beal; he was from Texas, and he owned the Rich People's House on Makaha Point. Owned as in "it's in the family." Turns out one Carlton Beal, his grandfather, built the house back in the early 1960s and christened it "Luana Kai." Stuart had spent a series of idyllic summers here as a kid, surfing, tide pooling, and learning many of his life's lessons at "Grandpappy's" knee.

The grandfather's tale was a classic: A jen-u-whine Texas oilman, Beal Sr. was also an intrepid sportsman who, while on a Hawaiian vacation back in the day, headed out to Makaha for a surf session. Caught inside somewhere between the Bowl and the Blowhold, Beal Sr. parted ways with his board, which banged him in the head for his efforts, sending him to the bottom, unconscious. Luckily for Beal (and, in turn, his descendant Stuart), Makaha's very first lifeguard was on duty. Buffalo Keaulana assessed the situation, plotted the underwater course of the drifting body, paddled out, swam down, and pulled Beal Sr. from a watery grave.

At once impressed and grateful, a recovered Beal Sr. subsequently helped build a house in Nanakuli for Buff and his wife, Momi, then built one for himself on the point at Makaha, their respective fates now linked. How Beal Sr. pulled off the dynamiting caper, shaping the exposed reef in front of Luana Kai into a semi-organic neighborhood swimming pool, is a testimony both to a more innocent era and the social dynamic of an authentic, hierarchal, clan-based Hawaiian culture in which the good graces of the *alii* ruling class—in this case the Keaulanas—ensure pervasive cooperation. In any case, Beal Sr. blasted his pool and dedicated it to the community with a plaque that once read: "Beal's Pond."

This was the sort of story I love hearing while sitting in the sand, and I guess it showed. "Why don't you paddle on over this evening," came the invitation from Stuart Beal. "Dinner's at seven."

Which is how I came to be seated before a feast at the Rich People's House, complete with linen tablecloths and attendants in white jackets poised for every remove. I had, in fact, paddled over from the Blowhold, cutting inside Sunn's Reef and eventually crawling up and into Beal's reef pool, then making my way through the gated portico and up into the immaculately landscaped yard. But don't let me make it seem stuffy. The newest generation of Beals were delighted hosts: unpretentious, good humored, and lots of fun. Dinner was a raucous affair, with stories and smiles from the whole Beal brood, including Stuart's wife, Kate, and his three sons, Alex, Phillip, and Thomas. After dinner and dessert, we moved to the lanai, the trade winds blowing down out of Makaha Valley and whisking the laughter out over the reef. A week or so later, back on the mainland, when I received an e-mail from a Texas oil company, I opened it with a grin. It was from Stuart, just a short, friendly follow-up note, with a file attached.

"Here are some old photos that my grandfather took of a big day at Makaha," he wrote. "Thought you might enjoy seeing them."

That's neat, I thought, and stored the file somewhere on my computer to be opened later.

Two years later, as it turned out, I was sitting with *Surfer's Journal* photo editor Jeff Divine assembling a collection of archival shots for an upcoming book when I came across the Beal file.

"Hey, here's some old photos of Makaha," I said. "Let's check these out."

Click. Scroll. Holy shit!

That's right. The file of "a big day at Makaha," which had been languishing on my computer desktop for the past two years, was a collection of photos taken by Carlton Beal during a big swell on December 4, 1969. Oh, yeah, that "Swell of '69" and that giant day at Makaha when Greg Noll caught what would be, for the time and for many years after, the biggest wave ever ridden—one of the most legendary single days of surfing in the sport's entire history.

It was a real Howard Carter moment as we scrolled through the images. They seemed to capture the entire day, shot with a medium-sized lens from a variety of angles, not quite pedestrian but not a pro's work either. This gave the shots the feel of witnessing the awesome swell event rather than covering it. Here it was: the smaller morning session in the Bowl, guys screaming in off the Point as the swell stepladdered. A sequence of Rolf Aurness. I think. A young Randy Rarick, dropping in late in front of Fred Hemmings. Big waves with surfers riding for scale. But then a series of images of giant waves, huge waves with nothing for scale but, compared with waves shot from the same angle, looking at least twice as high. Looking at them even all these years later, you got a sense of drama—a gut wrench—as with the rising swell those blue-gray monsters came growling down from Kaena Point, clearing the lineup of surfers one by one. Nobody left in these pictures, just massive waves exploding out past the back deck of Luana Kai.

"Hey, who's that?" asked Divine, pointing with a pencil at Beal's only shot of a surfer on the beach.

Click. Divine and I looked at each other. Of course. It had to be Greg Noll—who else could it have been? There's Noll, dashing down Makaha's steep, storm-gouged berm into the shorebreak, absolutely no hesitation in his step. His head is raised, the long, yellow gun tucked under his arm, just a hint of the jailhouse trunks peeking out from under the rail. Only one set of tracks in the sand. And in this single photo, apparently the only photo of Noll on the beach that December 4 (no still images of the humongous wave he eventually rode exist), the entire essence of that epic day is captured as no surf shot ever could. Surf history's only truly Homeric saga: one man heading out after everyone else had come in, daring to face alone whatever new terror appeared from beyond the horizon.

I looked at my watch. It was 2:30 in the afternoon on December 3, 2008. The following day, on December 4, exactly thirty-nine years to the day after Carlton Beal snapped this photo, three dozen or so intrepid surfers, with as many photographers, would take on what would later be called the biggest waves ever paddled into at Mavericks.

They followed this lone set of footprints in the sand, seen here for the first time.

A DEATH SENTENCE

There are waves out there that we surfers hope to ride before pulling into that big closeout in the sky: the super tubes at Jeffrey's Bay, the mile-long walls at Chicama, and the notebook-drawn perfection of Tavarua, to name a few. Shipstern's Bluff is not on the list and for good reason. Less than 1 percent of the global surfing population could navigate its steps, slaps, lips, and ledges well enough to consider the average session out there remotely fun. For you and me, it's a death sentence. This fact was driven home when Andy Irons, Joel Parkinson, Mark Matthews, Dylan Longbottom, and nineteen-year-old tagalong grom Laurie Towner from Angourie, Australia, made a surgical strike on the cauldron of Tasmanian hellfire. By day's end, all were perfectly amazed, none more than Towner, who blew minds by dropping into a hideously deformed right-hander some are now calling the biggest barrel ever paddled into. The swell continued to build and strengthen throughout the day, with the waves growing nastier by the set, to the point that even this extreme ensemble found the line between sanity and insanity blurring. As Parko put it, "You get only so much adrenaline."

—Jake Howard, "To Hell and Back"

TANGLED UP IN WAIMEA

as told by Maya Gabeira

That surfing lore doesn't include very many female big wave sto-
ries is understandable: There haven't been very many female big
wave riders. Until recently. Over the past ten years a small but
very determined cadre of waterwomen have worked their way into
the peak at heavy water breaks previously considered "for men
only." One of the most intrepid is Brazil's Maya Gabeira, who's
earned much respect for her commitment to the steep and deep.
But she's also learned that that sort of rep comes at a price—in
this case a near drowning at Hawaii's Waimea Bay.

I've had asthma since I was one year old, so I've grown up with
that feeling of struggling for breath. And the fear of suffocation.
Not the best situation for riding big waves. And the 2009 big wave
season ended up being the toughest one ever for my asthma. A lot
of the time I was struggling for air, sitting on a chair on land, so
it was an especially big challenge for me to be in the ocean, tossed
by huge waves, knowing I had such a serious limitation. I learned
to work around it. There were a few swells that I was actually 100
percent for and other days when I had to go cautiously and still
others when I couldn't be out there at all. And that was a hard
thing to live with because surfing big waves is my life.

But how do you face a big set with no air? If I was going to
surf on those really big days, I would have to control my breathing
and my heart rate, impossible demands during an asthma crisis.
To have an asthma attack during a long hold-down was one more
variable to deal with. I had to learn which days I could actually
manage, and that meant knowing my limitations. In a crunch, I
breathed slowly and hoped for the best.

On the 11th of January, a Monday, the biggest swell of the year hit the North Shore. I was just coming out of a bad asthma crisis and had been taking crazy amounts of cortisone for ten straight days. I wasn't anywhere near 100 percent. But I couldn't miss that swell. When Waimea Bay began breaking, I was there.

I paddled out at eight that morning. The bay was big but not out of control. I rode a few waves, but I wasn't pushing myself hard. Not yet. Every breath was important—and difficult. Those ten days on massive cortisone had left me at about half strength. I'd been out for about five hours and was tired enough when this huge set rolled in and caught everyone inside, just cleaned up the whole bay. The entire pack was scratching like crazy to get over this monster, and I'm stroking hard, trying to slow my breathing, trying to stay calm. But I was last in line when the lip curled over with about twenty boards and bodies all over the place. I had nowhere to go. I got sucked up and over the falls and driven down deep. I'd never experienced anything like it. Twenty feet down and all these boards are banging up against me, and I can feel people flailing underwater—total chaos. Then I'm tangled bad in leash lines, mine and several others as well. You can't see anything under a wave like that. Not up or down. After the first wave washed over, the ocean calmed slightly but I still couldn't battle to the surface. I was totally wrapped up in leashes, dragging along underwater and getting nervous about the whole situation, feeling like I was in a fatal accident happening in slow motion. Really slow motion—now fighting for air and for my life.

Then the second wave came. I remember thinking, *Wow. I've never been down for two waves before.* As the second wave pounded me deeper, along with the others wrapped up in those leashes, I knew if I didn't do something quickly I would die. And, yes, I had all the flashes in my mind—images of family, of people I loved, everything rushing up from the deep.

I was barely sixteen years old when I left Rio and flew to Hawaii. I told my parents I would stay on the Islands for a year, work on my

English, and return to Brazil and finish university. I was gone for three years. My parents hated me then, but loved me now. And now I was dying. So I had to do something. I had to get air. So I fought and clawed at my leash, one of those with a quick release—I'd almost forgotten. It never occurred to me that I'd have to use the quick release in an emergency situation. I reached down to my ankle and pulled the release, wiggled free from the other leashes, and finally could swim to the surface. This was the closest I've ever come to drowning.

I accept the risks. As a surfer with asthma I know the dangers every time I paddle out. All I can do is do it with love and passion and be dedicated to staying alive. But I'm not going to stop riding big waves because of a bad hold-down at Waimea. And I'm not going to stop because I'm scared to die.

Last year I was driving down Kam Highway at dawn with a Starbucks coffee, checking the surf. It was blown out and rainy, and I was disappointed that I wouldn't be able to shoot. There was no one in the water from Lanis to Waimea to Pipe. I drove by Sunset Beach, and to my surprise there were two little specs way out in the ocean. The swell was a huge washing machine of current and cross chop. I pulled over and watched as South African big wave charger Andrew Marr took a monster closeout in to the beach, riding straight until the wave clipped him. A few minutes later he plodded up the beach, retrieved his bike from the lifeguard tower, and slowly rode off. That left the other surfer out there alone. I waited and watched as the other surfer finally got a massive wall from the outside. It closed out, and then there was nothing. The person disappeared. After a few minutes of whitewater, to the horizon I saw the surfer on the beach coming out of the treacherous shorebreak: It was Maya Gabeira. I couldn't believe it. No one saw this; she didn't do it for money or fame.

—Dace Collyer

Ian Walsh and Makua Rothman share
a very heavy moment at Peahi.
PHOTO © ERIKAEDER.COM

REALLY GET YOU IN THE HOT CURL!

Waikiki, Oahu, Hawaii. In 1923 an artist named John Kelly sailed over from San Francisco with his young family to do illustrations and etchings for Waikiki's expanding hotel row. By 1928, Kelly's nine-year-old son, also named John, was learning how to surf on a miniature redwood plank shaped by David Kahanamoku, Duke's brother. The younger Kelly soon made friends with two other local *haole* surfers, a chalk-white scrapper named Wally Froiseth and a quiet, slender, well-dressed boy named Fran Heath. They rode all the Waikiki breaks and even discovered another half-dozen spots within paddling distance of Kelly's house at Black Point, on the east side of Diamond Head. When they weren't surfing, they hung out in an overgrown beachfront lot not far from the Moana Hotel; people started calling them the "Empty Lot Boys."

Kelly, Froiseth, and Heath watched and learned from the top beachboy surfers at Queen's and Public's, laughing in amazement at the manic wave-riding genius of Joseph "Scooter Boy" Kaopuiki, a former state welterweight boxing champion who ran, hopped, and pirouetted from stem to stern on a 15-foot fire-engine-red hollow board, stopping now and then to face the beach, spread his fingers, and waggle his hands like Al Jolson. By the time Kelly and his friends entered high school, however, they looked upon the Waikiki surf scene with a more critical eye. The old guard was just plugging along, doing the same things they had for years: taking the same angles, performing the same tourist-pleasing acrobatic tricks, and riding the same boards.

However, there was still a lot for the young up-and-coming surfer to admire in the beachboys: They dressed well, often got laid, and were the best-connected people in Waikiki. But the beachboys lacked the single-focus commitment to surfing of the Empty Lot gang. "We used to call it 'surf drunk,'" Froiseth later said. "We talked about it, slept on it, dreamed about it; surfing was practically our whole life."

The older surfers, in other words, didn't much care about advancing the performance standard, while the new kids cared about little else. This rarely caused any friction since there were waves enough for everyone. But occasionally the two groups collided—literally, in some cases. A middle-aged Duke Kahanamoku once made a leisurely descent into a wave that Froiseth was already riding, and the two surfers banged together violently. Froiseth came up swearing. A friend paddled over and in a quiet but urgent voice asked if Froiseth knew who he was yelling at—he did, of course—and Froiseth yelled back, "I don't give a fuck *who* he is!" On the beach, Froiseth was satisfied to discover that the collision had put a fist-sized ding in what, sixty years later, he still dismissively referred to as Duke's "big longboard."

The Empty Lot Boys didn't like longer boards. They didn't like hollow boards either—too buoyant and tippy. Heath was the best surfer of the group and from a wealthy family, and at age eighteen, he had a beautiful new Pacific System Homes Swastika model board freighted over from Los Angeles. On a summer morning in 1937, Heath and Kelly paddled out to a Diamond Head reef called "Browns," located near Kelly's house, to try to ride some overhead waves.

On wave after wave, both surfers kept "sliding ass"—spinning out—as they tried to hold an angle across the steep faces. Kelly stared down at his plank during a backyard lunch break that afternoon and came to what now seems like an obvious design appraisal: too much planing surface in the tail section. The faster the board went, the higher it rode in the water and the less "bite" it had. On an 8-foot wave, the boards were virtually uncontrollable. (Tom Blake had in effect already solved this problem a few years earlier by inventing the surfboard fin, but it hadn't caught on; the Hawaiian surfers were all still riding finless boards.)

Kelly, on the spot, convinced Heath to hand over his still-new Swastika. After setting the board on a pair of sawhorses, Kelly walked into the garage and returned with a small ax. He stood for a moment looking down at the board's stern and with a determined overhead swing buried the ax blade 3 inches into the rail. Both surfers then got to work, giving the blocky tail section a more streamlined profile. From corner to corner, the board's back end shrunk from about 18 inches to 5 inches, and Kelly and Heath blended the new rail lines to meet the original plane shape just below the board's halfway point. They also thinned out the edges and reshaped the bottom surface near the tail, giving it a boat-hull roundness.

Later that afternoon, with the new varnish coat still tacky, the two surfers paddled back out to a still-humping Browns lineup. Kelly had the new board, and on his first wave it bit into the wave face, and he was able to draw a high, fast angle toward the deep-water channel. Froiseth and Kelly customized their own boards the next day. Not long afterward, Froiseth shouted out, "These things really get you in the hot curl!" With that, the new narrow-tail design had a name.

The hot curl design, like the plank and the hollow, had no lift in the nose or tail; viewed from the side, the top surface was perfectly flat. Because it had less surface area, it paddled slower than the other boards and bogged down in small, flat waves. With a few exceptions—including a sharp-tongued little Queen's Surf dynamo named Albert "Rabbit" Kekai—the Waikiki beachboys had no interest in the hot curl; hollows and modified planks remained the rule in Hawaii for another ten to fifteen years. Still, Kelly's new board introduced continuous rail curve, thinner edges, and a rounded hull shape, all of which became standard board design features.

Kelly's new board was one of those developments that, in hindsight, seems both wildly modern and woefully overdue. Modern surfing begins at the turn of the century with George Freeth and Jack London, Alexander Hume Ford, and the Outrigger Canoe Club. Lagging by a full thirty years, modern surfboard design begins with the hot curl.

—From *The History of Surfing,* by Matt Warshaw

South Africa's Craig Bertish on the right side of the peak while Santa Cruz's Ken Collins prepares for a big letdown

HAMMER DOWN

by Evan Slater

The new millennium got off to a bang in California, where during the winter of 2001 a series of epic northwest swells slammed into the West Coast—and straight into a new era of big wave riding based 3,000 miles east of Hawaii. And who better to chronicle this massive attack than Evan Slater? Slater's role as former editor of Surfer *magazine belied his reputation as one of the state's most committed heavy-water surfers, having built considerable cred for his almost reckless charging behind the peak at Mavericks and Todos Santos. Back in 2000, Mavs was starting to firmly establish itself as home to the most consistent big waves in the world.*

Rrrrrrrmmmmmmm . . . ruddaruddaruddarudda . . . rrrrrrmmmmmmm!

What the hell's that sound? A swamp buggy in Florida Everglades? A British Columbian forest sacrificed to the almighty logging industry? A Modesto bikers' rally? Good guesses but no cigar. Believe it or not, that jarring, teeth-grinding noise is the clatter you're sure to hear this winter at the West Coast's marquis big wave spots.

Of course, this is nothing new at places like Jaws and the North Shore Outer Reefs, where ten years ago big wave superheroes like Laird Hamilton and Darrick Doerner replaced their Zodiacs and 10-foot brewer guns with Yamaha XL 1200s, high-tech life vests, and 20-pound, 6'10" pocket rockets. But tow-in surfers are no longer relegated to those faraway places. They're pulling off at the Circle K for a refill of Jumbo Java and asking you, as you sit in your favorite Jurassic Park catching one wave per hour, if you mind if they "tow."

The inevitable has happened. West Coast big wave surfing has loudly and boldly entered the machine age, and there's no killing the switch. Like the liberated sharecroppers or cobblers from 150 years ago, they're producing ten times the yield with a fraction of the effort, and they're laughing all the way to the channel. But historically, machines have always had an uneasy alliance with nature and have turned us into God. The Industrial Revolution was a win/win scenario for stamping out shoes in Hamburg or feeding the masses in Ireland, but when you're taunting 60- to 70-foot walls of water at the heaviest reefbreak in the world, one mistake can send you back down to Earth. Way down.

Tow-in trouncings are a risk that more and more surfers are willing to take when the surf borders on the supernatural. Take this past holiday season, when a late-December low-pressure spun over Hawaii and sprinted toward the West Coast. Buoys were off the scale—in the 40- to 50-foot range in northern California and Oregon—and only one swell in Mavericks' short documented history has come even close: October 28, 1999. This was the day deemed unsurfable by conventional means, the day Peter Mel, Ken "Skindog" Collins, and Jeff Clark inspired at least a dozen other Mavericks surfers to pick a partner, find some capital, and get their mitts on a WaveRunner. "If you would've stood on the cliff and watched those guys surf out there that day," said tow-in convert Matt Ambrose, "you would've gone out and bought a ski right then and there. I promise."

With the prototype deemed a success, this latest Mavericks blower—landing at dawn on December 22—kick-started the tow factory into production. No fewer than ten teams stomped all over the unridden realm during business hours, while only two paddle-in surfers (John Raymond and Mark Renneker) even made it out. The following day, Todos Santos caught a smaller but still-sizable share of the swell and faced a similar scenario: While a handful of young chargers were struggling just to make the drops, Mike Parsons and Brad Gerlach raged with their machine. Even with the engines on idle, the West Coast's fuel-injected big wave riders are still buzzing.

Mavericks, December 22, 2000: The Gambit

At approximately 7:00 a.m., big wave godfather Richard Schmidt, with the aid of partner Adam Replogle, towed into the first legitimate 25-footer of the morning—on a four-fin, 7-foot soft surfboard. Seriously. "It's one of those Surflight boards that Jim Richardson from Hawaii has been working on for the past few years," says Schmidt. "They have been a solid core, but they're soft, almost like bodyboard, on the outside. The best thing about them is that they flex a lot, and all along, I thought they'd make a perfect tow board because they tend to absorb the bumps.

"When we first pulled up, it was still really early," continues Schmidt. "I told Replogle that we should hang and watch a few sets, but he was like, 'Nah, nah. Let's get on it!' That huge one was my very first wave—it just lurched over that second bowl. It wasn't exactly the safest wave to test my theory, but luckily, I was right. The board worked."

The Wormhoudt brothers, Peter Mel, Ross Clarke-Jones (Mel's usual partner, Skindog Collins, was in Costa Rica for Christmas), Jay Moriarty, and Jeff Clark were also on the early shift, and as soon as news spread about Schmidt's mutant double-up, the fading game was on.

A Means with No End

Karl Marx warned us about the dead-aim efficiency of machinery way back in 1844. The more consistent output from the machine, he said, the cheaper the value of the product and of the worker himself. This might help explain why on this day no one seemed to even blink at the countless 40-foot waves detonating across the Mavericks bowl while antlike surfers skittered across the massive walls, carving and cutting back as if they were surfing a fun, low-ride day

A loose board leaps free of a closeout set,
having abandoned its rider to oblivion.
PHOTO © ROBERT BROWN

at Cardiff Reef. Thirty-footers are a dime on days like December 22; 40-footers, standard issue.

Amazingly, it's the 50- to 60-footers and beyond that guys like Mel and Moriarty now fend for, and this swell—too west to be ideal but ridiculously large—provided a few opportunities. First up (after Schmidt's predawn Loch Nessie) was Jay Moriarty. Jay has paid his dues. At sixteen, he probed Mavericks' deepest, darkest corners during one of the most famous wipeouts of the decade. Now, at twenty-two, he's teamed up with the marshal, Jeff Clark, on the tow frontier. Clark drove most of the morning since he separated a couple ribs surfing the left at Mavs earlier in the week, which gave Moriarty unlimited tow miles. Since tow-surfing is much about the driver's skills, it helps to have the Mavericks care-taker on the throttle, and Moriarty proved that when he launched into a Hollywood bowl from way back. One 50-yard bottom turn and a quick snap under the lip later, and Moriarty was safely on the shoulder after riding the biggest wave of his life.

"When I saw Jay get that one from the channel," says Pacifica charger Sean Rhodes, "I was like, 'He's got it, for sure [referring to the Swell.com XXL Biggest Wave Wins contest].' No one's going to top that."

But someone *did* top it—about five minutes later. Two-time Quiksilver/Men Who Ride Mountains winner Darryl "Flea" Virostko has a new theory about surfing Mavericks: He doesn't—unless it's off the charts.

"So many guys will hear the buoys are 10 feet at 17 seconds, and they'll get all jacked and go up there and battle it out in 12-foot surf," says Flea. "I'm not into that anymore. I know I can paddle in. I'm surfing the place now only when the buoys are like 15 at 17 or bigger."

Flea's only Mavericks session of the year began with one of the most gut-wrenching rides ever at the break. A couple weeks after the wave, Flea still acts as if it was no big deal.

"When [Josh] Loya and I got out there, I noticed that in order to make it more critical than any other wave, I'd have to get one and take it way back. That wave didn't look that huge, but as soon as it hit the bowl, I was like, 'Woah, this thing's making a run for it.'"

Virostko took a high line in an attempt to thread through the second bowl, but it was no use: A 30-yard slab, 8 feet thick and 20 feet wide, unloaded as he made his descent. For a moment, Flea stood at the bottom of a barrel that looked like a reverse Waimea shorebreak—to the tenth power. Seeing no hope for escape, Virostko straightened off, raced out to the flats as far as he could, and prepared, in the words of Laird Hamilton, for the cement truck to unload.

"It broke, I straightened out, and I remember seeing the cliff for a second just as all this whitewash started to fall over me. It was a pretty good doughnut: I was ragdolled, and my lifejacket ripped off a bit, but I was fine. Give me another one."

"Flea's wave was the first wave I saw that morning," said Noah Johnson, who had flown over the night before from Oahu. "And I thought, 'Oh shit. This is serious. I hope he comes up.'" But instead of playing it safe, Johnson hitched a ride with a surfed-out Replogle, who towed the Hawaiian straight up a bomb so titanic that it broke out beyond the normal Mavericks ledge and rolled right through the bowl.

"I towed on that big day at Outer Logs in '98," says Johnson, "and this wave had a similar kind of feel. It was so big that you really can't do anything on it. There's so much face above and below you that you just sort of have to . . . survive it. I played it pretty cautious on that one," continues Johnson. "I didn't want to fade too deep because I didn't think I could be mowed by a wave that big and come out alive. I was lucky, too. I barely made it around the first section. I could feel the whitewater nipping at my heels."

Those big days don't happen that often—few waves pass unridden by at least a few brave souls.

Both Flea's and Johnson's waves pushed the Mavericks width and height boundaries to comic proportions. Not surprisingly, though, they're not laughing. In fact, they're still striving for bigger, faster, and stronger.

"You definitely get caught up in it," admits Johnson. "As soon as I saw that Flea was okay, I started giving him shit. I was, like, 'Why didn't you snap under the lip on that thing?'"

Peter Mel also is admittedly caught up in it. He says tow-in surfing does that to you. You get a big one? You want a bigger one. And then a bigger one after that. As Mel found on December 22, this addiction is hard to satisfy when more than a half-dozen tow teams are in the water. The West Coast's most complete surfer happened to catch the next wave after both Flea's and Noah's top-billers, and although he tore both of them to pieces with tight, swooping arcs and commanding high lines, Mel knew he missed the highlight reel.

"It's a little frustrating," he says, "but you gotta show respect for your friends. So you take a number. A lot of it's positioning. On one hand, you're catching more waves than ever. On the other, you feel like you have to be on the biggest ones that come through."

"That one set that Noah was on—I don't know how it worked out like that," continues Mel. "Me and Ross [Clarke-Jones] were out of position and ended up in the back of the line. When there's stacks of guys, like on the 22nd, everyone tows from out the back and rides the swell in. With fewer guys, it's better: You can sweep in from the side or straight on, and it makes it far easier to judge the wave. I hate to say it, but those huge days like October 28, when it was just us and another crew—those days are gone."

Todos Santos, December 23, 2000: Hand-picked

Todos surfers have a distinct advantage. Instead of guessing the size of the next swell, all they need is to check what Big Leagues of the north did the day before and cut it in half. Half of 70 feet is still enough to scare the shit out of any mortal, but there's a young crew out of San Clemente and San Diego who are serious candidates for big wave beatification at *Isla Todos Santos* (All Saints Island).

Twenty-two-year-old John Walla, his friend Drew Card, teenagers Rusty and Greg Long, and Solana's Brian Conley went through the Todos ritual that morning believing they'd face the biggest waves of their lives: an ungodly wake-up call of 3:00 a.m., powering straight through to Ensenada and arriving by six. From there, they hired a *panga* from one of the hustlers in the alley and pulled up to *Killers* by 7:30.

The early morning lineup revealed inconsistent 15- to 18-foot sets, light offshores, hazy sun, and one tow team. Walla and the Longs gave Mike Parsons and Brad Gerlach another half-hour before killing their motor-assisted waltz with their 9'8" guns. As the swell filled in and sets continued to turn the Todos boil into the Colorado rapids, Parsons, Gerlach, and the young guns pecked away at their paddle-in wave count. But it wasn't easy.

"I caught only two waves, and I got worked on both of them," said Rusty Long. "I skipped down the face on one, and on the other, Greg and I both ate it on the boil. I just got pummeled. I was pretty shaken up after that second one, so I decided it was time to paddle over to the boat."

Walla had a better go at it but cut his session short after he hit a chop on a massive, white double-up.

"I don't know what happened," said Walla. "I hit a foam bump and just skipped across the flats. I ended up breaking my board on that one."

Parsons, naturally, maintained his kingpin status with a few late drops, but he's glad to see a new crew of surfers who are able to look beyond the "launch ramps" at their local beachbreak.

"It's so great to see a new, committed young crew out there," said Parsons. "Every time I see them out there, they've upped it another notch."

Laissez-faire

Mike Parsons and Brad Gerlach are true disciples of the tow-in faith. They're born-again big wave riders, surfing better and faster than they ever imagined possible when it was all about the drop. And at Todos Santos—save the occasional paddle-in crew—they're alone. Screw the feelings of emptiness, they're happily feasting off the tow-in tree. And the greed? Greed isn't part of the equation if there's no one there to share it with. Aren't they jaded if it's smaller than 90 feet? No way—they'll take all comers, from 2 to 200 feet. The truth is, Gerlach and Parsons—like all tow teams who click—are just getting their act wired, and they can't get enough of it.

The thirty-something duo was on it at dawn on the morning of the 23rd, long before the first *panga* even stirred in the harbor. "I rode the biggest wave I've ever ridden out there, easily a 40-foot face," said Parsons. "Granted, I towed into it, but it was definitely as big as that wave I caught in 1990. And this time, I actually surfed the thing."

Parsons and Gerlach towed for two solid hours in the morning and rode about twenty waves each. During the few hours they paddle-surfed, they could count their wave quota on one hand. After the paddle-in surfers cleared out around midday, the two former NSSA teammates went back at it again for another round of twenty each in the afternoon. For Parsons, just one day of tow surfing yielded more big waves than two winters' worth in years past.

Has West Coast big wave surfing made its official transformation from a labor of love to a labor of lube? Are gearheads destined to clutter the big wave lineups with that maddening buzz every time the California buoy hits 10 feet? Perhaps, but consider this: Most of those gearheads are the same surfers you worshipped when they were doing it the old-fashioned way.

"I still love to paddle," Parsons says. "But racing at the bowl at 30- to 40-foot waves on 6'10"s and riding thirty, forty waves in a day? Come on, it doesn't compare. Gerr and I are having the times of our lives right now."

Automated

Take pride in your labor, advised Marx, especially labor that is done by hand. For the more work is done by machine, the more you are removed from the production process itself and the less connection you will have with the final product. In the most extreme cases, you will become alienated from your labor.

Grant Washburn knows about alienation. He and his labor are doing just fine, thank you, but Washburn was one of the last of the core Mavericks surfers to resist the tow temptation. He's

Darryl "Flea" Virostko, bending
to fit the curve at Mavs
PHOTO © ROBERT BROWN

done plenty of driving and has whipped Jeff Clark into dozens of 20-plus-foot pyramids, but tow in himself? Nah. Something told the 6'6" San Francisco regularfoot that it just wasn't for him. During the opening ceremony for the Quiksilver/Men Who Ride Mountains event, Washburn even found a sympathizer in Brazilian charger Danilo Couto. "Fucking towing in!" Couto told Washburn. "You and me, we charge 50-footers with our bare hands!"

But if there were ever a day to set aside purist convictions, December 22 was the one. Washburn spent a good portion of the morning filming from a ski and helping with rescues, but after watching his usual paddle-in comrades ride upward of twenty waves each, he'd had enough. "All right," he said. "I'm in."

Washburn strapped himself into Jay Moriarty's board and let Clark return the favor after so many one-sided sessions. He motored out, not feeling entirely confident on Jay's board but resolved: "All I want is one, just to see what it's like."

When Washburn first released the rope, he couldn't believe he was on a big wave. "This must be a tiny one," he thought. "There's no . . . woah. Here we go." Planing across the face at speeds he never thought possible, Washburn couldn't resist. He faded when he promised himself he wouldn't fade; he turned when he told himself he wouldn't turn.

He . . . just then the wicked west bowl decided to end his fun and, faced with no other option, Grant ejected.

After a thorough spanking, Washburn popped out the back, relieved that it wasn't any worse. "I knew I shouldn't have faded," he said.

Then it got worse. Way worse.

About 30 yards beyond him, a wave—bigger than anything he'd ever faced—began to unload outside of the normal takeoff spot. "If it had been half the size, I still would have freaked out," remembers Washburn. "And I was right at home plate—couldn't have been in a worse spot. It looked like a 100-foot-tall whitewater coming at me."

Fearing retribution from the paddle-in gods, one of Mavericks' most loyal disciples hyperventilated for a few quick seconds, flutter-kicked under as deep as he could, and balled up. Violence. Whitewater demons taunted and pulled at him from all directions, trying to get him to fight. But Washburn stayed put, ten, fifteen seconds. Thinking the worst was over, he released his grip, but the beatings began all over again. Back in fetal position. Twenty seconds, twenty-five. At last, his somersault rotations began to slow, the turbulence gradually subsided, and he surfaced. Air.

Never mind the three more solid 15-foot combers that detonated on him before Flea could finally snag him; if he could survive that first avalanche, he could survive anything.

It's not easy finding a surfer who's towed and then pined for the paddle-in past. Granted, Washburn didn't exactly have a pleasant first tow-in experience, but after being amongst it for the past four years and finally clasping the rope on December 22, he knows where his heart lies, and it's not behind a WaveRunner.

"There's this feeling you get from paddling in," he says, "when your heart's in your throat, and you're just not sure if you're going to be able to claw over the ledge and make the drop. There's nothing like looking down the vertical ramp on a 20-footer. And to be honest, all of that's gone when you're towing in. You have to do so much more to even get any kind of rush—and even then, there's something totally missing in the tow-in equation.

"It was funny," Grant continues. "On that same day I saw Danilo Couto out there, and we both kind of looked at each other. 'Did you tow?' I asked. 'Yeah, but only a couple,' he said. 'Did you?' and we both just sort of held our heads down. So much for our pact."

German transplant Sebastian Steudtner at the bottom of
a Peahi left that measured out at 66 feet and earned him
a Billabong XXL Global Big Wave Awards nomination.

SPIRIT OF THE FOALS

by Leonard Doyle

It's an island whose northwest coast gets plenty of big swells, with reef breaks capable of offering 20- to 30-foot barrels, being ridden by a hardcore crew of hellmen who think nothing of hucking themselves over the ledge or towing themselves into some of the heaviest waves found in any ocean. Sumatra? Tahiti? Tasmania? Try Ireland, which, though it may be the Old Country, is big wave riding's newest frontier. Leonard Doyle, a reporter for the Independent *in London, penned an outsider's look at the Irish insider's awesome surf break.*

On the heart-stopping edge of the Cliffs of Moher, a few miles from Aran as the gulls fly, John McCarthy's enthusiasm is infectious as elfinlike he skips over a dry-stone wall and points down into the surf 800 feet below. Ignoring warning signs that read "Danger Cliff Edge!" combined with a pictogram of a person plunging backward off a precipice, he guides me toward a sandstone veranda overhanging the churning sea. We are inches from doom, and the hungry wind swirling up the cliff face threatens to suck us over the edge.

"There she is! That's Aileen's!" McCarthy yells over the gale. I make out that he is pointing toward a singular ocean swell coursing in toward the bottom of the cliff. As it passes over a submerged reef, the wave suddenly jacks up, its leading edge curling into a perfectly rounded C, as though thrust upward by a giant hand.

"That's our wave—the most perfect wave you'll find in Europe," says McCarthy. Moving toward the cliff face, the lip of breaking water is suspended some 20 to 30 feet above the surface of the sea as it races forward. Aileen's, as the local surfers affectionately call this monster, is a new discovery and until last October had never been surfed. A similar barrel-shaped wave called "Teahupoo" occurs off Tahiti—one of the crown jewels of big wave surfers. When the conditions are right here at Aileen's—usually a deep depression far out in the Atlantic and an offshore southeasterly— the perfect wave will come in regular sets of seven for hours at a time. When Aileen's goes off, it is a most elusive phenomenon, beautiful to behold but with the capacity to kill or maim as well. Only in the past six months has anyone dared to attempt to surf Aileen's. And it has been surfed only about ten times since.

Bloggers and podcasts have scatted the word across the globe, and now the west of Ireland is suddenly a center stage in the world of big wave surfing. Wikipedia enthusiastically lists Aill Na Searrach (or Aileen's) as one of the world's famous tow-in surf spots, along with Jaws in Maui, Teahupoo, and the giant Belharra off the Basque Country. Weatherwise, Ireland is not Hawaii. Mid-winter's wind-chill factor makes the sea unbelievably cold. Big wave surfers who head out in subzero conditions don 6-millimeter wetsuits, hoods, and gloves and have to combine the endurance of a mountaineer and the athleticism of a ballet dancer to survive the conditions.

The setting for the Cliffs of Moher could not be more dramatic. Paddling in is like entering a scene from *The Lord of the Rings*, says McCarthy. Off in the middle distance the three Aran Islands lie low and black in the water like great basking sharks. Closer to hand a great sea stack juts up beneath the cliffs, and humpback whales frequently break the surface within sight of the sandstone battlements. On shore, the Cliffs of Moher provide an unrivalled view across the vast boiling wildness of the Atlantic Ocean, a world unchanged since the pre-Celtic masters of magic, the Tuatha Dé Danann, ruled Ireland. In protest of the arrival of Christianity and the loss of miraculous rituals, the Tuatha transformed into horses and hid in caves for centuries. One day seven foals emerged from the caverns, and, frightened by the bright sunlight, they bolted. Galloping along the edge of the cliffs they met their fate at a spot known as Aill Na Searrach ("Leap of the Foals" in English). Today the surfers call it Aileen's.

"Maybe the spirit of the foals has been harnessed by the waves," says Katherine Webster, director of the Cliffs of Moher Interpretive Centre. The cliffs, one of Ireland's most visited places, attract more than a million visitors a year. On any given day, conga lines of tourists in bright raincoats stream out of buses to puff their way up the hill and gape out into the cold abyss.

A Recent Discovery
The west coast of Ireland has some of the finest, if intermittent, surfing conditions anywhere. Aileen's was a well-kept local secret until fifteen months ago when the acclaimed English surf photographer Mickey Smith brought some Australian body boarders to peer over the Cliffs of Moher. They decided on an immediate attempt. It is all but impossible to descend the sheer cliff face, so the Australians began an insane attempt to paddle from 2 miles away after jumping off a lower cliff face. There seas were treacherous, and it was getting dark and dangerous as they reached the wave. Exhausted, they turned back, guided by the flame from Mickey's Zippo lighter on the headland above.

In a nearby village, where McCarthy—Ireland's foremost surfer— was taking a break from coaching the next generation of surfers at his Lahinch Surf School, the idea took hold for a proper attempt on Aileen's. "For a year I watched the wave and could not get it out of my head," he recalls. "So many surfers told me they had watched it. There is even a girl from Maui who lives around here who goes up to look at Aileen's because it reminds her of Peahi [Jaws]."

Trying to Stay Alive
Last autumn, as the surfing season began in earnest, Mickey Smith showed up again in County Clare with Robin Kent, one of Britain's top big wave surfers. By chance world-renowned California

Makua Rothman is only 16 years old when he snags this six-story wall at Jaws and wins a Billabong XXL Global Big Wave award.

surfer Rusty Long (returning from a failed mission to the Hebrides) was also in the area, and they teamed up with McCarthy and his good mate Blount. McCarthy had just splashed out seven thousand pounds sterling on a jet ski, finally making an attempt possible.

Without the backup of a rescue vessel and with no real knowledge of the conditions, they set out. And like many a world first, whether bagging a mountain peak or crossing an ocean single-handed, this little expedition to conquer Europe's most terrifying wave would soon degenerate into controversy. It is one that still echoes through the world of big wave surfing.

On the fateful first attempt McCarthy launched his new jet ski into high winds and pitching seas off Doolin, some 2 miles north of the cliffs. Battered by waves, he was leading an expedition of surfers, body boarders, and Mickey Smith. When they arrived under the line of tall cliffs the group was awestruck. "It sounds clichéd," recalls Smith, "but it truly was like stepping through a portal into another world. Beneath the massive rock faces we were completely sheltered from the wind."

McCarthy remembers "an elemental feeling; we were like Lilliputians in a land of giants. Giant cliffs, giant rollers, and the thundering roar of water as the waves crashed against the caves under the cliffs—an unearthly boom."

Rusty Long was the most experienced big wave surfer among them, and he, McCarthy, Blount, and Kent spent their time trying to stay alive—avoiding more than riding the first tube-shaped monsters.

"You are not thinking about it at the time, but you realize that if this huge weight of water lands on your head, it can kill you," McCarthy remarks. "It's one of the biggest waves anywhere, but what makes it unique is its shape. It throws off this enormous oval-shaped tube, and that is where the surfer needs to place himself."

Several months after this first charmed day at Aileen's, an article was fashioned from whole cloth for the British surf magazine *Carve*. In this imperial farce the two Irish surfers were reduced to blathering Paddys, mere bit players to the heroic American and British surfers, and attributed with such expressions as: "Aye, fellas, d'ya know what? I've only gone and forgot to put some petrol in the bloomin' jet ski!"

Since that October day last year, McCarthy and Blount have been out in bigger seas catching enormous tubes. Towed in by the jet ski, the surfer whipsaws behind the peak of the wave, then stands tall in the pulsing chamber barreling headlong for the cliff. "It is an unearthly feeling, being inside a swirling tube of green water, moving at about 30 miles an hour with the terrifying sound of the collapsing wave behind," says McCarthy.

For the million visitors who puff their way to the highest point of the cliffs, there is now another extraordinary spectacle to be seen where the foals leapt to their doom at Aill Na Searrach all those millennia ago.

While the true danger factor might be low, the terror factor of getting caught inside in huge surf is off the scale.

BENEATH THE WAVES

by Chris Dixon

It was one of the biggest swells in modern surf history, with record waves from Hawaii to California. Such was the epic backdrop for Chris Dixon's tale of the death of a big wave rider and the birth of a legend. In particular, Dixon, a longtime surfer and New York Times *reporter, scored a major scoop with an account of Laird Hamilton's rescue of fellow Maui tow surfer Brett Lickle in 80-plus-foot surf, a feat that could be described only as Herculean—and one that didn't appear in any of the surf magazines.*

The wave was bigger than anything Laird Hamilton and Brett Lickle had ever seen—80, maybe 100 feet high. Though they were fleeing flat-out on Hamilton's personal watercraft (PWC), the great wave closed fast. "Our only words were Laird yelling *'Go go go!'*" Lickle remembers. "Then it was like hitting the eject button on a jet fighter."

Hamilton, riding the rescue sled towed behind the PWC, dove off at 50 mph as Lickle took the avalanche full force. Tumbling in continents of foam, Hamilton's twenty-pound surfboard rammed fin-first into Lickle's calf, flaying him open from his Achilles to the back of his knee. The pain of the bone-deep gash was blinding but irrelevant because if Lickle couldn't kick his way back to the surface, then somehow swim a mile to shore, he knew he was a dead man.

The monster wave that overtook the two big wave veterans was one of thousands that coursed across the northern Pacific ahead of a historic December 2007 storm, a cyclone that formed when a dying tropical depression over the Philippines met a frigid blast tumbling down the Siberian steppe, found warm water, and went nuclear. "The moisture supercharged the storm," says Sean Collins, chief forecaster of Surfline.com. "It was like throwing dynamite on a fire."

Within a couple of days, a 1,000-mile line of hurricane-force winds screamed east across the loneliest stretches of the Pacific. Mountainous swells piled up on one another, ripping weather buoys from their moorings. "Swell data showed 50-foot waves," Collins adds. "Occasionally there was a 100-footer." Bill Sharp, director of the Billabong XXL Big Wave Awards (the Oscars for surfing's top hellmen), says, "It's the most extraordinary week I've ever seen in big wave surfing."

In the underground world of big wave surfing, news of a great storm travels faster than the waves. Before dawn on December 3, scores of Hawaiians were tuning their PWCs and hitching the rescue sleds as forecasters predicted a swell that might flip the switch at Oahu's famed Waimea Bay or, better yet, a slew of outside reefs (which produced the legendary rides of 1998, then the biggest waves ever surfed). But Hamilton had a hunch that the forecasts were wrong, that the best surf would be at Maui, 120 miles east. By daybreak, with Maui's North Shore under siege from unsurfable 50-foot walls of water, Hamilton revised his plan. Mist and storm clouds obscured reefs farther out to sea that might translate the chaotic waters into titanic waves. So Hamilton and forty-seven-year-old partner Lickle set out on their PWC from Spreckelsville for a reef called Outer Sprecks.

"If anyone had any idea about the waves on the way, they would have turned on the tidal wave warning systems," Hamilton says. No small craft, much less surfers, would have been allowed on the water. In retrospect, Hamilton could have used the warning himself.

It took another day for the waves to make landfall in central California, but there, too, surfers were primed for a good old Pacific

Ocean beatdown. At the foggy crack of dawn on December 4, half a dozen tow-in teams left Half Moon Bay for Mavericks, California's most celebrated big wave venue. Another twenty-five teams motored out from Monterey Harbor, 100 miles south, to a remote corner of rock-strewn shoreline. Maps call it Pescadero Point. Surfers call it Ghost Tree.

The ominous name derives from bleached trunks of dead cypress at the end of 17 Mile Drive, the Monterey-to-Carmel road along some of the most dramatic coastline on Earth. On rare winter days with the proper westerly vector, waves focused by the deep Carmel Canyon rear upward of 60 feet in deadly proximity to black, car-size boulders. Don Curry, a chiseled forty-eight-year-old big wave master and personal trainer, forged his legend here at Ghost Tree and at Mavericks. "The waves are right there," he says. "It's the only place you literally feel the waves shaking the ground. If you don't make the drop, you'll bounce off the rocks. You're dead."

In the days before personal watercraft, a few brave locals paddled out to challenge Ghost Tree, but waves heaved in too fast and broke too close to allow anything beyond scratching in at the end. Curry, for one, charged other big waves nearby, and on the biggest days he could always count on one surfer to paddle out with him: a larger-than-life contemporary named Peter Davi.

Davi was a forthright, bearish surfer of Sicilian descent, one of the few who had paddled into big Ghost Tree surf. One of six children with roots in the Monterey Peninsula generations deep, his grandfather Pietro Maiorana was a pioneering seine fisherman during the days of Steinbeck's *Cannery Row*. Although not above accepting an occasional tow, Davi believed surfers should earn their waves—a quaint attitude tolerated by some and revered by others.

On December 4 longtime friends Anthony Ruffo and Randy Reyes gave Davi a ride on their PWC out to Ghost Tree, where photographers, resting surfers, and spectators were floating outside the big waves. Among them was Kelly Sorensen, owner of Monterey's On the Beach surf shop, who had sponsored Davi for twenty-one years with clothing and gear. Sorensen watched as Davi and Mavericks regular Anthony Tashnick tried to paddle in. "Tazzy" managed two short rides, but the waves were too fast and mostly rolled underneath them. Davi paddled his 8'6" board over and sat on the back of Sorensen's PWC, and the two gaped at the horrifying wipeouts of the tow-in boys and the barrels big enough to drive a bus through.

Curry, a tow-in regular at Ghost Tree since 2002, rode a 60-footer on March 9, 2005. That day's poundings were also legendary. Justen "Jughead" Allport broke his leg in four places, and Tyler Smith took a 50-footer on the head, his brother's rescue attempt nearly killing them both. Several of that day's waves, including Curry's, earned surfers nominations for the coveted XXL Ride of the Year award. So on such a colossal day at Ghost Tree, Curry wasn't surprised to see twenty-five teams vying for waves.

Up at Mavericks, Peter Mel had surfed two amazing waves and was up on his third when it hit an undersea ledge and jacked vertical, sucking the bottom out of the wave. As the six-story wall of water folded and detonated, Mel simply ducked, covered, and prayed. "It was like I was run over by Niagara Falls," he says. "I thought it was going to tear the limbs off my body." His partner, Ryan Augenstein, rushed in and stopped cold. The ocean was so churned, the impeller couldn't get a grip in the foam—like a car spinning its wheels in snow. As another wave bore down, the PWC suddenly caught, Mel grabbed the sled, and the two shot to safety. "It was one of the most amazing saves I've ever seen," Mel says. At 12:30 a rescue team motored out. A crab boat named *Good Guys* had foundered, its two fishermen lost to the waves.

Down at Ghost Tree, Anthony Ruffo had tow-surfed into four menacing bombs. Davi was determined to tow into at least one wave on his traditional paddleboard. "I'm forty-five years old, and I want one of the fucking waves," he said from the back of Sorensen's jet ski.

"Those were the last words I heard him say," Sorensen says.

Laird Hamilton had guessed right. The farther offshore from Maui he and Lickle got, the clearer it became that the storms' big swells were setting up hills of water 50 feet high, hills that were crashing over the reef and offering rides three-quarters of a mile long. "It was absolute perfection," Lickle says. "Not a drop of water out of place." As the waves grew, so increased the boils and chop on the face of the waves, and the pair found it nearly impossible to control their skittering boards. So they returned to shore to pick up Hamilton's favorite: a 6'7" hardwood missile shaped by Hawaiian Dick Brewer, thin as a water ski, heavy, and fast. By the time they returned, Outer Sprecks had gone mutant.

Helicopter pilot Don Shearer, who's flown film and rescue missions during Maui's hairiest swells, whirred in under the low ceiling and was completely awestruck by combers twelve to fifteen stories tall. "I've seen every big swell that's come in since 1986," he says. "This was far and away the biggest I've seen in my life."

"They were sucking the water off the reef, breaking top to bottom," Hamilton says. "We could barely get into them, even at full speed."

The aluminum fin on Lickle's board had bent, so Hamilton lent him his hardwood Brewer. The foot straps were too wide, but Lickle couldn't resist the opportunity to chase down "the two biggest waves of my life." But as he blasted down his third the entire wall reared up in front of him, ready to close out. With no chance to outrun it, Lickle dug a rail and desperately arced up the top, narrowly flying over the folding lip. He was done and took over the driving as Hamilton, the most celebrated big wave surfer of all

Big man on a big wave: Tow-in innovator Laird Hamilton is the flat-out best mega-wave surfer in the world.

March 9, 2005. It will be remembered as the day Ghost Tree, the Mysto deep-water break off Pebble Beach, California, went huge, perfect, and nearly homicidal. And if personal watercraft are eventually banned in the Monterey Bay Sanctuary, tow-surfers may look back on March 9 as the most memorable day of a short-lived golden age.

—Ryan Masters, *Heroes and Ghosts*

time, grabbed the hardwood board and the tow rope and readied for a few bombs. Then the horizon went dark: It was a rogue wave, straight out of *The Poseidon Adventure*. Not surprisingly, Hamilton wanted the rogue. Lickle pegged the throttle.

After releasing the rope, Hamilton felt as if he were flying. Plunging down the wall, he violently bashed over dire ledges and warbles, barely staying upright, focusing far ahead for the line. Suddenly the wave lurched up into a closeout. Tearing along at 40 knots, Hamilton's only hope was to dive into the wall, kick like hell, and pray he didn't get sucked over the falls as the wave thundered shut.

Lickle, tracking behind, was horrified when the wave closed out. Then his buddy popped up unharmed but waving frantically: The next wave was even bigger. Hamilton grabbed the sled, and Lickle nailed the throttle, shooting toward land at 50 mph. It wasn't fast enough.

"The wave hit us like we were going backward," Hamilton says.

Lungs near bursting, Hamilton and Lickle finally surfaced in choking foam. "I could barely keep my chin above the surface," Lickle says. Another wave followed, then another, dragging the pair a third of a mile until they reached calmer water. Then Hamilton heard Lickle say something like "tourniquet." Pulling his leg out of the water, Hamilton was shocked by the carnage. "It had to be taken care of right there," Hamilton says, "or he was going to bleed to death."

Almost a mile of sea and shorebreak lay between them and safety.

Shearer's helicopter flew over, but he couldn't see the pair in the continents of foam. Hamilton ripped off his wetsuit and tied a sleeve tight around Lickle's leg. Then he spotted the watercraft a quarter of a mile away, floating perfectly upright. He gave Lickle his vest and said, "I've gotta go."

As Hamilton swam off, Lickle came to know what it means to be alone.

"I had bled out to the point of weakness," says Lickle, who could only drift, wondering if he'd ever see his family again. "I've got kids, twelve and seven."

Lickle's light-headed fog broke when the PWC arrived with his butt-naked buddy at the helm. The ignition lanyard gone, Hamilton had used stashed headphone wires to MacGyver a replacement. When he punched the ignition, the waterlogged engine fired right up.

Hamilton yelled into the radio for EMTs as Lickle knelt on the sled, trying to hold his calf closed for the grueling twelve-minute race to Baldwin Beach Park. By the time the watercraft ground into the sand, paramedics were waiting.

To hear locals tell it, Peter Davi was the most loved, feared, and respected surfer from the Monterey Peninsula. He chased wintertime swells from Big Sur to Santa Cruz to Mavericks. In his teens he'd left for Oahu's North Shore to take on the world's most towering waves—and outsize egos. With his size, talent, and force of will, he befriended Oahu's most imposing watermen, from Marvin Foster and Johnny Boy Gomes to Michael and Derek Ho to Garrett and Liam McNamara. "Because Pete charged hard and was so big, he could have been a bad boy if he wanted to," Liam McNamara says. "But he was a gentle giant, a soft-spoken family man who earned respect. He took care of you like a brother."

In the mid-1980s Davi lived on Sunset Point, where he earned the nickname "Pipeline Pete." "I had my most memorable sessions at Pipe with him," says McNamara. "I remember him and Derek Ho coming out of double barrels together, waves no one else could have made."

"He was a good surfer, built like a lumberjack," Hamilton says. "There weren't many bigger. And he was always a gentleman."

"The big Hawaiians really loved the guy," says Ruffo, whom Davi called "Ledge," for "Legend." "He was a big *haole* [foreigner] who had their respect when the locals were still punching people out. He opened the door for a lot of Santa Cruz guys like me and Peter Mel."

With money he earned fishing in 1986, Davi and his girlfriend Katrin Winterbotham bought some Big Sur property, where they planted fruit trees, fertilizing them with the guts of fish he hauled in. Two years later they had a son, Jake, who grew up with his dad hunting wild boar, surfing lineups from California to Oahu, and scouring the beaches and hills for shark teeth, arrowheads, and slabs of jade. A picture in Jake's room shows Davi wrapping a burly arm around a towheaded little kid in a pink wetsuit.

At Ghost Tree, Reyes handed Davi the rope and towed him off Sorensen's ski onto a wave—no monster but plenty dangerous on a paddleboard with no foot straps. The big man played it safe, riding near the top beside Reyes. Ruffo feared Davi would be trapped between the whitewater and rocks, but Davi somehow raced around the corner. "Everything was cool," Ruffo says. "We laughed about it."

Davi told Ruffo he was going to paddle back to Stillwater Cove, a fifteen-minute arm-powered journey. Ruffo offered him a ride, but Davi refused. "He was almost mad at us for suggesting it," Ruffo says.

What happened next is unclear, but a friend of Sorensen's claims he saw Davi catch a wave near the end of Pescadero Point, only to wipe out, snapping his leash. "He knew what to do," says Sorensen. "He was so big he could float just sitting in his buoyant wetsuit." But Stillwater Cove is full of shelf rocks, with a particularly bad one in the middle. As Davi drifted toward it, Sorensen's friend saw him rise on a swell. Then a sheriff ordered spectators off private land on the point.

Fed up with the crowds, Ruffo and Reyes called it a day. "Every time a set came, five teams would go for the same wave," Ruffo says. Rounding the last rocks 200 yards from Stillwater Pier, Ruffo saw something bob up in the wake of another jet ski. A seal? Then he saw a body floating facedown. He thought it was a diver until spotting the snapped leash. "I wasn't ready for that moment," Ruffo says. "I'm thinking, *Is that Pete?* We were just confounded. At a moment like that you don't know what to do. I jammed to the pier and yelled to someone to call 911."

Ruffo was back in less than two minutes, jumping into the water and pulling the stiff body of Peter Davi up onto his ski. When he steamed in over the rocks, paramedics were waiting and administered CPR for twenty minutes but to no avail. Peter Davi was declared dead at 1:28 p.m. An autopsy revealed he drowned after blunt force trauma to the head and chest.

"I've taken a lot of shit for saying this," Don Curry says, "but on that day, Pete just wasn't in the shape you need to be to go out there and paddle for waves. I'm not slandering the guy; I'm just stating the truth. That's the tragedy: His death was unnecessary. Pete didn't need to go down."

Another surfer, speaking on condition of anonymity, pins the blame elsewhere: "On a day like that, you have to pay attention to people in the water, no matter what," he says. "Pete had been in the water for two hours, he lost his board, and there were huge seas and currents and rocks. There were more than twenty skis out there, with five teams resting out the back, drinking water and talking on cell phones. And all these media guys clicking away." When word spread through the water of Davi's death, some of them continued surfing. "A crew of Santa Cruz guys shut down their skis and formed a circle, but others acted like nothing had happened. That was fucking wrong."

"Peter Mel called me that morning on his way to Mavericks," says Ruffo. "He said, 'I just want to tell you to be careful today.' Pete usually tells me anything but that. I was like, *What the fuck was that, dude?* It was in my head all day. It's what made me go in. We all like living on the edge, but not to the point of doing things that are stupid. That's what made me mad about what Don Curry said. This wasn't stupid. Davi was out there way before this. He was a solid waterman and fisherman. There was no reason to think he was doing anything wrong."

It's the night before Christmas Eve, and Jake, Katrin, and Ruffo are hanging out at Peter Davi's Monterey home. It's a modest place, decorated with artifacts from a life on the water. Jake shows off a thirty-pound rock of jade his dad unearthed, a replica of Peter's grandfather's grandfather's fishing boat, and a palm-size fossilized shark tooth his dad found up in the mountains. "Dad should've had a museum," his eighteen-year-old son says. "If you liked something, he'd give it to you, even if he'd never met you."

Jake says Pete looked out for everyone, no matter how big or small the waves. "'Two feet to twenty,' he always said," Jake says, recalling a day in 2002 when his dad pulled four tourists from the freezing waters off Carmel Beach. The fifth, a kid, died in Davi's arms. Davi did time in 1998 on drug and firearms charges, but Ruffo says jail was a wake-up call. "We all do crazy shit," says Ruffo, who was busted in 2005 for selling meth. "But Pete paid his debt. He worked hard, fishing every day." He may have turned his life around, but there was another factor in Davi's death. The toxicology report, issued on January 10, revealed that at the time of his death Davi had methamphetamines in his system at a level of 0.75 milligrams per liter—more than enough to make him intoxicated and potentially impair his ability to survive an accident in dangerous surf.

The evening of December 3, as Peter Davi prepared to head out to Ghost Tree, Jake and some friends were sitting on Oahu's North Shore, watching waves crash in the twilight, when a pair of surfers were sucked out by a rip current. Commandeering a jet ski, they charged out and saved the kids from being lost at sea. The next morning Jake was trying to sleep, but his phone kept ringing. "Around twenty people called me," he says. "They told me something bad had happened; my dad was lost at sea. I'm thinking, *Lost at sea? No fucking way. Not my dad.*"

Jake assumed his dad's fishing boat had simply failed to report. "'Think positive,' I said. 'He'll make it in.' But then I found out he was surfing."

Jake stood in Saint Angela Merici Catholic Church in Pacific Grove two days later, listening to friends eulogize his father. Hundreds turned out at Lovers Point in Monterey that afternoon for a paddle-out memorial. Jake watched from the rocks until his friend Darryl "Flea" Virostko paddled by on an 11'7" Dick Brewer board that Peter had given Jake. Jumping into the frigid water in his full Versace suit, Jake rode the board as the crowd cheered.

Ghost Tree wasn't finished wreaking havoc. In late afternoon, Russell Smith towed his brother into a monster. Unaware of the prodigious beating he was about to take, Tyler styled straight down the beast's massive face. The crowd assembled on the adjacent cliff moaned and yelled in horror as Ghost Tree dropped a 50-foot ax on the elder Smith. Without hesitation, Russell raced into the impact zone but couldn't snag Tyler before the next wall of whitewater blew him off his ski and into the sea alongside his injured brother, who had torn a rotator cuff in the wipeout.

—Ryan Masters, *Heroes and Ghosts*

Drained but unable to sleep, the next morning Jake drove to the mortuary to say a few final words to his father. There was stuff that Jake wishes he'd told him. He wishes he hadn't been so embarrassed by things his dad did when Jake was a kid, like dropping him off at school in posh Carmel with no shirt on. "He was a fucking caveman, and he'd embarrass me all the time," Jake remembers. "And we fucking butted heads. He knew how to yell because he was a fucking Sicilian. But he was one of a kind. He fucking raised me right and taught me a lot of good lessons. And I'm thankful for it all."

Jake was angered by Don Curry's claim that Davi wasn't in shape to be out in the waves and by another person's suggestion that it was the drugs that allowed his father to fish through the night. "My dad worked his ass off fishing," says Jake. "If he hadn't, he wouldn't have been able to afford a million-dollar house. He had to fucking take care of shit, and he did."

On the way to the mortuary, Jake fell asleep at the wheel going 85 mph. Driving behind him, Liam McNamara was horror-struck to see Jake's truck drift into oncoming traffic. At the last instant, Jake says, he felt a slap to the face that could have come only from his father. He swerved, avoiding other cars but plowing into trees. Sure that he'd broken his neck, paramedics airlifted Jake to San Jose, but aside from a load of glass in his head, Jake and his dog Hueneme miraculously escaped unharmed.

It was part of a string of signs, Jake says, that began on December 4. Shortly after Davi disappeared, Flea Virostko endured what onlookers say was the heaviest wipeout they'd ever seen, sucked into the lip of a huge wave and augured in deep. "He told me he should have died on that wave," Jake says. "He said my dad grabbed him and brought him to the surface."

With medical bills and his father's mortgage, Jake knows he has to get serious about life right now. He wants to start up an outdoor equipment company and one day earn invitations to the Mavericks and Eddie Aikau big wave contests.

A few days after Davi's funeral, Jake, his sister, the McNamara brothers, Kealii Mamala, and a few other friends held a private memorial above the Carmel River mouth. As they sat, the biggest red-tailed hawk they'd ever seen perched nearby and stared at them for thirty minutes. "Dad was sitting right there," Jake says. "He never got recognized at Pescadero Point, and they named it Ghost Tree. Now it's Peter's Tree. If you read the Bible, *Peter* means 'the rock.' Peter was a fisherman, and he was a fucking legend. Just like my dad."

In a hospital bed a week later, Lickle has had time to reflect on the most intense experience of his life. "With these high-performance aluminum fins, we've always said if anyone gets hit, it could be nasty," he says. "It was a lot nastier than anyone expected.

"I'm getting too old for this shit," Lickle says. "This was the big one. The near-drowning taught me that I can make it. But do I want to go through that again? No."

Hamilton might wish he could make that decision, but he can't. "A lot of it, truthfully, is out of my hands," he says. "When I see giant surf, it's not like, *Should I go?* It's automatic."

Exactly one month after Davi's death, an even stronger storm hit California, bursting levees and dumping 10 feet of snow on the Sierras. Another group of top-drawer big wave surfers—Brad Gerlach, Mike Parsons, Grant Baker, and champion Greg Long—found it impossible to resist the pull of the great waves and on January 4 headed out to a legendary spot called Cortes Bank, an underwater mountain range 100 miles off the California coast, and plunged down 80-foot faces in the middle of the ocean. One speeding wave caught Gerlach and Parsons's PWC, burying them underwater. But their flotation vests brought them back to the surface.

"I've never had a more adventurous day," says Parsons, forty-two. "I'm way more calculating now than when I was twenty-four and would drop in on anything. I know my days are numbered, but days like this are so special, you don't ever want them to end."

BIG WAVE SURFING'S MOST DRAMATIC EVENT (1958)

Big wave riding advanced to a new and terrifying place during a two-day run at Makaha on January 13 and 14, 1958. The weather was hot and windless as Makaha shuddered from the output of a gigantic North Pacific storm, which meteorologists later estimated covered nearly a million square miles.

A day earlier, the West Side had been flat. On the evening of January 12, Buzzy Trent had gone to sleep in his Makaha Valley home after drinking two or three Primos, only to snap awake just after midnight to the thundering noise of incoming surf. He ran outside and spent two hours watching huge moonlit waves roll through before going back to sleep.

Paddling out not long after daybreak, Trent was thrilled and a little spooked to find the deep-water channel adjacent to the break, normally a calm zone on even the biggest days, slowly rolling and shifting, while 20-footers looped over in the Bowl section. Paddling farther outside, he found George Downing already sitting at the far end of the takeoff area, waiting. A few more surfers would paddle out as the day progressed and ride with varying degrees of fortune and mishap. (Not long after catching a screamer from the top of the Point all the way through, filmmaker John Severson blacked out underwater during a wipeout and nearly died.) But Trent and Downing, already known as the era's ranking big wave masters, owned the day.

Of the two, the Hawaiian Downing was the more accomplished surfer. But Trent was more compelling. At the beginning of a ride, after snapping up into a wrestler's squat, he'd launch his board like a missile on the highest possible line across the wave face and hold position until he either coasted into the channel or was deep-sixed by whitewater. There was more technique involved than met the eye, but Trent's style looked like surfing's version of power-lifting. Downing, strong but wiry, had a lower angle of attack and was able to make small, fluid adjustments as he raced forward. Unlike Trent, he wouldn't sacrifice himself to a lost cause; once the ride began to fall apart, Downing would quietly step off the back of his board, tuck into a ball as he plunged beneath the surface, and avoid—usually—the worst of the explosion that followed.

Makaha during that mid-January swell was perfection on a never-seen-before grand scale. Trent, grabbing the only point of reference he had, often described it as looking like a "giant Malibu." Even so, the waves were generally so fast as to be unrideable. Most of Trent's rides came spectacularly undone at some point, but he got at least a half-dozen keepers from the top of the Point, through the Bowl, and into deep water, each one a catapulting 300-yard race where maximum board speed was an exact match for the chasing speed of the wave.

Wave size climbed steadily on the 13th, leveling off in the midafternoon somewhere around 30 or 35 feet and still smooth as cream. At about 3 p.m. Trent repositioned himself near the channel to watch six or eight sets of waves funnel slowly down the coast from distant Keana Point. Each wave seemed to inflate as it hit the top of the Makaha lineup, just before the curl arced out and down to create a huge, black, pinwheeling hole of a tube, the size and diameter of which remained unchanged from the top of the Point through to the Bowl. The waves weren't getting much taller, but a line had been crossed. Trent later claimed his whole existence had led to this moment, and the realization that the waves before him were in fact too big and fast to ride, he said, was "terrible . . . just terrible." Humbled, he turned and caught a smaller wave to the beach.

Downing's run ended the next morning after he sprint-paddled over four progressively bigger waves and was caught out by the fifth. He pushed his board away and swam for the bottom, felt his sinuses rupture from the pressure change as the wave moved overhead, and broke the surface a few moments later with blood pooling in the back of his throat and rushing from his nose.

The 1958 Makaha swell was big wave surfing's most dramatic event to date, but it passed by largely undocumented. John Severson shot a roll of film over the two days, but the quality was poor. A few rides were used in *Surf*, his first movie (the only copy of which was either stolen or lost), and a few 16-millimeter "frame grab" prints were made. None of the images, though, really showed off the surf's true height and amplitude. In decades to come, Trent, Downing, Severson, and a few others, without fail or hesitation, would all say that Makaha during that two-day swell had served up the finest big waves in the sport's history.

Yet, it never really became part of surfing lore. Makaha remained the anchor of West Side surfing, and huge Point Surf would always be an incomparable surf-world challenge. But by 1958 it was in fact already losing its place at the fore of big wave surfing to Oahu's North Shore—surfing's own beautiful, tropical, hostile mecca.

—From *The History of Surfing*, by Matt Warshaw

Brock Little's epic Waimea
Bay drop during the 1990
Quiksilver/Eddie Aikau contest

REFLECTIONS ON WAIMEA

by Brock Little

It happens to every surfer: Eventually you've ridden enough waves, been there for enough classic swells, watched the sun set on enough memorable days that you begin looking back as much as you used to look forward. Call it age, call it perspective . . . call it wisdom. Big wave heroes like Hawaii's Brock Little call it difficult to experience something as a man that they once lived for as a boy. In this case, a big, scary day at Waimea Bay.

I missed the Eddie because of a hurt rib. Anyway, here we are six weeks after hurting my rib, and I'm ready to go. I've surfed three or four times, swam a little in big surf, and feel pretty confident. By the way, lying on a hurt rib and trying to paddle a surfboard is not pleasant. The point of these excuses is I haven't surfed much.

The good part is I'm back home in Hawaii, ready to start surfing again, feeling pretty good and about to go to bed. I decide to take a quick look at the buoy readings at Waimea Bay before knocking off. It's 25 feet at 17 seconds. For people who don't speak buoy language, that's *giant*. It's as big as the Bay can handle and still hold some kind of shape—or possibly too big. I have no reason to be nervous. The Eddie is over, and I've proved myself enough times. But I still can't sleep.

When I wake up in the morning and drive down the hill, I see it's really big. I have a doctor's appointment I shouldn't blow off, so I go. Driving around the Bay I'm seriously hoping it will drop by the time I get back. When Waimea is this big, it's not fun; it will kill you, or me.

When I get back from town around eleven, it's as big as it gets. I'm not sure why, but I have to go out. Waimea has nearly killed me twice at this size, and I'm afraid. When Waimea is huge like this I never watch it before I go out. I get down to the beach and paddle out. People usually follow because I've been around a while, but paddling out when I do is a dangerous idea.

This time my friend Arnold Dowling followed me out. He paddled toward the channel; I stuck next to the rocks. He got his ass kicked in the middle of the Bay; I got tossed around by twenty waves with 5 feet of whitewater next to rocks. When the waves finally let up, I paddled my ass out to the lineup. All the way out I was worried about a closeout set. When I made it out, I was winded.

I knew I shouldn't be out there. I was not in shape, mentally or physically, for maxed-out Waimea. And this was maxed-out. Usually when I'm on the beach, I'm scared. I feel sick in my gut. On my way out, though, those feelings start to change, and by the time I reach the lineup, I'm fearless. This day was different. When I got out I could think only, *Shit, it's going to be hard to catch a wave in.* With that mind-set, you're just asking for it.

All of my life I've seen that when people surf closed-out Waimea, and I'm talking about champion-level chargers here, very few want a real wave, one of the true monsters. They paddle out thinking they want one, but when they get out it feels like a bad idea. On this day there were twenty guys out, but only three or four who wanted a 20-plus-foot wave. Kahea Hart surprised me: He charged. Arnold, and also one of the South African *brahs*, was big game hunting. Pretty much everyone else looked like they'd seen a ghost.

I was on the fence and not sure which way to go. I told myself many times, when I became one of the guys not wanting a set wave, I'd quit. That's the session I realized that I might be one of those guys. I'm forty-two, I have a great wife, and I can't achieve much more, wavewise, than what I've already done. Why am I out here when I know it can kill me? I also know that when I'm out in the thick of things, I make bad choices in regards to my well-being.

1989. Dawn at Waimea, one day before the famous Eddie Aikau contest. Titus Kinimaka paddles out into the 18-foot swells and spends several hours catching bombs. His final wave closes out, the lip collapses on top of him, and his surfboard "chops" into his right leg. "I dove under and got tumbled around again," Titus says, "and when I finally came up there was something hitting me on the side of my cheek, back by my right ear. I was kind of dazed, wondering, 'What is this thing?' and I grabbed it and was looking at it, and then I realized it was the bottom of my foot." After a steel rod was inserted through his right hip and he spent four months in bed healing himself, the first thing Titus Kinimaka did was go out and surf 10-foot waves at Hanalei Bay.

—Maura O'Connor, "Big Wave Surfing: Tales from the 'Unridden Realm'"

So all this crap is going though my head, but I'm starting to get my wind back. I've been out about ten minutes, and a set starts to form way out in the ocean. Horns are honking; everyone is paddling for the horizon. I don't paddle out because I know if you want to catch one, you have to stay close to the reef. For some idiotic reason, all of a sudden my mindset has changed, and I'm going to get one. When the set rolled through, I was too far in for the first one, out of position for the second one, and the third and biggest was steaming right at me.

I turned around and took off, knowing I'd make the wave. It was outside the main reef, so catching it wasn't hard. A wind chop pushed me in, and before I knew it I was halfway down the face. Then the wave hit the regular Waimea reef and created a little bump. I went over that and knew I had the wave made. I sighed with relief. My board slowed down, but my body did not and crashed shoulder first into the bottom of the wave face. No big deal. I'd be under a while; I've done it before. I got worked. And when I made it up, I felt fine.

Then I noticed that although I was swimming with two arms, one was just floating. I freaked out, screamed like a little girl. I dislocated my left shoulder, and it was heavy to see my arm just dangling. A 20-footer was bearing down, so I had to start thinking about functioning with three limbs instead of four. I took off my leash because I didn't think it would be a good idea to drag my arm through the water with the leash pulling me. The wave thrashed me around pretty good. Underwater I swam like I had two good arms; it didn't feel much different than normal. When I popped up, both arms were working. I was actually swimming. Did that just happen?

Somebody out on the shoulder came in and let me jump on the back of his board. I'm sure he heard me screaming because before that wave I was howling like a big pussy. Clyde Aikau came over to help push me into the channel. Everybody was waving for the jet ski. The weird truth was I felt fine. I was paddling on the back of some guy's board, and my arm didn't even hurt. Lifeguard Abe Lerner came over on the ski and had me climb onto the sled. He took me in and dropped me perfectly right on the sand. End of story.

But I don't know. I've come a lot closer to drowning, broke my kneecap, blah, blah, blah. But I keep asking myself if I should keep surfing giant Waimea. For years I was usually the best guy out, and there's still some truth to that, though Shane Dorian and a few others are definitely better than me now. But I can't pass up a closeout if I'm in the spot and in the mood. I'm forty-two with nothing to prove. No decision made just yet, but leaning toward walking away. We'll see.

I just saw the photo. Kind of a nothing wave and a nothing fall—not so good for my ego. If my shoulder pops out on a medium wave at the Bay, what'll happen on a real wave? It makes me think about Mark Foo's medium wave at Mavericks, his last one.

I think I think too much.

THE BIGGEST, THICKEST,
MEANEST WAVE OF THE DAY

A dozen or so California pioneers saw to it that the North Shore replaced Makaha as surfing's big wave capital. Each year they returned in slightly bigger numbers, with a slightly raised level of confidence. Informality was the rule. With few exceptions, California surfers on the North Shore didn't come off as determined sportsmen, like bullfighters or mountaineers, grimly pursuing their dangerous dance with fate. Rather, they acted like frat boys on spring break.

They climbed to the top of Waimea Falls and double-dared each other to jump 60 feet to the lake below. When it rained, they hiked into the backcountry and went mud-sliding down pig trails. After a few beers, somebody might walk out to the porch and fireball a mouthful of lighter fluid onto a lit match. They went shirtless, stole chickens, played poker, and broke wind with the kind of volume and frequency that comes only from twice-daily servings of canned beans. John Severson bought a rusted '41 Chevy sedan for $19.95, painted it from bumper to bumper in swirls, scrolls, and curlicues (tires included), hand-lettered "Sunset Special" across the passenger doors, then drove the car for months before selling it for $15.

One of the new mainlanders was a lanky, sad-eyed board-maker from La Jolla named Pat Curren. For his second visit to the North Shore, Curren rented a three-bedroom beachfront house at Sunset for himself and nine other San Diego-area surfers, removed all the furniture, demolished the partition walls in the front of the house, installed horizontal floor-to-ceiling surfboard racks along one side, and built a long trestle down the middle of the room. Curren had a passing interest in Norse legend, and he called the new digs *Mead Hall*. Normally the quietest and most reserved of the California surfers, Pat Curren was so inspired by the renovation that he'd preside at mealtime wearing a thrift-shop Viking helmet, pound his fist on the tabletop, raise one foaming beaker of mead after the other, and exhort his friends to do the same in a broken Old English–surfer dialect.

Along with Greg Noll, Curren became one of the acknowledged leaders of the North Shore pioneering effort. Back in California, while most of the other mainland big wave riders were attending college, Curren worked as a draftsman and a carpenter and did some underwater repairs on the Santa Barbara Channel oil platforms; he had an air of offhand but absolute mechanical competence. Curren's high rank on the North Shore had a lot to do with the specialized big wave boards he made—sleek, perfectly crafted 12-foot balsa pintails, described by one surfer as "a cross between a work of art and a weapon."

[George] Downing and [Joe] Quigg invented the finned big wave surfboard, but Curren improved on the design with subtle but crucial adjustments to the rocker curve and bottom contours. Curren was also the slouching, near-mute apotheosis of surf cool: draining an afternoon beer, flicking a cigarette butt to the side, then taking down Malibu golden boy Tommy Zahn in a paddle race; flying to Hawaii one season with no luggage save a ten-pound sack of flour for making tortillas; sailing the 3,000-mile Great Circle route from Honolulu to Los Angeles on a 64-foot cutter and posing for a photo en route, bearded and watch-capped, a huge Havana cigar jutting from a corner of his mouth, left hand on the wheel, right hand holding a shot glass of *crème de menthe.*

Cooler than all these images put together, Curren would invariably pick off and ride the biggest, thickest, meanest wave of the day. With Zenlike patience he'd sit on his board at least 10 yards beyond anybody else, then wait an hour, two hours, three hours if necessary, for the grand slam set wave. The ride itself was stripped down and fluid, as Curren went into a deep crouch, spread his arms like wings, and led with chest and long chin; tearing across a huge wave face, in circumstances where other riders dropped automatically into a survival stance, Curren often looked like an Art Deco hood ornament.

"And he didn't give a shit if anyone saw it or not," fellow big wave charger Peter Cole said. "The rest of us would run around, chasing photographers, 'Did you get the shot? Huh? Did you?' While Pat would just grab the wave of the day, walk up the beach, and vanish."

—From *The History of Surfing,* by Matt Warshaw

Grant Baker taking an optimistic line at Dungeons, off South Africa's Cape of Good Hope

DUNGEONS TIME

by Rusty Long

It was called the Cape of Good Hope, some kind of cruel joke when you consider that seventeenth-century Dutch mariners applied the moniker to the storm-battered, monster wave–lashed southern tip of the African continent. But over the past decade a new breed of ocean explorer has flocked to the Cape Town region with the hope of tackling the very same storm surf that sunk fleets of Dutch Indiamen. More specifically, to ride a scary, inhospitable spot known as Dungeons, which breaks big and often enough to make devotees out of Californians like Rusty Long, who provided this battlefield account.

Shark Alley is so-named because directly in from the farthest west section of the Dungeons reef is a seal island with thousands of blubbery snacks frolicking at all times. The place is a drive-through for the lurkies. Local fishermen think we're nuts for surfing out there.

The pioneers of Dungeons used to paddle across that channel to get out and, in some instances, swim back in because of broken leashes. Pierre De Villes is the most notorious pioneer and respected big wave surfer of the area. He owns a surf and art joint called the Dream Shop. I met him there a day after he returned from a dive trip in the Natal area. "A hell trip," he called it. The visibility was subpar, and a bestial grouper snagged his catch and took him for a ride, nearly drowning him. He likes diving during sardine runs when the food chain is in full effect—that's how he gets his adrenaline fill. "You ever come across sharks out there?" I questioned. "Are you fucking kidding me? This ocean is full of

Sparkly, warm afternoon lighting belies the serious nature of every go-out at Dungeons.
PHOTO © NIC BOTHMA

'em! They usually give you a once-over, but sometimes a pissed one will grind your catch." That's the breed it took to initially surf out there without boat or safety crew. Try and imagine that.

It seems the world's most majestic waves are backed by equally majestic landscapes. Dungeons is no exception. A densely forested valley surrounded by mountains with only one winding road through leads to the bay, with massive homes interspersed throughout. The place is the Beverly Hills of Cape Town. Red Bull [a company sponsor of big wave riders] didn't mess around with accommodations either. We were set up on the valley floor on a two-acre property with a big house and some small cottages with a couple of pools and spas.

It was a bit of an animal house commune, but what else is expected when a handful of frothing, big wave hellmen live in such close quarters? Twiggy and Antman lived together in a cottage. Twiggy is from Durban, a jack of many trades. He works for a few months a year as a Billabong rep in the Natal region. He's one of the best kiteboarders in the world, an expert tube rider, and a smooth romancer of women.

Antman Patterson, from Yallingup, West Oz, is a legend. He'll ride any wave, take any bet, and cook up a gourmet meal to finish the day. He turned his 2,000-rand contest appearance money into 20,000, the equivalent of $2,000, which would last months there. We were all in awe, but he coolly explained it as "standard procedure; woulda had way more, too, but I was handing off all the small chips to an old boy hanging around."

Also at the pad were Rudy Palmboom, a country legend from Durban; Jon Whittle, who in his younger days partied harder than anybody but now has no fear "because the Lord is watching over me"; Grant Washburn, the animated giant from Mavericks; and the godfather, Gary Linden, who directs the event and is the only fifty-three-year-old I know still paddling into 20-footers.

Dungeons helps establish Capetown as the home of seriously heavy waves.
PHOTO © NIC BOTHMA

The entire month was an incessant run of big waves. Unfortunately, most swells arrived with the brutal fronts that created them, resulting in uncouth conditions. Aside from one ultra-clean 15-foot day that was too inconsistent to hold the contest (a day Jamie Sterling smacked his head on his board for a concussion), most sessions were amid a mess of wind and chunky swell. Even on its prettiest day, the wave is unpredictable, and on its uglier days, well, nightmarish. The waves pop up sporadically along a 200-yard stretch of reef. The outside and inside sections are the gnarliest. The top section is a folding slab impossible to paddle into—it honestly mimics reverse Teahupoo. When somebody eventually tows

into it, heroic tubes will manifest. The bottom section is another shallow shelf that contorts the waves into boxy, boily mutants. In between these sections is where the proper waves break, which shift drastically and show a different form for every wave. You never really know what will unfold.

On one of the big messy days, Gary made the wise decision to not run the event, but a handful of crew was amped for a surf anyhow. I was with Sterles as we watched. I asked him, "If Waimea was this out of hand, would you go out?" "No way!" he replied. "What about Todos?" "Not a chance!" But we couldn't be the princesses left on the boat.

Greg Long got out a bit before me, and I paddled up to him for a synopsis. "It's fucking sketchy; I'm catching one and getting out of here," he hollered.

My session went like this. A macker caught me inside, and my leash was pulled from the strings and washed into Shark Alley. The safety ski grabbed me, we fetched my board, and I reattached and paddled back out. Anticipation time was about half an hour until a macker swung right to me. I stroked in, and the wave jumped simultaneously. I looked straight down, my board clinging vertically to the face, realizing I'd put myself into "a predicament." A chop caught the nose of my board at the top and swallowed it, sending me cartwheeling forward onto the pitching face. I flew backward with an upside-down look at Sentinel Cliff, thinking for an instant, *Wow, neat view.* There was a tranquil moment, then a long "Ohhhhh, Shiiit!" then a vicious explosion that compressed my head, shooting yellow and white fireworks through visual darkness.

Luckily, the hold-down wasn't too long, maybe twelve seconds, but the impact was the most brutal I've experienced. I surfaced and couldn't judge up from down, in from out. My head was spinning like it does when you jump in bed after a night of boozing and stare at the ceiling. My board was, amazingly, still in one piece. Sterles wiped out on the wave after mine just up the reef and ended up right by me. He realized I was dazed and headed me to the channel. Another wave on the last section nailed us and pushed us into deep-water safety. My neck tightened immediately, and my head spun circles for a good fifteen minutes. I was fortunate to come out with just a concussion and a weeklong stiff neck. That's exactly where flexibility comes into play. After that, no more out-of-control days for me.

James "Billy" Watson drops into a hole in the ocean while riding a remote, offshore "bommie" in Tasmania.

PHOTO © TONY HARRINGTON

FISHERMAN'S HUNCH: FIRST TRACKS AT THE BOSENQUET BOMBORA

by Tony Harrington

Going surfing Down Under used to be easy and mostly fun: the casual stroll through Norfolk pines to the jump-off spot at Queensland's Burleigh Heads; cruising along backcountry roads on the way to Angourie's fabulous point break; the short jog across the sand from the parking lot to the tubes of Sydney's North Narrabeen. Key phrase: used to be. *Once a new generation of full-throttled Aussie surfers looked up from their sunny beaches to the outer realms of their Pacific and Indian Ocean shores, the monster wave discoveries came fast and furious. Mostly furious, as revealed by this expedition account in which an intrepid team of watermen confront a true Tasmanian devil.*

Saturday, Day 1. The Gathering

The offshore wind had been picking up since dawn. The breeze was light enough in the beginning; the early arrivals reveled in some 12- to 15-foot morning glories before it turned punishing, forcing us back to the beach. We didn't know what punishment was.

Jamie Mitchell and Billy Watson had just accomplished a mammoth driving task, towing their ski for twenty-four hours from the Gold Coast. I had picked up Bra Boy Richie "Vass" Vaculik and his mate, John "Bones" Dwyer, from Bronte, in Adelaide, the night before. This was Bones's first real trip away from Sydney chasing bigger waves than he was used to, something of which Bungy, his friend from home, consummated when he sent a text to Bones en route exclaiming:

"Here are the three scenarios: Bones overestimates his ability and gets hammered by massive waves; Bones dies. Bones faces his worst fear in the cold southern Australian waters when he meets an 18-foot great white shark, and after a very brief struggle, Bones dies. Bones is exposed as the coward he is when he refuses to leave the boat the entire trip; Bones lives (although sadly, he later takes his own life when he realizes he's been exposed as a soft cock)."

With a rumpus cackle from Vass and myself and a worried look on Bones's face, we cruised through the night, finding ourselves at base camp at 1:00 a.m. Five hours later we are in the water for day 1 of the Search for the Bosenquet Bombie.

Shipsterns guardians Marti Paradisis and James Hollmer-Cross flew in later, along with Mark "the Shadow" Visser. We all regrouped at the dock to meet up with legendary fisho and surfer Jeff Schmucker, his seventeen-year-old son, Josiah, and Dave from Oregon, Jeff's long-time surfing buddy, the two having first met years before at some exotic break overseas.

After loading the deck of the 22-meter prawn trawler with a seemingly endless supply of food, equipment, and Coopers, we transferred down to our bunks set up in the fish freezer room. It resembled a jail with all the caged enclosures but was clean as a whistle and smelled nothing of fish despite having thousands of tons of prawns dumped there over the last few years.

At 5:00 p.m. the wind backed down, and we decided to give it a shot. We blasted across the tricky bar and headed 30 miles out to an island that offered some protection from the weather should it turn heavy.

One thing my science teacher always told me, and one thing that has bitten me on the butt more times than I can poke a stick at, is *never assume*. Within an hour of setting sail, the winds kicked back up: 25-30-35-40-45-50 knots. Storm-force gusts beat down as darkness fell. We were towing three skis, had another on deck, plus the aluminum dinghy. It didn't take long before the violent rocking started striking the team. Billy was the first to go puking, with everyone else feeling the effects in some form.

Our typical four-hour trip would obviously take much longer. I took watch of the towed skis, less for the machines and more because continued sitting meant upchucking for sure. Equally sickening was watching our skis getting smashed by swell and storm. They looked like corks thrashing around. I shudder to think what the captain saw as the trawler smashed through raging seas, but I didn't dare claw into the stale wheelhouse. Instead, I braced against a bulkhead for six hours, staring into the maelstrom. Waves crashed over the bow, hosing three levels of the boat, cascading over to the stern just in front of me. Several times I saw my ski get picked up and dropped on top of the others, but there was simply nothing we could do. We couldn't stop, couldn't turn—just had to punch on. After three or four hours of this madness, had the tow ropes snapped, which seemed likely, I wouldn't have minded. I was past the point of caring.

Jamie Mitchell's take on the moment: "We were about four hours into the trip, and I remember going up into the captain's quarters and checking out the conditions, and it was wild. It reminded me of *The Perfect Storm*. Then I told the cap that he must see conditions like this all the time, hey? He just looked at me and said, "Nah, mate, we stay at home when it's like this," and then just focused on punching through the swells.

At around 11:00 p.m. we pulled into somewhat calmer waters, but the wind and ocean still boiled. As we anchored up for the night, we noticed that Jeff's ski was sinking. Billy dived into the dark and shark-ridden ocean at 1:00 a.m. to throw a rope around it so it could be retrieved. The ski was hauled out of the water and drained, and the engine fired first go.

With the first—and heaviest, we'd hoped—part of the journey over, we hankered for some shuteye. But a mad chorus of snoring made sleep impossible for some, so I dragged myself into the dining room and collapsed on the floor, finally copping some kip.

Surfing miles from shore means
no point of reference other
than the waves themselves.
Marty Paradisis, Tasmania
PHOTO © TONY HARRINGTON

Sunday, Day 2. Sanctuary Found

The second day of the journey once more awoke to a torrid ocean, but, being on the leeward side of the wind, at least it was offshore. We cruised around to a point break, which had been surfed before, but for the stiff offshore we needed skis slingshot onto the waves. Such a serene setting: a tranquil bay, reeling rights, ominous cliffs rearing in the background, separating a lost piece of land from the continent, and a sense of complete isolation—a desert in the middle of an ocean. Now this felt like home.

Toward dark, the point started to really fire. Vass was the standout, pulling into the longest and heaviest of pits, but not far behind was Josiah, a seventeen-year-old with a huge future on his plate. Billy and Jamie had engine trouble. They hauled their ski onto the deck, where a couple of gallons of saltwater were found in the fuel tank. How the hell that got in there we had no idea, but given the punishment of the tow-out, anything was possible.

With an abating wind at dusk and rising full moon on the horizon, the location turned surreal as a horde of pastels enveloped the sky and landscape. The sanctuary had been found. We retreated to the safer anchorage around the corner, cracked open the Coopers, and feasted on a few kilos of legendary Venus Bay prawns. It was a ritual that we'd repeat each afternoon of the trip.

Monday, Day 3. The Big Blow

We were expecting this to be the wildest weather of the trip. The deep low sitting several hundred kilometers below us was the strongest of the winter. The swell had certainly jumped, and if it weren't for the blustering side-shore conditions, the 10- to 12-foot waves would have been epic. If it's this big on the eastern side of the island, how big would it have to have been on the side open to the brunt of the storm?

Most of the day was spent siphoning the spoiled fuel in Billy's ski from the tank, cleaning, resiphoning, and refueling again and again. Seeing the spontaneous stroke in his eyes when the ski roared to life and then the exasperation and disappointment when it died again was heartfelt by all. This happened several times in between the hours of tireless drudge work.

By the end of the day they believed it was running well enough to go surfing. We had a thirty-minute steam in the trawler to get to the point, so Billy and Jamie put trust in their handiwork and went ahead, battling a raging ocean to claim some waves before the rest of the crew arrived. As they charged forward, they disappeared in the ungodly looking ocean. We feared for their safety. If the ski broke down, they'd have been blown into the 400-foot-high cliffs and smashed to pieces, ski and bodies both.

We arrived at a windswept point, the wind not quite offshore enough to keep it from being epic. Ten- to twelve-foot lines poured down the rocky foreshore, but it was more a mercy surf for the sake of getting off the trawler. Still, a few fun waves went down, and the location showed the potential at a bigger size.

Day 4. Finding the Bosenquet Bombie

The weather was still up at 6:00 a.m. My heart sank. I'd known all along that this was the day we'd score—if at all. We still had another 10 miles to the reef Jeff had seen years ago while shark fishing. Given his surfing background, the hunch was more than enough to set up this mission. But at this point, I truly thought we had bitten off ten mouthfuls.

We pulled into a stretch of deep water near a *bombora*, an area where waves break over a submerged rock shelf, sand bank, or, in this case, a reef. A wave came through, and my heart hit rock bottom. It looked 6 to 8 feet and little more than mush. Jeff's face lit up, saying, "No, it's an easy 15 feet."

Despite the thrashing the skis had received, mine was running perfectly, and it was time for a reconnaissance. With Billy and Jamie on the back, we motored around the impact zone. A solid 20-footer loomed, reeling off left and right. The ocean was still as raw as hell. Huge lumps appeared from the deep and belched over the reef, disappearing as they passed into the deeper water off the backside.

Finally knowing we weren't in for a total skunking, we watched a behemoth lurch up and across the horizon. The next second we found ourselves drawing up the face of a 15-foot wall, the top half capping. I punched through the whitewater, narrowly escaping getting sucked back over the falls. Wow! Now it would be a case of just wait and see what the boys might get their fins into.

Jeff dragged Jamie into the first set wave, coming up short on speed and location, leaving Jamie teetering on the top of a 20-plus-foot crest peering down into the bowl. Next wave he's in, and things looked good for the first part. Not for long, though, as it closed out. Jamie bailed, trying to punch through the wave and out the back. He was sucked up and over, the curl detonating like a bunker buster. Jamie got worked satisfactorily.

As the morning unfolded, the wind died off, and the sea calmed, though it still was a warbled mess out there. But at least the faces were smooth, helped out by the drawing of so much energy off the reef as each wave rolled through. Sometimes the ocean would go silent, and with no obvious markers to line up on, it was impossible to tell where we were until the next mountain shouldered up. Fortunately for Marti and James, I was in the right position to nail a couple of beauties.

Bones managed to contradict the text messages by staying entirely alive. The Bronte surfer who works on the docks had his first taste of big wave surfing.

Visser was dubbed "the Shadow" because he was never seen until it was time to surf. Even though the wave was a two-way peak, I concentrated on the right-hander, as that's where the majority of the waves were ridden. We did see him drop into a lefty—apparently he scored a massive tube (so he says). Perhaps he did, as there were some solid ones out there.

Billy got a pit. Jamie's take: "It was the second-to-last wave surfed of the day. It was the wave before the sick shot Harro got of Billy, and this one looked especially thick. As soon as I saw it, I remember whipping him in and being able to look over the shoulder; I just saw this thing drawing off the reef. I got the best view of him bottom turning, and the thing was so square and hollow, I swear you could have fit two kombis in it. I just remember thinking, 'Fuck, man, you got to make it,' 'cause I was scared when I saw what was behind him, and, yeah, he pulled it off. I'll never forget it."

The storm had passed, there was no wind, and the angst of wondering if we'd even score a new wave was gone. More Coopers were cracked, and the Venus Bay prawns were grilled. The five-hour journey back in was glorious. There was a soft, rolling ocean, a beautiful setting sun, and dolphins taking flight all around us.

Day 5. The Aftermath

At 5:30 a.m. the next morning, we were up again, charging 4WDs down the coastline and around dirt tracks to a hidden wave in the middle of nowhere. The swell was still pumping and the wind offshore—a blue-bird day. For the next few hours, the boys traded spiraling pits. It was the ultimate detox from the head-splitting dose of adrenaline and punishment of being thrown around the trawler twenty-four hours a day.

I spent eighteen hours driving home along the coastline of Australia, my mind now even further fueled by the possibilities available for the next trip. Crikey, could it get any better? I aim to find out.

Oahu's North Shore enjoys that rare combination of sublime weather and ferocious waves. Going right at Pipeline epitomizes the latter.
PHOTO © JEREMIAH KLEIN

HARSH REALM:
FIFTY YEARS ON THE NORTH SHORE

by Sam George

By 2003 Sam George, then editor of Surfer, *had spent twenty-six consecutive winters on Oahu's North Shore, the 9-mile stretch of golden sand and scary waves long considered surfing's ultimate proving ground. He was joined by just about every notable surfer on Earth in what over the past half-century has become the sport's greatest gathering of the tribe, a mighty clash of big waves, big boards, and big egos. Yet, having first surfed these waters as a twelve-year-old gremmie back in 1967, George developed a long-running fascination with the history of the North Shore's remarkable surfing culture and offered up some highlights (and lowlights) in this loosely arranged timeline.*

1700s

Hawaiian folklore tells of an adventurous *alii* from Kauai named Kahikilani, who sailed the treacherous 90 miles from Lihue to the North Shore of Oahu with the express purpose of riding the thundering waves at Paumalu, the site today's surfers call Sunset Beach.

There the handsome, daring surf-prince ran afoul of a beautiful bird-maiden who, furious at how he rushed from her arms every time the surf came up, made Kahikilani at least promise that he would never kiss another woman. But while out surfing the inside bowl he attracted the attention of another beautiful *wahine* strolling on the beach. So taken was she by his performance that when Kahikilani beached a ride she approached and gave him an *ilim lei*—and a kiss. But the bird-maiden's spies were on the wing, flying back to tell all to the bird-maiden. She rushed down from her cave in a rage of jealousy, tongue-lashing Kahikilani for his faithlessness. The hapless surfer, protesting his innocence, chased the bird-maiden back up the hill toward her cave, but a few feet shy, she turned him to stone.

Kahikilani, having played out a romantic melodrama that would repeat itself countless times in surfing's centuries to come, sits to this day on the North Shore, his stony face peering out of a *kiawe* patch alongside the Kamehameha Highway, just north and across the road from the A Taste of Paradise Grill.

2002

Jon-Jon Florence, age ten, walks into the back yard of an opulent, beachfront home that looks down on Ehukai Beach Park, known to all as "Gums." Next to Florence a surfer over twice his age waits for an assessment, deferring, perhaps, to the little blond-haired grommet's nine years of experience surfing these waters.

"How's it look, Jon-Jon?"

Jon-Jon pushes the hair from his face, shades his eyes with a tiny hand, and looks out over the shoreline, his view taking in a panorama that stretches from Kaena Point to the west—the Mokuleia coast hazy and indistinct, Haleiwa, Laniakea, and Waimea Bay hidden by a curve in the coast—to the wide, sandy beach fronting the surf of Log Cabins, Rockpile, Off-the-Wall, Pipeline, and Gums and then around to the north toward Pupukea, Gas Chambers, and Rocky Point, Sunset Beach smoking in the distance.

"It's insane," he says.

1832

Having survived the long, arduous sea voyage from Boston, Protestant missionaries Reverend John Emerson and wife Ursula Sophia embark on a circumvention of the island of Oahu in the brigantine *Thaddeus*. Putting in near the mouth of the Anahulu River in Waialua Bay, the Emersons come across a village known as Hale'iwa (*hale*, home, of the *iwa*, or frigate bird). The Emersons are met and welcomed by Haleiwa's Chief Laanui, who convinces the Protestants to establish a church in the village, backed to the southwest by lush, rolling hills rolling down from the plains of Wahiawa, and facing, to the north, the wide, blue Pacific. The Emersons' journals make no mention of what the surf was like that first day in 1832, but it would have to be imagined that the New England couple witnessed plenty of North Pacific power during their years in Haleiwa. Their Liliuokalani Church still stands, as does the structure of their original adobe home located in Haleiwa across from Matsumoto's Shave Ice.

1994

After more than five years of detailed analysis, costly feasibility studies, and countless design proposals, the Honolulu Department of Transportation installs a sign on the H1 Freeway, located approximately 2 miles west of Pearl City, just past the last exit for Waimalu and Waipahu and in conjunction with the Wahiawa/Schofield Barracks off-ramp. In familiar green backing with white lettering, the State of Hawaii's newest and certainly most poignant freeway sign reads, simply: NORTH SHORE. One hundred sixty years after the Protestant missionaries' arrival, it's finally official.

1932

Andrew Anderson Jr., son of the manager of the Bank of Hawaii's Waialua branch, takes up surfing at the nearby Army Beach. The ten-year-old Anderson borrows a redwood plank from a local Hawaiian named Solomon Kukea, who, by all recorded accounts, is the first surfer to ride the North Shore in the modern era.

1951

Phillip "Flippy" Hoffman and Bob Simmons rent a small, clapboard house tucked between palms and *pandanas* in the Paumalu neighborhood, several miles west of Kahuku and adjacent to the reef break already known as Sunset Beach. Although surfed tentatively in the early 1940s by pioneers like Woody Brown and Fran Heath, then more regularly in the decade by island greats George Downing and Wally Froiseth, the newly dubbed "North Shore" has yet to be colonized by intrepid mainland surfers as has Makaha, located on the west side of the island. Hoffman and Simmons, avoiding the communal Makaha camp, which included early frontiersmen like Flippy's brother Walter, Buzzy Trent, Jim Fischer, and Billy Ming, hole up on the sparsely populated North Shore, first-surfing many of today's popular lineups by day, eating rice and fish and arguing over fierce chess games at night. Innovations abound, including Flippy's attempt to control the drift of his wide-tailed balsa board in the grinding sunset peak by affixing a thick hawser to the transom, letting it drag behind like a sea anchor. Almost forty years later surfers would make a similar performance leap by towing into waves on a rope rather than towing one behind.

1943

Having been trapped outside by a fast-building northwest swell at Sunset Beach, Woody Brown and Dickie Cross make the wrenching decision to paddle down the coast to Waimea Bay, which, though unridden at the time, has never been seen to close out. Both make the journey through and around offshore cloudbreaks that today would host numerous tow-in squads, arriving off Waimea Bay in the late afternoon. Caught inside the point by a huge set, Brown barely crests the bowl, while Cross disappears, perishing somewhere under the avalanche of whitewater. Brown makes it to shore; Cross's body is never found. Big wave surfing retreats to Makaha for the next decade.

1957

Greg Noll, Pat Curren, Bing Copeland, Del Cannon, Mickey Munoz, Mike Stang, and Bob Bermel ride Waimea Bay for the first time, paddling out en masse on a clean "15- to 18-foot" day. Aside from the specter of Cross's drowning, Munoz remembers, the bay's ominous reputation is that of being shark infested. Locals line the rim of the bay to watch the crazy *haoles* deal with the steep drop and run for the shoulder. Munoz, riding his balsa Malibu hotdog board, shows plenty of gumption but wipes out on every wave he catches. A relatively anticlimactic session, it is still a landmark day. A session much less mythologized, however, comes later on the same day, as under stormy skies the swell builds to a solid 25 feet. Late in the afternoon, as the setting sun fires the tops of the dark-bellied clouds, a very game (considering his earlier performance) Munoz joins the more experienced Stang in legitimately terrifying, maxed-out conditions. Dodging clean-up sets, Munoz clings to life on his Malibu board while the bearded Stang sits up and hurls Shakespearean taunts at the elements: "Once more unto the breach, dear friends, once more; / Or close the wall up with our English dead!" Munoz survives the go-out, returning home to the Mainland the next day to resume spring semester of his high school junior year in Santa Monica.

2002

A mid-December, west-northwest pulse peaks in the small hours at 30 feet. Dawn reveals a confusing mix of swell on the water, most of the strip roiling with unruly whitewater and messy sections. Waimea Bay is just breaking on the boil; the outer reefs are awash. Confounded by the conditions, Californians Mike Todd and Dan Malloy decide to paddle out north from Waimea, back toward Sunset Beach with plans to beach themselves through the surf at Gas Chambers, near Pupukea. Together the duo, who both distinguished themselves paddle-surfing the Bay during a late-November swell, route-find their way through a labyrinth of booming offshore reefs and cloudbreaks, unknowingly re-creating in reverse the desperate journey of Brown and Cross some fifty-nine years

Pure Hawaiian juice—for the surfer,
the Islands' greatest natural resource

PHOTO © ERIKAEDER.COM

earlier. Todd and Malloy, however, both make it to the beach alive and in time for supper.

1958

California transplants Fred Van Dyke, Peter Cole, and Rick Grigg, all North Shore pacesetters, share a house on Ka'Waena Street. Between charging big winter waves from Avalanche to Outside Velzyland, Cole and Van Dyke find work as teachers—math and science, respectively—at Honolulu's prestigious Punahou School. Students include Paul Strauch Jr., Fred Hemmings, Gerry Lopez, Jim Blears, James Jones, and Jeff Hakman, all of whom would eventually graduate with honors in their teacher's North Shore classroom.

1960–2002

While its history seems dominated by the exploits of West Coast transplants, and there are other regions of Oahu with larger populations of Hawaiian ancestry (Waianae, on the West Side, has the greatest percentage), a number of notable Hawaiian surfers have followed in Kahikilani's footsteps, modern bird-maidens notwithstanding. A partial list includes Kealoha Kaio; Paul Strauch Jr.; Eddie Aikau; Clyde Aikau; Ben Aipa; Tiger Espere; Barry Kanaiaupuni; Tom Stone; Tom Padaca; Reno Abellira; Larry Bertlemann; Michael Ho; Dane Kealoha; Louie Ferriera; Buttons Kaluhiokalani; Tony Moniz; Max Medieros; Derek Ho; Johnny Boy Gomes; Sunny Garcia; Myles Padaca; Malia, Mikala, and Daniel Jones; Tory and T. J. Baron; and Mason Ho.

2001

Primary location photography begins along the North Shore for Universal Pictures' feature film *Blue Crush,* the latest in a long line of Hollywood surf and romance epics—this time around from a female surfer's point of view. Appropriately detailed actresses are assembled and posed against suitably dramatic backdrops at power spots like Avalanche, Pipeline, and Makaha, while a team of top women pros Taft-Hartley their way into well-paying double work. Injured while riding decent-sized Pipe, go-getter Rochelle Ballard, doubling for lead actress Kate Bosworth, is relegated to the beach. She is replaced by diminutive former Quiksilver/Eddie winner Noah Johnson, surfing in a blonde wig and bikini, who provides the film with its climactic—and, in fact, its only successful—Pipeline tube ride.

1962

Having convinced producers of Columbia Pictures' *Ride the Wild Surf* that he is a true big wave legend, Malibu stylist and merry prankster Miki Dora must now join the film on location on the North Shore and surf, for the first time, Haleiwa, Sunset, and Waimea Bay. Dora, his back to the wall, so to speak, performs creditably at every venue, including a big day at the Bay, where his midface, turn-and-trim approach, while snickered at by the gun-and-run heroes of the day, closely approximates what will be considered high performance Waimea surfing for the next three decades. Stealing the *RTWS* scene, however, is Dora's ersatz friend Greg Noll, who barges into so many waves that filmmakers later write a character named "Eskimo" into the script, played by almost-famous James Mitchum, resplendent in Noll's trademark "jailhouse" striped trunks.

1965

Fred Van Dyke is approached by Honolulu night club promoter and entrepreneur Kimo Wilder McVay, who pitches him the idea of a "professional" surf contest to be held on the North Shore. McVay calls it the "Duke Kahanamoku Invitational." Not coincidentally, McVay owns Duke Kahanamoku's, a struggling night spot located in Waikiki's International Market Place. While no actual prize money is offered, appearance fees are paid to a select list of twenty-four elite invitees, the whole group being feted about Waikiki in grand style. With Van Dyke at the helm, the inaugural Duke runs on a single day in perfect 10- to 12-foot Sunset and is won by sixteen-year-old Jeff Hakman, who shocks the established North Shore riders with his "New School" approach.

2002

Jamie, the nineteen-year-old son of North Shore fixture Mick O'Brien, competes in his second Pipeline Masters trials. The previous year Jamie, who grew up on the beach at Pipeline, surfed his way to a berth in the main event finals. In this year's trials, the blond regularfoot is a berserker, charging heedlessly into long barrels and unmakable sections. Despite his electrifying performance, O'Brien places third and is eliminated from further competition but is described by the event commentators as a promising representative of the North Shore's "New School" performers.

1980

Larry Blair, a charismatic young goofy foot from Maroubra, Australia, having won back-to-back Pipeline Masters in '78 and '79, arrives on the North Shore in fine fettle. Rocketing onto pro surfing's center stage after winning Sydney's prestigious Coke contest in 1978 as a complete unknown, the theatrical, if often ungainly, McCoy team rider (who actually attended acting school and once played a corpse on a popular Australian soap opera) is described by a leading Australian wetsuit manufacturer as the "hottest kook in the world." A proprietary cross section of North Shore locals, unimpressed with both Blair's acting credentials and bold claims to take out yet a third Pipe title, deal out their own response. Accosted on the beach at Pipeline before the contest, Blair gets punched out and has his boards stomped on. He is later gang-blocked in the Pipe semifinals, eliminated from the event, and is never again a significant presence in professional competition.

1962

Having been ridden first by Phil Edwards, who the season previous paddled out and caught several fast curls at the urging of surf filmmaker Bruce Brown, the Banzai Pipeline quickly becomes one of the North Shore's premier arenas. On the period equipment, wild wipeouts dominate, but from amid the carnage Honolulu local John Peck stands out on his backhand. Utilizing the novel approach of crouching to grab his outside rail while still dropping in, Peck can avoid the speed-scrubbing bottom turn and trim high in the curl through the middle of the wave. Fourteen years later, during the fabled "Free Ride Era," South African Shaun Tomson would use the same approach to "redefine" Pipeline surfing. Six years later still, Hawaiian Michael Ho would add his touch to Peck's line, winning the Pipeline Masters with his right hand, the one that holds the rail, in a fiberglass cast—rumored to be the result of a pre-event brawl.

1966

In an interview for *Sports Illustrated,* Waimea regular Fred Van Dyke theorizes that most North Shore big wave riders are latent homosexuals. Van Dyke later claims he was quoted out of context, while everyone else is busy looking up the word *latent.*

1980

Steamer's Disco in Haleiwa establishes itself as the North Shore's only real night spot, where, during the height of New Wave, a pro surfer can still wear skin-tight Jordache jeans and not get beaten up. Or at least not on purpose. During one nocturnal foray into Steamer's pink and black zone, the ever-stylish Shaun Tomson, striding manfully across the dance floor, is caught in the middle of a catfight between a prominent Australian professional and her irate lover, the latter apparently incensed about the blond goofy foot's particularly charged performance with another *wahine* to A

Taste of Honey's "Boogie-oogie-oogie." Tomson catches an elbow with nothing latent about it in the face, sustaining a black eye that would later require explaining.

1965

In a social climate previously lubricated with Primo Beer Mateus Rose, acid hits the North Shore, adding new significance to the term *big drop*. Younger generation stars like Jeff Hakman, Jock Sutherland, Herbie Fletcher, and Jackie Eberle turn on and drop in, but it's Old Guard member and early '60s Sunset superman Paul Grebauer who really establishes the Rainbow Bridge, passionately espousing LSD's mind-opening qualities a full two years before the Summer of Love. By that time Grebauer had already dropped out to seek further enlightenment in Up Country, Maui.

1982

With Hawaii's statewide, DEA-backed Operation Green Harvest eradication program in its second year, the North Shore's *pakalolo* supply withers considerably. Cocaine fills the gap, bringing with its flurry a significant increase in violence, theft, tension, and bottle-blonde *haole* girls willing to do anything for blow. This influx of available, compliant women, the first in the North Shore's history, has a major social impact, bringing elements of Da City to Da Country in the form of a proliferation of shirts with collars and lowered Honda Accords.

1967

Jackie Eberle, the stand-out goofy foot of the season after ripping both Sunset Beach and Waimea Bay on clean, pretransitional-era Harbour guns shaped by Dick Brewer, is discovered one night by Jeff Hakman and Jock Sutherland in a catatonic acid trip from which he never returns. Even as MacGilivray-Freeman's newly released *Free and Easy* highlights his clean lines, Eberle remains institutionalized.

1986

Hawaii Kai's Tim "Taz" (as in "Tasmanian devil") Fretz, a standout in the Pipeline fray for both his buzz-cut, white-blond hair and penchant for riding Pipe on a 6'2" twin-fin, dies in what Honolulu police call a "drug-related suicide." In explanation of why Fretz was discovered with two bullet wounds to his head, police sources merely shake theirs. "He must have had considerable resolve," they admit. "Hey, it can happen."

1961

Former Mainland hot-rodder and model-plane designer Dick Brewer opens the North Shore's first surf shop. Located in Haleiwa and given the somewhat grandiose name Surfboards Hawaii, Brewer's shaping room becomes an epicenter for big wave gun production, including the construction of the prototypical Buzzy Trent Model, 11 feet of pure trim.

1969

Bill Stonebreaker, Mike Turkington, and Mike Hobak open the North Shore's second surf shop, Country Surfboards, located in the old 1935 M. Yoshida building on the west end of Haleiwa. While cultural scholars have difficulty pinpointing when the term *country* was first used to describe Oahu's North Shore, Country Surfboards, with its trippy peace symbol/pot leaf/palm tree logo, is the first to institutionalize the term.

1969

The biggest winter swell in recorded memory hits the North Shore, generated by a massive 960-millibar low-pressure system whose cyclonic winds cover almost a third of the entire North Pacific. Storm surf estimated in the 30- to 40-foot range (60 to 80 feet by today's standards) batters the coast between Kaena Point and Kahuku. The National Guard closes down the Kam Highway in

Waimea Bay is still the spiritual home
of traditional big wave riding. And
for all the right reasons.
PHOTO © JEREMIAH KLEIN

Haleiwa as during the swell's peak at midnight of December 2, a number of beachfront homes are swept off their foundations and back onto Ke Nui Ka'Waena Roads.

1977
Kua Aina Burgers opens in Haleiwa and is an immediate hit with locals and visiting surfers alike, despite exorbitant prices that include $3.50 for a plain burger with lettuce, tomato, and grilled onions.

1969
Riding a series of bladed-out, wafer-thin pocket rockets, Hawaiian icon-to-be Barry Kanaiaupuni becomes the first surfer to successfully interpret the power-surfing capabilities of what are now being called "short boards," reinventing the bottom turn at Sunset and Haleiwa.

1994
Riding a series of bladed-out, wafer-thin pocket rockets, Floridian icon-to-be Kelly Slater becomes the first surfer to successfully interpret the power-surfing capabilities of what are now being called "glass slippers," reinventing both frontside and backside surfing Pipeline and Backdoor on his way to the first of three successive Pipeline Masters victories.

1941
At approximately 8:02 on the morning of Sunday, December 7, fifty-one Aichis Type 99 dive-bombers from the Japanese Imperial Navy carrier *Akagi,* led by Lt. Cmdr. Kakuichi Takahashi, fly in low over Haleiwa en route to their attack on the 6th Pursuit Squadron barracks at nearby Schofield Barracks, coordinating their bombing run on the North Shore with the more extensive strike on the U.S. naval base at Pearl Harbor, 20 miles to the southwest.

1972

Burleigh Head local Paul Neilson muscles his way to first place at the Smirnoff Pro, surfing in sizeable Haleiwa against the cream of the new North Shore regime, including Jeff Hakman, the Aikaus, James Jones, and Barry Kanaiaupuni. Narrabeen hot grom Grant "Dappa" Oliver places fourth in a show of force that predates the more traditionally accepted Aussie North Shore "invasion" by almost four years.

1971

Laguna Beach goofy foot Mike Armstrong is out surfing a windy, 6- to 8-foot day at Pipeline. Groomed in the Brooks Street shorebreak, the eighteen-year-old "Army" has the weighted-front-foot, hunched-back tube stance down. On this otherwise unremarkable afternoon, a man with a clipboard and a bullhorn who looks surprisingly like 1968 world champ Fred Hemmings Jr. flags him in and ask him if he'd like to compete in a new, ABC-televised surf contest called the Pipeline Masters. Armstrong is apparently to replace Gerry Lopez, who, thinking the contest was called off for the day, is home in Niu Valley watching TV. Army says, "Sure!" and paddles back out with Jeff Hakman, Corky Carroll, Jim Blears, Bill Hamilton, and Jock Sutherland. Jeff Hakman wins and takes home $500, while Army, signed up on the beach, places second. Lopez, the undisputed Pipeline master, hears the results on the evening news. Livid, he wins the next two Masters contests in succession.

2002

At the $250,000 X-Box/Gerry Lopez Pipeline Masters, Andy Irons beats Shane Dorian, Kelly Slater, and Australian Mick Fanning in shifty, 6- to 8-foot Backdoor barrels, taking home $30,000 for his first-place finish. Irons's earnings represent a 6,000-percent increase over Jeff Hakman's haul thirty years earlier. One needs to compute both inflation and cost-of-living increases to appreciate how much progress this amount truly represents.

1971

Two well-known California/North Shore surfers—one of them a primary, if seldom-acknowledged, architect of the minigun movement—flee the island when felony arrest warrants are issued after a girlfriend is caught passing counterfeit $20 bills at the Ala Moana Shopping Center and names them as the source.

1974

At the Hang Ten American Pro at Sunset Beach, contest director George Downing's innovative new objective scoring system represents a brave attempt to improve over the "biggest wave, longest ride" format that had been the standard in Hawaiian surf competition for over twenty years. Sadly, however, a serious flaw is later revealed. In the semifinals, maneuver-spotter Jack McCoy, whose job is to call out completed maneuvers, each assigned a certain number of points, is apparently very liberal with his zigs and zags in the case of South African Michael Tomson. Tomson, his score padded with six extra zigs and at least four superfluous zags, advances to the final. McCoy, never suspected of passing the counterfeit zigs, eventually moves to Australia and becomes one of the sport's greatest cinematographers. Tomson, ironically, goes on to form a successful surfwear label called "Gotcha."

1980

Foodland supermarket opens across the street from Three Tables in Pupukea. Built on the site formerly occupied by renowned glasser/airbrusher Kelly Main's Waimea Bay Surf Shop and the Canaday family's feed-and-grain store, Foodland, with a swoosh of automatic doors, provides North Shore residents living north of Waimea Bay instant access to meat, produce, dairy products, and cold beer.

Previous alternatives were restricted to a trip through the claustrophobic aisles of Kammie's Market at Sunset Beach or the long haul to Fujioka's or Haleiwa Superette in Haleiwa proper. This sudden abundance provides an unforeseen challenge in the shape of increased calories, both solid and liquid, as more than a few prominent surfers' waistlines expand uncomfortably beyond the confines of sponsors' trunks. The trend is especially noticeable after Foodland begins selling Häagen Dazs ice cream.

1990

The state of Hawaii's Department of Transportation, responding to increased traffic congestion on the two-lane Kam Highway wandering through Haleiwa Town, begins construction of a 1.8-mile bypass that will completely skirt behind the site of Chief Kaanui's old village, emerging on the north end of town. To complete, it would eventually take a year for each of the seven minutes that North Shore commuters would save, including long delays when it is discovered that the new freeway runs through both an ancient *heiau* (temple) and nesting sites for an endangered species of plover. When completed, it introduces the North Shore's first traffic light, the very first between Wahiawa and Kailua.

1970–2002

Relatively unknown North Shore shapers, with proximity to both some of the most powerful waves on Earth and the equally powerful surfers who ride them, design and build some of the best surfboards in history. Some of these foamsmiths are Larry Felker, Ryan Dotson, Buddy Dumphy, John Mobley, Bosco Burns, Rick Irons, Harold Iggy, Don Koplien, James Turnbull, Jim Turner, Randy Rarick, Tom Nellis, Chuck Andrus, Dennis Pang, Bill Barnfield, Mark Angell, Charlie Smith, Jim Richardson, Gerry Smith, Cort Gion, Jeff and Don Johnson, and Kirk Bjerke.

1977

The ride of the decade, or at least the second half, comes down on a big day at Off-the-Wall when all-around nice guy Aussie Mark Richards uncharacteristically drops in on '77 world champion-to-be Shaun Tomson. MR, feeling very involved himself, industriously weaves and poses through the curl of one of the heaviest waves to be ridden that season at this photogenic stone/coral-bottom beachbreak just a flying kick-out away from Pipeline's notorious Backdoor. Unbeknownst to Richards, however, is the fact that Tomson survives the rather brutal stuff job, pulling up into the barrel behind him, successfully negotiating both MR's twin-fin wake and the grinding tube. With only about a hundred cameras firing off sequences, MR emerges from the curl triumphant, acknowledging the hoots and whistles. Then someone tells him. Shaun goes on that season to establish the single greatest performance gap that has ever existed on the North Shore, surfing virtually a decade ahead technique-wise of such luminary contemporaries as Richards, Bartholomew, Cairns, and Ho. MR, even after winning four subsequent world titles, still bristles whenever the topic of the great wave comes up.

1981

Narrabeen surfer/shaper Simon Anderson effectively changes the shapes of things to come with a groundbreaking performance on one of his three-finned Thrusters in the finals of the Pipeline Masters. Whipping around deep on a set wave, Anderson bottom-turns deep and pulls up into the tube standing upright, the inside fin allowing the big backsider to climb and drop in the barrel, emerging from under the curtain in the channel to win the event. One week later a less publicized but no less significant affirmation occurs when shaper Dennis Pang takes his first, hastily built 7'4" Thruster out on a good-size day at Sunset and stylishly proves to the still-skeptical North Shore cognoscenti that the design is no fluke.

1989

Enjoying dinner at Pizza Bob's in Haleiwa, twenty-two-year-old Brock Little, the North Shore's top young gun, mentions that he'd someday like to surf Waimea in the moonlight. Dinner partner, the late Jack Denny, suggests there is no time like the present, especially considering the moon on that evening is almost full and, at 9:30 p.m., just rising over the hills of Pupukea. Little, who will later go on to forge a career responding to dares as a Hollywood stuntman, wolfs down his last piece of Sicilian Special, drives to the bay, entourage in tow, and not only goes out but also actually jumps in off the rocks on the point rather than paddle out through the bay—a route considered suicidal even in the daytime. While his awed fans watch from shore—hooting only when they make out his tracks shimmering in the moonlight—Little enjoys what he calls "fun Waimea. About 18 foot."

When the following morning word of his nocturnal session sweeps the Strip, Little's transformation is complete: He is now officially a hellman.

2001

Thirty-five-year-old Brock Little, fresh from the Mainland and sporting an uncharacteristic wax rash on his pale chest, sits on the beach under the Pipeline lifeguard tower, shaking his head. He has just been asked a question in regard to his romantic life—more specifically the May-September romance Little struck up with *Blue Crush* star twenty-year-old Kate Bosworth during the last season's filming and has been continuing, somewhat problematically, to this day. Little's rueful response gives the impression that compared with surfing Waimea at night, dating a Hollywood actress just out of her teens is a much more daunting challenge.

1990

The Weatherly family moves into a modest beachfront house just to the west of the Pipeline right-of-way. Sons Jason and Benji take advantage of their proximity to the most torrid stretch of surf on Earth to develop into fine performers in their own right. It's their friends, however, who really establish "Benji's Backyard" as the epicenter of a progressive surfing movement later dubbed "the New School." Kelly Slater, Shane Dorian, Ross Williams, Pat O'Connell, Taylor Knox, Rob Machado, the Malloys, Kalani Robb, Akila Aipa, and Todd Chesser are just a few of the yard's denizens, all of whom benefit hugely from both the unobstructed view of Pipeline, Backdoor, and Off-the-Wall and the inevitable push from the hypercritical gallery up in the grass. Also living in the yard is a penniless, fresh-faced young videographer from Solana Beach named Taylor Steele, whose unblinking eye would go on to provide the new movement with plenty of momentum.

1980

In one of the strangest episodes in the North Shore's complex social dynamic, California insurance junior mogul Ray Keller of UIAA Insurance, looking for some sort of entry into the island surf scene, decides to personally bankroll an attempt to produce a Hawaiian world champion. Keller's campaign involves a liberal expenditure of funds, deemed as "sponsorship" of a number of notable local surfers, including actual contenders Buzzy Kerbox and Hans Hedemann. This deluge of cash, vast surfboard quivers, and free automobiles, combined with Keller's shrill cheerleading, produces an intimidating air of entitlement that simmers over at the Pipeline Masters. There, following the semifinals elimination of UIAA-sponsored Buttons Kaluhiokalani due to an interference call, a battery of incensed locals storms the judge's tower, sending the frightened judging panel scrambling for a nearby beach house. From a position of relative safety the decision is then made

Waimea surfing has changed little over the years: make the drop, edge off the bottom, and outrun the whitewater to the shoulder.

to reverse the decision and put Buttons back into what has since been called "the Seven-Man Final." During that heat—featuring Bobby Owens, Simon Anderson, Al Byrne, Wayne Bartholomew, Shaun Tomson, and Chris Barella—Kaluhiokalani inadvertently drops in several more times but—surprise!—still places third in the event.

1991

In what is considered by many to be the decade's single greatest day of surfing, the '91 Eddie is held in super-clean, maximum-size Waimea, brushed to perfection by uncharacteristic southwest winds. Peak moments abound, including one spectacular over-the-falls high dive by Haleiwa's Kerry Terukina. But it's Brock Little who provides a one-man highlight reel, pulling into and almost out of the biggest tubes of the biggest Waimea waves ever attempted, freefalling midface for a horrendous beating. Little eventually finishes second behind Keone Downing on a day that is still the benchmark against which all paddle-in sessions are measured.

1992

By this time the annual Thanksgiving dinner at the single-story, ranch-style home of the Hill family, just down from Laniakea, has become the North Shore's coolest tradition. Gathering for turkey and stuffing with son Ronald is the cream of the New School generation, including Kelly Slater, the Malloys, the Weatherlys, Brock and Clark Little, Matty Liu, Shane Dorian, Rob Machado, Todd Chesser, Seth McKinney, Akila Aipa, Donnie Solomon, and just about every other connected young star on the strip. In the next few years, however, tragedy will leave the dinner table with two notable vacancies.

1982

In November Hurricane Iwa roars over the Hawaiian Islands in the middle of the annual winter surf season, devastating portions of

Oahu with 100-plus-knot winds and high storm surges. The North Shore is especially hard hit, left without power and water for nine days. The scenes and disaster are shocking, trees and telephone poles toppled, roads flooded, and the ever-dapper Shaun Tomson seen with a beard for the first time in his life. (He should've listened to his visiting mother, who hoarded cases of Perrier from a nearby liquor store at the first sign of storm clouds.) Surfers, nothing if not adaptable, adjust quickly, lining up at Foodland when it opens its useless freezer section and distributes free Häagen Dazs rather than let it melt and descending en masse on the nearby Kuiliima Hotel to bathe in its resort pool.

1990

Pipeline ace and rising Billabong promo-star Ronnie Burns is found dead in the hills behind Velzyland, lying next to his motocross bike. The surf scene is stunned at the loss of the affable, talented goofy foot, and rumors fly. An autopsy later reveals, however, that Burns in fact died from a pulmonary condition complicated by asthma.

1995

One year to the day after Mark Foo's death while surfing Mavericks in northern California—and following a memorial service held that morning at Waimea Bay—Ventura surfer Donnie Solomon is sucked over the falls on a closeout set and, in an eerie repeat of Foo's demise, is found floating facedown in the channel. Desperate attempts to revive him are unsuccessful.

1997

Hired as a stunt double on the production of Sony's *In God's Hands*, North Shore legend-in-the-making Todd Chesser dons a skullcap and doubles for writer/producer/actor Matt George in serious Off-the-Wall, one of Chesser's favorite breaks. During a big swell later in the production schedule, however, with the film crew moving to Jaws on Maui for its climactic final segment, Chesser opts to call in sick, choosing instead to paddle to an outside reef west of Waimea Bay. Surfing with only a few friends, including Kauai goofy foot Cody Graham, the popular, fearless young hellman actually laughs when they are caught inside by a freakishly huge set but then is held down for two waves and loses consciousness. By the time his shaken friends reach his body, it is too late. Chesser's death sends shock waves through the tight-knit New School and reinforces the revelation following Solomon's death: that a big wave can hold you under until you drown.

1974

Reno Abellira, Hawaii's most successful surfer/shaper/competitor, wins the Smirnoff Pro, held in giant Waimea Bay. Much will be made of the fact that when faced with closed-out Waimea, even many of the veteran Hawaiian competitors are reluctant to paddle out until shamed into doing so by contest organizer Fred Hemmings. Hemmings, faced with a big wave boycott, claims that if the pros won't, he'll go out and prove that the sets are rideable (a strategy he admits in a later autobiography was all bluff). But more indicative of the challenges faced by those early pros is the response that Smirnoff victor Abellira receives when, stopping by Kammie's Market on the way home from his epic win, he asks proprietor Mr. Kammie, who in the course of his long career behind the counter knew virtually every surfer on the North Shore, for a celebratory bottle of champagne, gratis. Fat chance.

1998

The biggest swell since the winter of 1969 hits the Hawaiian Islands, except this time under blue skies, with light trade winds grooming the massive walls to perfection in what the still-delusional North Shore experts describe as "35- to 40-foot" surf. In some cases it is almost twice that, a point made clear by North Shore vet Ken Bradshaw who, during a monumental tow-in session at Outside Log Cabins, drops the rope on what looks like a 75-foot version of Queen's surf: a perfect, smooth peak that, if not for its extreme height and mass—and its ability to kill you—looks almost fun. To the delight of the crowds of more mortal surfers who take to the roofs of their houses and the Pupukea Highlands to get a view beyond the horrendous shorebreak, Bradshaw rides the behemoth to perfection, the culmination of his long, vaunted big wave career. Other surfers aren't so lucky. Brock Little, who has been waiting for this sort of swell his entire life, is denied access when the State Harbors and Beaches Division shut down the harbors and beaches, including PWC launches. And at Waimea Bay, after the Eddie is cancelled because of too much surf, police for the first time in history declare the surf off-limits, a decision that infuriates more than a few danger-surfers, keen to vie for the $50,000 offered in the XXL Big Wave Award. North Shore resident Jason Majors slips past the police barricade to the cheers of the crowd that lines the bay and paddles out into the seriously closed-out lineup. After rolling under several waves that gapped the entire bay, Majors washes back to the beach, where he is arrested by waiting police.

2002

On the biggest day of the 2002 winter season, twenty-one-year-old Mark Healey parks in the lot next to the Catholic church overlooking Waimea Bay, takes his 10-foot gun, and negotiates his way over the black lava rocks to Waimea's sandy crescent. There he spends a few charged moments regarding the swell's size and direction, waits for a gap in the legendary shorepound, sprints down the berm into the water, paddles through the deep, unsettled center of the bay, makes his way out past the black lava and green palms of the point, takes his place in a knot of fellow surfers waiting restlessly on their boards and, with the approach of a massive, broad North Pacific swell, turns his big board and paddles for all he's worth, digging deep as the impossibly steep wall looms up behind, stroking hard as the water beneath his board turns to sky. He finally leaps to his feet and drops into the one situation that, despite the changing decades, styles, and surfing sensibilities, will forever and always remain quintessential North Shore.

BLACK BUTCH AND THE BIGGEST, FASTEST RUSH IN SURFING

Phil Edwards rode Pipeline first (1961), but it was John Peck and Butch Van Artsdalen, two more southern Californians, both younger than Edwards, who set the early Pipeline standard.

Peck was the more innovative surfer. Tube-riding is easier to do while riding frontside (facing the wave), and Pipeline is a left-breaking spot, which meant that a right-foot-forward "goofy footer" had a big advantage over a left-foot-forward "regularfooter." Peck, a gangly teenage regularfooter, not only figured out how to reduce the backsider's handicap but also did it pretty much all at once, on New Year's Day, 1963, with a vicious hangover.

Peck came up with two basic techniques. First, he dropped his back knee toward the deck of the board on takeoff, almost like a sprinter in the blocks, which gave him added stability during the ride's first few crucial moments. Then, while in trim, he swung his right hand forward and clamped onto the outside rail. This low and solid "rail-grab" stance reduced Peck's exposure. If the curl *did* whip down onto his head and shoulders, he might still hunker down into an even tighter ball and ride it out.

Peck was a finesse man. Butch Van Artsdalen, a goofy footer from San Diego, was surfing's own Raging Bull. He'd already proven himself fearless in La Jolla's hard-breaking reef waves and was virtually impervious to pain; his back and shoulders would be raked and bleeding after a wipeout at a shallow break called Big Rock, and Van Artsdalen would crane his head around for a quick look, swear, pick his board off the sand, and stroke back out. He was chatty and friendly as a rule but a street-fighting terror when drunk, which was often. Friends and foes alike called him "Black Butch," and the surf world in general gave him a lot of room.

Van Artsdalen flew to the North Shore in October 1962 and moved into a dry-docked boat just west of Pipeline. He'd been there the year before—his first visit to Hawaii—but left a few days before Phil Edwards rode Pipeline for the first time. Van Artsdalen heard the stories and saw the photos and knew Pipeline was his break even before he rode it.

That November he paddled out for the first time, on a new fire-engine red Hobie; before the month was out he was the break's dominant surfer. He matched power with power. Nobody charged into waves with as much speed and force, and the advantage from this running start alone was enormous. Beyond that, Van Artsdalen had a genuinely intuitive feel for the break. He knew which waves to ride and which to let go. The line between a perfect Pipeline tube and a malformed closeout is so fine it's nearly invisible, and Black Butch had a jeweler's eye for picking out the narrow vertical seam that would get him from crest to trough in one piece. The drop was the hard part. Tube-riding itself, for Van Artsdalen, was comparatively easy: turn, crouch, extend the arms, and floor it.

That December he late-dropped into a cavernous 10-footer, found his line, and vanished behind the curl, with just a foot or two of his bright red Hobie board sticking out from the mouth of the tube like a toothpick. Two seconds passed. Three seconds. Then Van Artsdalen shot back into daylight, while cheers went up from the beach gallery. Someone shouted out, "Nobody does that!" Another surfer fell dramatically to the sand, as if he'd been shot, and rolled around muttering, "Oh my God." It was the ride of the year, and Van Artsdalen, improvising as the wave now fizzled out, sat back on his board, grinned, and rubbed his hands together.

From then on, the surf media devoured "Banzai Pipeline." Waves broke close to the beach, the color and lighting were beautiful, and each ride was like a miniature rocket launch, with a better than even chance of blowing up spectacularly. By the mid-1960s, Pipeline was well on its way to becoming the sport's most-watched, most-photographed break. Phil Edwards's opening-day experience had been edited into a perfect little two-minute epic for *Surfing Hollow Days*. John Peck's New Year's Day performance earned him a *Surfer* gatefold cover. A surf journalist called Butch Van Artsdalen "Mr. Pipeline," and it stuck. Meanwhile, the Chantays' 1963 surf instrumental "Pipeline" reached number 4 on the charts, making the break only slightly less famous than Malibu and Makaha.

Long before anybody died at Pipeline, surf journalists and moviemakers did their best to present it as a killer on the loose. *Surf Guide*'s first article on the break was called "Rest in Peace at the Pipeline," and it predicted this little stretch of beach was about to become "a surfer's graveyard." Bruce Brown chilled *Endless Summer* viewers by describing the Pipeline bottom as studded with coral heads that "stick up like big overgrown railroad spikes," and he showed a clip of Australian surfer Bob Pike, after a bad wipeout, being helped off the beach with a broken collarbone and three broken ribs. Waimea Bay heavy Peter Cole said he wouldn't ride Pipeline because of the "coral pinnacles that could actually sever my head from my body." In truth, the Pipeline bottom is cracked and fissured but relatively flat and coral-free, but the legend persists.

Joaquin Miro Quesada of Peru slammed onto the reef in 1967, broke his neck, and died a few hours later. It was the first Pipeline fatality. Thereafter, about every three years or so, Pipeline would claim another surfer. Lesser injuries were common: cuts and abrasions, plus the occasional broken bone, dislocation, or concussion. Most of the time, though, surfers who took horrific wipeouts at Pipeline came up without a scratch.

But the risk was always there, and Pipeline had everyone psyched out like no other surf spot in the world. The break defeated newcomers by the dozen. Some sat on the beach, unable to screw up the courage to paddle into the lineup. Others made it into the channel, stared into the pinwheeling tubes, and were frozen in place. Most first-timers who took a big hit left the water immediately, trembling and relieved, never to try again.

Each year a few stuck it out for reasons that were embedded in that clip of Phil Edwards getting shot like a cannonball from his first big Pipeline wave. *Time* magazine was completely wrong. Tube-riding wasn't like smoking hashish. There was nothing opiate-like about it. Pipeline was the biggest, fastest rush in surfing, the aquatic equal of hitting a crack pipe. Surfers who got a lungful couldn't get enough.

—From *The History of Surfing*, by Matt Warshaw

PAT CURREN COFFEE BREAK

by Mike Davis

File this one under the heading of stories that, although they may be hard to believe, are of the sort that surfers really want to believe. Because when given the choice between the truth and the legend, surfers will take the legend every time. Mike Davis's epic tale of a particularly epic ride during one of the most epic swells in history is a perfect example. Are we really to believe that the legendary Pat Curren actually surfed a wave across two different zip codes? Davis never winks, so you'll have to figure this one out for yourself.

"Humongous!" was Larry West's weather-forecasting guru dad's response when I asked "How big?" in relation to the "Big One" in '69. He'd predicted it days before it even showed up on the earliest weather maps or any mention of an especially deep front and the resulting northerly swell that'd arrive Thursday afternoon or Friday morning, 5th of December 1969—"Never seen anything like it—huge—perfect conditions, 21-2-second intervals—Friday latest."

I spent Thursday afternoon with Renny Yater sandbagging an old lady's backyard on the point at Rincon, which gets clobbered every time there's a big swell and any kind of tide. We spent the afternoon with one eye on the job and the other on Indicator for the slightest hint of anything.

It was still flat at Coral Casino when I checked it before my night class at Santa Barbara City College. Still nothing. I checked it again after City College at ten. Nothing. The ocean was strangely serene at sunrise and the hour following on Friday morning. Eerie calm.

I checked it again at ten o'clock from the end of Coral Casino pier, just north of Hammonds Reef. There was nothing for the first twenty-five minutes.

I was about to leave when a 6-foot set broke—crisp, clean, and perfect as you please.

Before I could turn around, Pat Curren appeared next to me, eyes keen on the horizon. A few minutes later a 10- to 12-footer lapped the decking underfoot.

"Get a couple?" I ventured.

"Tide's too high for anywhere else," he answered absently, eyes still scanning the horizon. "May's well," he grumbled after a second, banging my arm as he turned toward his pickup and the 11-footer.

We were waxing up on the wall when the shriek of protesting metal and cracking timber beckoned us to the pier. We watched in awe the death throes that marked the end of the still-unused, brand new VIP landing platform. The bits of which would be pulled out from under houses at Miramar, a mile distant, or as small flotsam and jetsam at Summerland beach several miles west.

After we'd thrown our boards off the end of the pier and jumped in, Pat led the way on his 11-foot gun toward what we hoped was the takeoff at Hammonds Reef. I followed on a nearly new 7'9" Yater Hawaii. I swallowed hard, more than once, because each set was way bigger than the last and continued to increase until every wave we paddled over was bigger than the previous one.

Then there'd be these absolutely still lulls. It was eerie, not a whisper of wind, dead glassy, and yet strangely alive. Awesomely alive. Conditions couldn't have been better. Except for the fact that we'd paddled into the unknown zone. At least I had. I'd never seen waves forming this far out even under the wildest of storm surf conditions, and I'd been looking hard for ten years by that time.

When Pat crested the biggest wave yet, my heart stopped as he suddenly changed direction in midair. He'd shifted up another gear and swung south, heading way wide as I cleared the clifflike wall of water. As bad a sign as you can get if you're out there with Pat Curren. Consider yourself caught inside.

He was 50 to 70 yards outside me when he wheeled around and paddled for a monster. He took it early, got to his feet, and began his slide. It was way, Way, WAY overhead.

As he passed outside, he motioned frantically for me to come in behind him, in no uncertain terms. His insistence told me that we'd never make it over the next one, so without hesitating. I spun around, dug deep, and clawed my way into this thing.

By the time I'd caught the wave, Pat's wake had already been drawn up and over the face, leaving me a clean wall, bigger and more perfect than anything I'd ever seen or in fact dreamed of. Not a ripple. No wind jewel or anything. Pure, green glass.

We rode that wave from outside Hammonds into the area outside of Miramar Point, way outside. The wave had no taper. The wall in front of us was as big as the takeoff had been. Amazing!

At the end of the boardwalk, Pat straightened off and motioned for me to follow. Still climbing and dropping, I had plenty of altitude and speed, so I climbed as high as possible and drove toward the bowl forming outside of Fernault's Point. Just one more bowl; I had to do it. I rode the wave hard. Way past parallel and extremely steep and late.

Halfway through the bowl, I realized that if I didn't make it, I'd be in that monstrous current that was sweeping the point, where I'd then be dragged into the rocky groin. I pumped again. Held my high line and squirted past what would have been a fatal trajectory. Perfect!

Miraculously, I made it just as Curren would've breached it, but I wasn't watching anything but the next bowl forming outside of Sharks Cove, and it was even heavier. It looked like the takeoff at insane Indicators. I swear I could hear it growling.

Carrying a lot of speed, I hung high before running straight down, aiming for the tiny patch of sand just beyond the point at

The fearsome slab at Tasmania's Shipsterns Bluff has redefined what is rideable. For waves like these, thick as they are tall, judging a Billabong XXL Global Big Wave award-winning ride is as tricky as catching a Shipsterns right.

Sharks. Then I realized that if I got caught in the current beyond that little triangle of sand, I'd be driven onto the rocks they'd dropped at the base of Summerland Hill to protect the railroad line from days like this. And that would be it.

I squirted out as far in front of the whitewater as I could and drove hard left until I had to prone out, still driving hard toward that 30-foot-wide patch of sand in the corner.

I beached it safely enough, only to confront an 8-foot wall of sheer sand and mud scoured out in a matter of minutes. A vertical wall between me and safety.

I ran to the base and heaved my board up onto the berm, backed down to get a running start, not even daring a furtive glance over my shoulder because if I failed I was dead. There was no doubt in the world that next wave would sweep me into the base of the cliff, where everything in the water—for half a mile up, to 200 yards out—was getting dashed against the gigantic granite blocks strewn along the shore line.

Gasping, I made it up the mud wall first try. I grabbed my board and sprinted for the ice plant below the cyclone fence that separated the railroad line from the beach, running as far up the squelchy green ramp as possible before throwing the 7'9" Yater onto the ice plant, diving onto it, and wrapping my arms and legs around it and as much ice plant runners as I catch hold of.

I glanced over my shoulder when the next wave of whitewater smacked the berm, shooting at least 30 to 40 feet in the air before rushing across the sand and creaming, then up over me, clinging to the ice plant like a crab.

I hung on for grim death for a long and turbulent time.

When the wave receded, even as I sucked in that first breath, I was untangling myself so I could grab my board and bolt for higher ground before the next wave, knowing it would wash even higher than the last one.

I didn't stop until I was safely on the road behind the beach, where Ricky Vogel met me with a hot coffee.

"Saw the whole ride from the balcony. You okay?"

"Yeah . . ."

"Next wave wiped out all that sand in the corner! GONE! Just like that!"

My jaw went slack. Trying hard to comprehend how much water those monstrous waves were moving.

"El Cap?" He suggested hopefully in the next breath, eyes going beyond wide.

I shook my head, "Rincon."

We spun to the sound of whitewater crashing over the rocks on the point in his back yard, dragging a picnic table and chairs across the yard, then back over the far wall, never to be seen again. And the tide was still going out.

"Where's your car?" he asked finally.

"Coral Casino."

"Wow! I wondered how you got out."

Ricky strapped my board onto his VW and dropped me off at Coral Casino on his way to El Capitan Point; it was 3 and a bit, maybe 4 miles by car. A mile and a bit by beach. Except now, there's no beach.

I was hurriedly strapping my board onto my Mustang when Curren approached from behind.

"Made it?" he inquired darkly.

"Radical ending!" I chuckled, making light of my little ordeal in the ice plant.

"Thought so," he muttered before grumbling, "Damned lucky!" and looking at me like I'd just run over his dog.

"Low-tide Rincon?" I ventured quickly, changing the subject.

"Campus might afford a safer exit," he said after some thought, adding, "Long's you hit the beach before gettin' strained through the fuckin' pier."

"Rincon. If the tide drops enough. Only safe bet at this size, surely," I said, hopefully to his back.

The southern tip of Africa is a veritable graveyard of ships. Grant Baker discovers why off Capetown's notorious Tafelberg Reef, where he towed into this 60-foot-plus rogue, becoming a Billabong XXL Global Big Wave Awards contender.
PHOTO © BRENTON GEACH/BILLABONGXXL.COM

"Better take the afternoon off," I advised Stu Fredericks from Yater's factory. "I just rode the biggest wave I've ever seen at Hammonds. All the way to Sharks. Dunno how big in feet. Curren and I were the only ones that got a wave. Rincon's gonna be unbelievable!"

By the time we arrived at Rincon half an hour later there was a big surf-generated mist rising from the ocean that smothered the hills behind La Conchita. It was weird and almost smelled like a raw petroleum product. Probably comprised of gases stirred up from the deep and layers of sand that hadn't been disturbed in years, irritating the hell out of our eyes and burning our lungs.

We surfed huge Rincon that afternoon. Rennie Yater, Stu Fredericks, Miki Dora, Jeff Boyd, and Kevin Sears were standouts. Yater stopped me as I jogged back up the point after I'd ridden the biggest wave I've ever seen.

"I've been trying for that wave for twenty years." His smile said it all.

Somebody told us later in the afternoon that thirty-five boards had been broken before it got too big for most to want to tackle. And they were the ones they'd been fortunate enough to recover.

It wasn't until the swell was over at midweek that I realized how close I'd come to having my ticket punched. How lucky that I'd been able to hang on to that ice plant or I would've joined the unfortunate PT boat crew that'd drowned trying to move her into deeper water off Summerland at exactly the same time I was clinging to the green squelchy stuff.

The following week some guy Yater knows dropped off some photographs that had been taken of us at Rincon.

"Twenty-plus feet, any way you want to measure those waves," was his only comment.

I was still puzzled by Curren's "funny" attitude after our Hammonds session until the final postmortem was considered fully. My little indiscretion really had been a lot more than a minor infraction. I should've listened to Curren, who'd had years of experience in really big waves. He knew beforehand that he'd have to exit at some point and knew exactly where that point was. I, on the other hand, had been shortsighted and screwed up big time but managed to survive. I'd been extremely lucky that morning.

That was nearly thirty-nine years ago now. The fact that I'm still around probably has a lot to do with Curren's dark scowl. 'Cause, if things had really gone bad that morning, Pat would've probably come after me, and there's no way either of us would've survived. And if there was one man whose dog I'd really hate to have caused to go hungry or be harmed, it'd have to be Pat's.

WHAT THE HELL WAS *THAT?*

Against the sunset glare reflecting off the placid Bay of Biscay, they darken the gilded banquet room of the Biarritz Casino. Oxbow, the European surf clothing company, has flown in film footage of Laird Hamilton's recent tow-in adventure at Teahupoo in Tahiti.

At first it seems like a cartoon, the scale between rider and wave so ridiculously out of proportion as to look digitally enhanced. Hamilton, who measures 6 foot 3, 215 pounds, resembles a Malibu Ken doll getting blown through a mammoth water conduit. The crowd visibly recoils, as if watching a 3D tiger leap off the screen. The wave is a freak, more lip than wall, with a boxcar-thick over-hang of vaulting water that impacts the shallow reef with the heft of melted lead.

Hamilton's tow-in entry is at least 75 feet deeper than the traditional paddle-in takeoff point—an insolent, suicidal move. The room erupts with wild hoots and nervous involuntary laughter. Just before he reaches the channel, Hamilton is apparently reduced to atoms by a huge explosion of spray. But he emerges unscathed, blown out the maw of what he later described as ". . . something large with giant teeth." In the aftermath, Laird is later seen recov-ering in the channel on his jet ski, hunched over and speechless. He rubs his eyes, presumably wiping away tears of relief.

Looking around the room, I see that same body attitude mir-rored by many of the contest pros—now hunched over their dessert and rubbing their eyes as the lights come on. The mood becomes strangely morose, the initial thrill of surf lust quickly giving over to morning-after pragmatics tinged with resentment. Was it envy or? Or fear?

A well-known media surfer sitting at the table with me strug-gles with an alien concept as he fretfully stirs his mousse into brown slurry.

"Did you just see what I thought I saw?" he begs from across the table. "I mean, what does that mean? Is that what I have to do now to be a pro surfer? I mean, really . . . *What* the hell was *that?*"

—Steve Barilotti

DISLOCATED: MAVERICKS AND ME

by Taylor Paul

Surfers have traditionally been reluctant to talk about wipeouts in any great detail, as if those frantic moments of breathless oblivion are best left unexamined, let alone recounted in full, so traumatic are the memories. This, of course, bewilders the casual spectator who, upon witnessing a heavy big wave wipeout, invariably asks, "How come more surfers don't die?" The truth is, although not many surfers do die in five-story waves, plenty come close. One of those was big wave rider Taylor Paul, who, in a feature published in The Surfer's Path, *breaks the code of silence to describe in exacting detail a particularly bad wipeout at northern California's fearsome Mavericks.*

The wave doesn't look perfect—windswept and chunky, a three-story building about to tumble. But nobody else is going, and I can catch it. That's rare at Mavericks these days. I must take advantage. I turn, put my head down, and go.

Not five minutes ago I jumped off the boat and paddled away from the Long brothers, Grant "Twiggy" Baker, Mark Healey, Shane Dorian, and Nathan Fletcher. I was in a hurry. I wanted to get out there before they took all the big ones. And because of that, I skipped my normal routine. I didn't watch and count the waves in each set. I didn't notice the wind rippling the wave face. And I didn't exchange so much as a head nod with anyone out there, let alone a "How is it?"

If I had done any of these things, I wouldn't be paddling into this wave.

I put my weight onto my front foot to hasten the journey down the face. It looks like a keeper, but a third of the way down, chops appear on the face. I come to a virtual stop when my inside rail sticks on a lump.

I'm bucked off my board, flying toward the trough, Superman arms extended. I hit with brutal force; the water feels unbelievably thick, like quickly setting cement.

I penetrate the surface instead of skipping like a stone; under the water my left arm dangles at my side. I've dislocated my shoulder. I can't think about that, though. First I have to make it through the hold-down.

I don't know why I'm on this boat of superstars. I'm an imposter, but they treat me like one of the gang. Big wave surfing is my hobby. It's their job. They train for it. They travel for it. They live for it.

Which brings them here, to Mavericks, to paddle and pull into waves that a few years ago people were nervous to tow. Why am I here? Greg Long is my friend, and now I'm everyone's friend. That's how they make me feel, anyway. Greg and his crew are engaging, unassuming, and inclusive. They remind me of "that one bomb" I got last year. They ask about my recent travels. I've traveled a lot. So have they. You see? You're one of us! It's implied. But their graciousness is a double-edged sword. If I'm one of them, then I can do what they do. I can keep up with them. I should keep up with them. I must keep up with them. God forbid I warm up with a couple of medium-sized ones. How could I return to the boat with my head up?

The wave overtakes me and thrashes me hard. I'm terrified with every foot I descend, with every flip that disorients me so much more. My body is balled in the fetal position except for my left arm, which cuffs about limply, a thread in a hurricane.

Deep, deeper—until the jolting subsides. It's my cue to start up. I flutter-kick my legs and sweep down with my right arm. Progress is slow. I try to use my left arm, but it won't respond. Gone. I continue with my limited resources. Up. Up. I break the surface. My head spins on a swivel to check my surroundings. Where's the second wave? Four seconds before impact. I look for the rescue ski . . . *three* . . . the nearest ski is a dot in the distant channel . . . *two* . . . I raise my right arm to signal that I'm hurt . . . *one* . . . Oh, God, please say they saw me . . . *impact.*

I have certain rules for myself when I surf Mavericks: Don't sit on the inside, don't go out alone, and don't take the first wave of the set. The latter is the most important and one that until recently I'd adhered to. You don't cast off on the first wave because if you miss it, you take the rest of the set on the head. If you do catch it and fall, your situation is even worse. And, without previous waves grooming and flattening the water, it's usually the bumpiest.

It's best to use the first wave as an observation deck. Paddle over it, count the many lumps on the horizon, and adjust your strategy from there—position yourself for the rest of a six-wave set, for example.

But a couple of weeks ago I broke that rule and kicked out in the channel in time to see the only other surfer in the lineup get caught inside. I'd made a lucky and foolish decision. And once you break a rule, especially with favorable consequences, it's easier to justify breaking it once more. It's a slippery slope.

The second wave hit me with as much ferocity as the first. It's almost worse because I have time to anticipate it, to consider the repercussions of a 25-foot wave. What happens if it drives me as deep as yesterday, when I took all my energy and two arms to get to the surface? I was down for nearly two waves. What if I hit the bottom? What if . . .

The wave twists and spins me. Like unexpected airplane turbulence, I drop 15 feet. Flip upside down. Or right side up? My mind wanders. Why did I have to injure myself on the first wave? Now I'll have to sit out the rest of the day. I feel bad for Caroline, my girlfriend, she was so worried when I'd left the boat. It's Valentine's

Taylor Paul catches his edge and a quick breath before going down hard at Mavericks.

Day, and this is a bad present. Is my board broken? I'm embarrassed. I picture the boys shaking their heads, muttering something about me not belonging out here. I've wiped out on my first wave for the second consecutive season. Two days. Two waves. Two falls.

I'm hoping for two rescues. I surface and gasp for breath, clearing the foam in front of my face. But the oxygen relief is fleeting— a leftover whirlpool sucks me back under like a liquid vacuum. As it pulls me down I tilt my head toward the sky for one more breath. You never know how long these aftershocks will last.

Luckily it's just a jolt, and I'm up in a few seconds. White surrounds me. The sun blasts off the foam and whitewater like an overexposed photo. Dreamy. I scan for a jet ski, but there's nothing. No boats. No surfers. Just me. The next whitewater gains momentum as it passes the inside bowl. I prepare for impact with rapid breaths. Every bit of oxygen counts. It's on top of me now. I don't even dive. One more breath. The avalanche smothers me.

I was thirteen years old when I decided that I would surf Mavericks. Naïve and impressionable, the epic winter of 1994 fresh in my head, I dedicated my life to preparing, much to the dismay of my mother. She, too, had '94 in her head—more specifically Mark Foo's death. But I was unwavering. I did what I read other big wave surfers did: I swam laps underwater, I jumped rope, and I ran with rocks on the sea floor. I lived cleanly. I didn't smoke. No drugs. I wrote papers about my desire to surf Mavericks (I'd heard Jay Moriarty did that). I visualized it. If I were to have a relationship with this wave, it deserved my respect and preparation.

Then, at seventeen, I got out there, and my ideal didn't match reality. I had expected to find a crew obsessed with training and leading healthy lives. But while many guys trained, most just surfed. Some even surfed under the influence.

So my thinking changed. I didn't need to train to surf Mavs, I just needed to surf Mavs. Confidence was key. I had a big board and faith that I wouldn't become Mark Foo. I even convinced my mom to stop being so dramatic—I didn't need her doubt in the back of my head when I turned for a 40-footer. And the more I surfed there, the more I realized it wasn't so bad. Trips through the rocks were rare. Two-wave hold-downs even more rare. But that confidence (or denial) is dangerous. Mark Foo didn't paddle out for his last session thinking he was about to meet Davy Jones.

It feels like I'm boxing Ali with a plastic bag over my head, my lungs a raging fire. I move quickly with the underwater river—I have to be approaching the rocks. Where's the surface? A thicker wetsuit would help me float, or a life vest. I should have grabbed one. Almost there. I break through the water and taste the air—it's cold and salty.

After a couple of breaths I see two things—rocks and a jet ski. Fuck. Hallelujah. I'm parallel with the rocks. Next to me a small waterfall cascades off a shallow rock shelf. I pull the emergency release on my leash. I don't want it to snag on the rocks and stick me in an endless river. Photographer Fred Pompemeyer is waiting on his ski on the inside of the rocks. But where's his rescue sled? When I reach him, he tries to pull me up by my right arm, but it doesn't work, and we don't want to flip the ski. Desperate, we try again. This time I use my left arm as leverage while pulling up with my right.

"AAAARRRGGHHH!" the pain manifests itself in a primal scream. I let go and fall back into the water. Fred hits the throttle and turns toward shore. Wait. Where's he going?

Jet skis are banned at Mavericks because environmentalists say that they pollute the water and hurt sea otters. What they overlook is that they save human lives. People still use them on bigger days for both rescue and/or photography, but that won't last when the authorities start to crack down and give fines. The skis will disappear, and surfers will be left to swim ashore with dislocated shoulders. It's going to take someone dying to shake the foundation of the bank, to make people realize what a utilitarian tool the jet skis are. Why do we have to wait for this to happen? Will it be a friend? Or will it be me?

I'm alone again. The waves that pass over me are small, less than 6 feet, and they hold me down for just a few seconds. Then I see Mavericks photographer Frank Quirarte. He has a sled. He always does. Frank volunteered during Hurricane Katrina. He fought in Desert Storm. And for years he has watched over the surfers at Mavericks. He takes your picture from his ski, then rescues you if you're in serious trouble, like now.

He approaches on the ski, and I hold up my good hand. "Left hand," he instructs. "Can't. Left shoulder is dislocated." "Okay, climb up the back on the sled if you can." But I'm already halfway up.

"All right, Taylor, here's what we're going to do." His voice is steady, his eyes are calm. "You're going to leave your left arm at your side and then wrap your right arm tight around me. Got it?"

I've never been so happy to embrace a man.

He drives gingerly back to the boat. Fred follows with my board under his arm. Frank talks the guys on the boat through the transfer. It goes smoothly. One perk of being around big wave surfers is that they keep their cool. Rusty Long and Nathan Fletcher are genuinely concerned and fuss over my comfort. Their kindness dissolves my embarrassment. I sit on the bow of the boat, shock wearing off. My body, with an ample supply of air, can now concentrate on my arm. The pain pulsates with my heartbeat. By the time a harbor patrol boat fetches me, it's excruciating. The only thing I want in the whole wide world is to make it right, and I suffer a kind of temporary insanity waiting to get that bone back into the socket. I've never felt something so strange and terrible. The boats are clumsy in the rough sea. They bump into each other, and the harbor officers seem panicked.

"We got no time. We gotta make this quick," the officer says to me as I position myself on the rail for the transfer. As if I'm lollygagging? The boats clank together, and I leap in before I'm ready. I bump my arm and wince, making sure the officer sees that his haste caused harm. Luckily, Frank is still here to help transfer Caroline. With the ski she easily goes from boat to boat.

I lie on the deck of the boat as we bounce slowly toward the harbor. Caroline stabilizes my arm and pets my cheek. I'm glad she's here. The harbor patrol officer crouches next to me and gets my information for his report. I look down at my shoulder; it's hanging below my left pec. If I can't get it back in place, I'll lose my mind.

I wake up sore and swollen. The painkiller hangover and fitful night's sleep cloud my head. I have to use the bathroom. Left. Right. Left. Right. Concentrating. My steps are short and labored. At the toilet, I pee, and my head spins. I will pass out soon. I imagine falling and hitting my head on the porcelain. I walk to the nearest chair and collapse.

The next day, when my mom flies home from a conference in southern California, she coddles and kisses me. She is so glad I'm okay. Am I okay? Yes, I'm fine. It could have been worse. She knows this; it's all she's been thanking God about since she got the call. It could have been much worse.

But after the initial once-over, she says something I know is well rehearsed. It would have to be, from any mom who's lost sleep over her child surfing big waves. She speaks up, as if a higher volume will muffle the tears forming in her eyes.

"Well, we're just going to have to get you better so you can be out there again soon."

We'll see.

Garrett McNamara armed and dangerous in Alaska, where he and his tow partner ride the wave caused by a calving glacier

PHOTO © ROBERT BROWN

THE RUSH: A PROFILE OF GARRETT MCNAMARA

by Kimball Taylor

One of the more flamboyant of the modern big wave riders, Hawaii's Garrett McNamara (Gmac) isn't shy, not when it comes to riding five-story waves and certainly not when it comes to making sure the rest of the world sees him doing it. But this didn't make Kimball Taylor's job any easier when penning this Gmac profile, having to sift the profound from the promo. Taylor rose to the occasion, revealing a surprising complexity behind the daredevil's bravado.

On October 2, 1978, twelve-year-old Garrett McNamara and his nine-year-old brother Liam arrived on the North Shore of Oahu. As if stepping out of the Hawaiian vacation special of a *Partridge Family* episode, the boys wore matching white pants and sharp white '70s collared shirts brought together under vibrant orange velvet vests. The boys came in tow to their footloose mother Malia and a long-forgotten musician boyfriend. Malia McNamara had actually made the boys' outfits for the occasion. This arrival was important, even though it represented only one of many new starts. So far the unit had bounced from Massachusetts to California, Mount Shasta to Berkeley, Mexico to Belize—and finally Sonoma County, where the McNamaras developed an impromptu sort of commune. But after Malia spent time at another commune in Kauai's Kalalau Valley, where she earned fame as a cook for the eighty or so semiclothed inhabitants of the valley, she returned to California, collected Garrett and Liam, and made for the Islands.

"We were supposed to go to Kauai and run around naked," Garrett remembered.

Yet, on a fateful North Shore stopover, the family ended up finding an apartment in a corner of Waialua nicknamed "Haole

Camp." The boyfriend soon split for greener musical pastures. And the idyll of a '70s Kauai existence quickly faded into island-style poverty on what was fast becoming surfing's most important stretch of coast. The McNamaras, of course, held no conception of what that would mean to them or their new home. "'They're surfing,'" Garrett remembered his mother offering—an attempt to settle the boys' fears of displacement. "'It's like skateboarding but on the water.'"

"We were urban kids," Garrett said flatly. After the boyfriend left, "We were alone and living on welfare."

Liam remembered that the small family could afford one pair of shoes a year for each of the boys. Underwear wasn't in the budget. When the local kids harassed him because he wore no "Baybee Dees," it took Liam a while to understand that to mean no "BVDs" and only a bit longer to understand where that placed him in this new social order. On his first day in their new school, Garrett fought the biggest kid in class. "Coming up on the North Shore as a *haole*," Liam remembered, "it's a hard life."

When I contrast this image to my first encounter getting to know Garrett McNamara—on his attempt to surf a wave created by the decay of a 300-foot-tall glacier in a southern Alaskan river—I struggle to join the beginning to maybe the most pivotal moment in an aquatic daredevil's career. In little more than six years, a thirty-something surf shop owner would develop one of the most reputable tow-in careers going. His trajectory followed the insipient rise of competitive tow-surfing itself and continues to beg the question of where it could possibly end. And maybe even how insane surfing can possibly become along the way.

It's facile to draw the Evel Knievel analogy, that once a professional daredevil jumps ten buses, the next step is to jump twenty and eventually a canyon and then the Grand Canyon—which the real Knievel had threatened to do for many years. For professional big wave surfers, the only way to guarantee a career is to keep surfing the next-biggest wave—50, 75, 100 feet and climbing. True, the Alaska stunt may have been a sideline. It appeared ridiculous on the face of it (a barreling wave created by a calving glacier? In a river?). In person, however, it was the most terrifying wave-riding activity I'd ever seen. The mere attempt may turn out to be equally McNamara's V-Day—or his Waterloo. My sense is the distinction will take considerable time to sort out in this new golden age of the big wave radical. For as the forty-one-year-old McNamara said at home again on the North Shore, "I will be surfing massive waves professionally until I'm fifty years old, minimum." But of the glacier attempt, he said, "Alaska changed everything."

In October of '08, a year after Garrett's mission at Child's glacier, I met up with him on the North Shore. Since we'd last met, Garrett had towed giant Teahupoo and survived tremendous wipeouts. He'd made barrels at Pipe and Puerto Escondido on a stand-up paddling (SUP) board, paddled into Mavericks and even long-boarded Malibu. His career and life were diversifying, his big wave career pushing at the limits of the possible—yet his plan for this meeting was a tour back through the years to his roots along the Seven Mile Miracle. Garrett brought along his twelve-year-old son Titus and his thirteen-year-old daughter Ari. Neither of them had experienced this tour either. Members of a now-extended McNamara family, they're healthy and quiet groms, a little removed from and in awe of their father's boisterous energy and need to connect in social settings. As Greg Long said recently, "I think Garrett's stoke factor is sometimes intimidating for some people."

At the Café Haleiwa, while the kids found a booth, Garrett greeted various tables and struck up conversations. When he joined our table, he sat as if he'd carried something heavy across the restaurant. Then he spilt a secret that seemed to have occupied his thoughts since entering the cafe: His wife Connie was pregnant again. Titus and Ari already knew this and also that he shouldn't be telling anyone. Appraising his son a while, Garrett then began to discuss Titus's surfing prospects as if picking up the thread of an old conversation. "I hope he doesn't want to one-up me someday. If he did, I'd be horrified." This pronouncement hung between them and caused me to think Garrett may harbor a bit of horror for the job himself. "But if Titus does want to do what I do," he added, "I'll make him train hard."

Both Garrett and Liam know something about preparation and the power of desire. Despite their relatively late entries into the sport, their unavoidable *haole* status, and childhood poverty, by the time they reached their teens the McNamaras had become contenders on surfing's toughest proving ground. Admittedly, at that time they weren't the hottest surfers around. Some of the guys their age from the North Shore—Kalohe Bloomfield, Jason Majors, Brock Little—"surfed circles around us." The difference was that Garrett and Liam wanted it more, and they more often employed attitude to get it. "They had each other to bounce off of," said Randy Rarick, team manager with their first sponsor. "To be honest, they were wise-ass little prick kids. I saw that trait in them early on, and I liked it."

The boost to Garrett's development actually came as an economic necessity. When he was thirteen, his mother found a $400-per-month apartment at Velzyland, a semislum fronted by world-class surf. Haleiwa may have been the best possible place to learn, Garrett said, but "Haleiwa was light-years behind." V-Land offered the power and complexity the young McNamaras needed to mature. Liam began to hang out with some of the North Shore's heavies. Garrett hung with another set, a difference of degrees maybe, but as Garrett said, "I was a 6-foot-and-under-wonder guy." A couple of milestones then occurred in Garrett's late teens. In 1985 he placed in the money-making ranks of the Triple Crown. At that time, accepting $250 or more automatically garnered pro status, which pushed Garrett into the professional sphere. But he also found big waves—at Sunset and then the Bay. "Once I got a taste of Sunset, it was all about big waves," he said. By nineteen years old, "My goal was to get a 20-foot barrel at Waimea."

As Rarick pointed out, "Experience on the North Shore makes a huge difference. It gives locals an edge over surfers from other places." Both Garrett and Liam benefited from proximity. But Rarick added, "I think Liam had a little more talent and used his ability to be out in those lineups. He also specialized [at Pipeline] early on."

Garrett had to work harder, and he knew it. Sometimes this meant going where others would not. Yet, he also possessed an ability to dream of lines where others could not. Out in a by-then familiar lineup at twenty years old, Garrett spotted a Waimea bomb looming that promised to offer the elusive two-story tube. "I air-dropped and punched hard for the barrel," he remembered. The single fin beneath his feet, however, cavitated while the board drifted ever straight. The lip smashed him. He felt his ankles and feet strike the back of his head. Pounded fathoms underwater, he believed for a moment that his body had weathered the beating. As he made for the surface, however, a black tunnel enclosed upon the surrounding blue and the sunlight above. This tunnel increasingly pinched into darkness as he reached for the surface. Luckily, fresh oxygen and light snapped him back to consciousness. Garrett didn't know it yet, but the pummeling exploded a disk in his spine. Somehow he drove himself home from that session. The pain had become so intense once he arrived there that Garrett donned a snorkel and mask and climbed into the bathtub just to achieve some of the weightlessness he felt beneath Waimea—an effort to suspend the pressure on his ruptured disk. At some point Liam showed up and tried to lift Garrett to his feet. Garrett blacked out completely.

"I woke up to my brother crying," he remembered.

After two months "on the floor becoming addicted to codeine," Garrett admitted, "I wasn't focused on big waves anymore. I didn't know what the hell I was going to do." A summer and another winter passed before he surfed again. It took five years before he felt himself in the water. "I wasn't a competitor anymore; I lost that. I lost the tour," he said. And that loss "shattered me emotionally."

Over the following years, Liam's career took off. Garrett would keep on charging, and he did compete—in the Triple Crown, Excel Pro, and HIC Pipe events on an annual basis. As Rarick said, "Garrett tried and tried to be a presence on the competitive front." He wasn't a natural competitor, he knew, and felt he had to work harder than most just to be "good." The exception, however, was his prowess in big waves.

On our tour of his life along the North Shore, we eventually came to a little house wedged between Sharks Cove and Waimea Bay where Garrett lived during some of the most important years of his life. It is so close to the bay that its windows tremble during any swell that brings Waimea to life. I wondered what that rattling sounded like to a man whose dream since nearly ending his life there had been an invitation to the Eddie.

Soon enough, however, Garrett's tour led us to another of his loves, Sunset Beach—the wave that began and also reignited his passion for big waves. Around 1994, while checking the surf at Sunset, Garrett spotted Laird Hamilton and Buzzy Kerbox using a Zodiac to pull each other into set waves at an outer break called Backyards. The sight mesmerized him. He ran to grab a board so he could paddle out and be that much closer to the action, but then he just stopped there on dry land and watched. Not long afterward he bought his own Zodiac and began experimenting with this new sport. These were potent times on the North Shore. New generations of surfers boiled up under the old, and older surfers reinvented themselves and surfing itself. Garrett and Liam seemed to realize both sides of this coin; as they evolved their own careers they also mentored local grommets, including a pair of brothers from the Kauai—Andy and Bruce Irons. "They were our older brothers, chaperones, everything," said Bruce of his first stints on Oahu. "Garrett and Liam took us out to big Pipe and Sunset for our first times."

While we sat at Sunset that October day, an older fan misheard a snippet of Garrett's conversation and inserted himself to ask, "What's the goal?" It's hard not to sense that Garrett's charisma acts like a magnet, repelling personalities of a certain charge while unavoidably attracting others. This random attraction occurred several times during our interview, but knowing his own magnetism, Garrett never hesitated to engage.

"The number 1 goal is to keep surfing," Garrett replied to the older man. "How to do that? It's for you to figure out." Through the late '90s Garrett's scrappy, survivalist style in the water earned him the odd photo in the surf mags, which he knew would appease his sponsors a bit longer. "I got to surf; that's all I wanted to do. Financially, it was tough, just barely making it at the end of the month." By the close of the decade, however, Garrett had gained a wife, two kids, and a new venture: a surf shop in Haleiwa called Epic Sports. The business took up all of his surf time. "I barely surfed. I worked the store, and it was all about the family, becoming a nine-to-five guy." The man who feverishly talked about, and searched for, the "rush" suddenly found it only in his morning coffee.

Despite the obvious coincidences that might have led Garrett to an inevitable big wave career—the popular tow spot Hammerheads lay just outside his family's first apartment, and the beach that lured him into big waves, Sunset, also served as ground zero for the insipient tow community—oddly enough, it was the pissy landlord of his surf shop whose nearly two years of needling convinced Garrett. He needed to ditch the shop and give big wave surfing another go. And the timing seemed perfect. The inaugural 2002 Tow-in World Cup at Jaws lay just ahead. The only problem was that neither Garrett nor his new tow partner, Brazil's Rodrigo

Resende, had ever surfed Jaws. They practiced towing into 2-footers on the North Shore days before the event (reasoning that accuracy on a 2-foot wave was much more critical). The competition, however, opened with 50- to 60-foot faces.

"I was scared shitless," Garrett remembered. Uncertain of his first wave, he kicked out early, realizing later that he'd thrown a good one. That feeling didn't sit well, so he and Resende began to charge a series of bombs that led to their eventual victory despite a ten-point barrel ride negotiated by rival Mike Parsons. The win ignited a golden year for the thirty-five-year-old. He garnered magazine covers air-dropping into Waimea and spreads featuring his lines through giant Teahupoo. In November he returned to Jaws for what is recognized as one of the gnarliest big wave barrels ever. Needless to say, the surf shop was closed.

"For years there, Garrett had to tell people he was my brother before he got that respect," Liam said recently. "Now I have to go around telling people I'm Garrett's brother."

The elder McNamara solidified his streak in 2002 with a near-maniacal gamut for big wave celebrity—in Chile, at Cortes Bank, at home. In '07, he landed both the Billabong XXL Big Wave Award as well as performance of the year. In that stretch, though, he'd also taken some of the heaviest wipeouts imaginable. One in 2006 earned the dubious "Golden Donut" award. For a daredevil blessed with a young family, the question of motivation always looms. This is not a big wave surfer unaware of the consequences; he's rescued near-fatalities at Ala Moana and Pipeline. And in 2000, when Tahitian surfer Briece Taerea was caught just inside a rogue Teahupoo 15-footer and thrown over in the lip, Garrett held the unfortunate distinction of performing mouth-to-mouth on a man who'd lost portions of his face and neck. "I worked on Briece as hard as I could." He remembered seeing a man who looked a lot like Marvin Foster suffering before him. "I was head-to-toe in his blood, and I had cuts all over my feet . . . so we're blood brothers."

In surfing, coming to terms with death—or at least the possibility—is an ongoing crisis in big waves. The set is building outside, and it's so beautiful aesthetically. People are watching in awe from the beach: the blue water, the stiff offshore winds, the 40-foot walls charging in from the open ocean. If you're out there with nothing but your body, your wits, and a surfboard, that set can be your coffin.

—Bruce Jenkins, *North Shore Chronicles*

Taerea later died of the injuries. The question of whether that harsh confrontation with the consequences of both decisions and luck at this level became unavoidable. I asked Garrett if he thinks about Taerea's death even as he attempts to push the limits at Teahupoo himself. "I'm actually more comfortable," he said. "I worked as hard as I could for Briece. He's always there watching over me. I'm safe there. I'm set."

Clearly, there is an element to Garrett's motivation that pushes beyond career security. Billabong XXL winner Brad Gerlach said, "He's got something to prove to the point where you get the sense that he'll die for it."

One of the best heavy barrel riders in the world, Bruce Irons, said, "Yeah, he's definitely going for the scary wave realm."

Last year in Alaska, even as the film crew unloaded and the jet skis were prepared for long hours in 37-degree water, the idea that this was "the wave" that would put Garrett and his tow partner, Kealii Mamala, over the top seemed ever-present. This was bigtime. Talk of the "rush" waned and ebbed. I began to suspect that this rush Garrett talked about—almost as if it were a rare bird that may or may not alight on his shoulder—represented some portion of his motivation. It wasn't the part desperate to make a good living for his family on the North Shore or to continue fulfilling dreams within the sport he loved or even the measure of approval that twelve-year-old *haole* kid deeply desired from his new community. I wasn't so sure it was "stoke" in the traditional sense. The "rush," I suspected, was just that sliver of something *other* that made the risks worth it.

So a few days into their Alaska trip, when Garrett and Kealii witnessed a thirty-story tower of ice fall into the impact zone of the wave they proposed to surf, the "rush" definitely suffered an effect. The surfers became a bit more shy at the throttle of their jet ski, more leery of leaning chunks of ice. Beautiful river-brown barrels went unridden, even as Garrett and Kealii looked for some entry that resembled "safe." On film, when *The Glacier Project* is released, viewers will see Garrett breaking down on the phone with his family. At the time, I thought I was witnessing a couple of daredevils who stepped a touch beyond their courage. Now that I've met that family, I suppose I see something else. After that session, Garret approached Kealii—a lot was riding on this project for both of them. "I'm over it," Garrett said. "This is not worth the rush. My family losing their father is not worth the rush."

The pair did continue their bid on a Childs glacier wave. They've also continued to push at the boundaries of tow surfing. But depending on when you catch him, Garrett may or may not allude to the fact that the "rush" received a mortal blow that day.

Last summer Kealii towed Garrett into some frightening Teahupoo bombs and equally incredible wipeouts. As Garrett emerged from one of the best waves of the day, Kealii swooped in on the ski to pick him up. Kealii was ecstatic. "I didn't get the rush," Garret said.

"What?!" Kealii shouted. "Are you nuts?"

BUZZY TRENT, KING OF THE BIG WAVE BEASTS

George Downing, Wally Froiseth, Woody Brown, and a few other Waikiki surfers were all riding finned boards at Makaha by the end of 1951 and stroking with confidence into 15-plus-foot waves. The new equipment was fast and stable and miles ahead of the hot curl in terms of traction. If the boards weren't all that maneuverable, it didn't really matter. A high, tight, cleaving line to deliver you from the Point through to the Bowl on the heaviest wave of the day—*that's* what mattered.

The big wave push was further boosted when a small and equally committed group of California surfers turned up at Makaha. It was a nice, quiet, easy scene. Apart from the occasional beered-up weekend scuffle, everybody got along well. Makaha was too remote and provided too much surf for there to be any territorial problems, and plenty of bonding opportunities were generated by shared moments of big wave terror and accomplishment.

The mainlanders were led by Walter Hoffman and Murray "Buzzy" Trent, both of them young Malibu regulars in the early postwar years. Hoffman was a big, strong, corn-fed nineteen-year-old who got along well with everybody. He'd met and befriended George Downing in 1949 at Malibu and later that year sailed to Waikiki for a three-month summer visit. He returned the following year. In 1951 he extended his trip into the winter season and began surfing Makaha regularly.

Hoffman had an 8-millimeter movie camera, and he mailed a few rolls of Makaha footage back home to his older brother Phillip ("Flippy" to friends and family) and Trent, both of whom watched and rewatched the grainy color film until the projector bulb finally blew out. All three surfers flew to Hawaii the next winter, in 1952, along with a revolving crew of another half-dozen Californians. They camped on the beach at Makaha

Buzzy Kerbox, one of the original tow-in surfers,
getting loose on a "smaller" day at Jaws
PHOTO © ERIKAEDER.COM

for days at a time in army surplus tents and lean-tos made from tarps and scavenged wood. They ate triple-decker peanut butter sandwiches and went through a few hundred cans of VanCamp's pork and beans.

Just about every photograph Walter Hoffman took that year embodies the frontier surfing ideal: empty waves, coconut palm-frond hats, boards scattered along the beach, a nine-surfer group shot with everybody tanned and smiling and barefoot, arms draped over each other's shoulders. It was all that. It was also consecutive days of flat-surf boredom, violent bouts of diarrhea, staph infections, and an assortment of tropical-borne skin conditions. "We all got sick," Flippy Hoffman remembered. "We all had boils. Carbuncles. It looks pretty in the pictures, and it was. But a lot of the time it was awful."

Living conditions were much improved the following year when the Hoffmans rented a pitched-roof wooden shack a few hundred yards off the beach at the foot of Makaha Valley. More southern California surfers showed up, including surfboard designer Bob Simmons in his first and only visit to Hawaii. (Simmons drowned less than eighteen months later while surfing Windansea in San Diego.)

Walter Hoffman and Trent had by that time distinguished themselves as the company's two most gung-ho surfers. If they were both well off the mark set by Downing in terms of skill and wave knowledge, they matched him for raw courage. Hoffman, in big surf at Makaha, was as cheerful as he was fearless, paddling out like it was a mess-around summer afternoon at Queen's or Malibu. Trent's focus on big surf, on the other hand, had shifted from intense to monomaniacal.

Trent made a lot of other surfers nervous. He was a chatterbox and liked attention, and on a lazy afternoon among friends he'd hold court for hours, telling jokes and stories, pulling faces, and making big sweeping gestures with his arms. Everybody laughed—but Trent was a little off somehow, as if all settings had been turned up to "10" and left there. Raw ass-kicking masculinity came off him in waves. Trent had cinder-block arms and shoulders, a tiny *danseur* waist below a row of corrugated abs, and a smash-nosed face set low on a huge, blunt head. He was a fighter and a bully in high school as well as an all-state fullback who could run a ten-second 100-yard dash. Trent's birth father taught Buzzy that "suffering makes you like steel." With a note of approval, Trent later said his father was a "mean son of a bitch" who used to turn loose the family dogs on any Depression-era poor who made the mistake of stopping by the family house to ask for food. Trent's stepfather, meanwhile, passed on a deep and abiding love for German military history and Teutonic glory in general.

During Trent's Malibu apprenticeship in the forties, he came under the tutelage of Bob Simmons. They sometimes drove out to ride the winter heavies at a break near Santa Barbara called Ventura Overhead, and Simmons told the younger surfer, "You ride *anything*, got that? You're a big *chicken* if you don't take off on these waves!" Trent nodded and did as instructed. He became a tight, clenched surfer. He couldn't swim very well, but he'd been diving for years, and he could hold his breath underwater for three minutes—wipeouts weren't especially scary to him. Plus, every bad wipeout, he believed, made him that much harder and tougher.

Trent arrived in Hawaii in late 1952 and never left. Although the big surf meant a lot to all the visiting Californians of the era, and three or four others would also move to Hawaii permanently, nobody took it on the way Trent did. He lifted weights, skipped rope, shadowboxed, and took long thigh-burning runs through the sand at a time when training was nearly unheard of among surfers. He closely examined other surfers' big wave equipment and had new boards built that were even longer and racier. He also formulated a grim, heroic, death-or-glory view of big wave riding—an attitude that was passed on virtually unchanged to each succeeding generation of big wave surfers.

This last bit was a remarkable one-man achievement. George Downing, Wally Froiseth, John Kelly, and a few others had built specialized equipment and pointedly gone out to ride oversized waves. But none of them saw the need to redefine himself as a surfer. They invented big wave surfing; that was enough. Trent invented the big wave surfer.

For reasons that can only be guessed at—a natural show-man's instinct, a bully's insecurity, a genuine belief that conquest is the transcendent human experience—Trent's *beau ideal* wave-rider viewed the sport almost exclusively in terms of battle and combat.

The Makaha board that Trent got from Joe Quigg, a wicked 12-footer with a black dagger painted on the deck, was his "Sabre Jet." That name didn't stick, but Trent's description of big wave boards in general as "guns" did. He idolized World War I German flying ace Baron Manfred von Richthofen and told friends that while paddling into the lineup during a huge swell he imagined himself as the Red Baron banking through a hive of Allied planes above the French countryside. Here in the big waves, and *only* here, Trent believed, could surfing rise above the level of sport and recreation and offer the surfer a chance to drape himself in glory, honor, and valor.

"We're warriors," Trent once told a big wave comrade, sum-ming up their time together in heavy surf. "We didn't have to kiss anybody's ass. We came, we saw, we conquered. *We're Caesars!*"

—From *The History of Surfing*, by Matt Warshaw

Archie Kalepa, adhering to the Hawaiian
warrior code of "no fear" at Peahi
PHOTO © ERIKAEDER.COM

THE 100-FOOT WAVE

by Evan Slater

For fifty years surfers were bound by the 25-foot ceiling—no wave, however big, could be described as being bigger than 25 feet. No one is quite sure why this was so, but in the early part of this millennium, big wave riders cautiously began describing waves by their actual height. Once they did that, the sky became the limit. Former Surfer *and* Surfing *editor Evan Slater, who has ridden more than a few 40-footers himself, examined this new obsession with size—more specifically, the concept of a rideable 100-foot wave. Anything approaching such magnitude was strictly tow-in fare, but the largest day in Mavericks history had some contemplating tow-in surfing's "unridden realm."*

The world's best big wave surfers have been scanning depth charts of the world's oceans and speculating where the next tow-in frontier may be when all along they should have just asked Jeff Clark. The man who unveiled Mavericks to the world in 1990 knows that you don't need maps, scouting missions, or passports to find the 100-foot wave. You head to Mavericks, where once-a-year megaswells continue to rewrite the record books. And on Wednesday, November 21, 2001, Mavs added yet another chapter.

According to Sean Collins of Surfline.com, a "complex low" formed in the Aleutians (meaning a mother of all tempests with a few smaller storms circulating around it) and sent a one-two punch of northwest swell steamrolling toward the West Coast. Mavs was a 15- to 20-foot paddle-in gunfight on Tuesday, but when news of an Oregon buoy reading of 42 feet at 20 seconds surfaced midday, Clark knew the real showdown would be on Wednesday. "By my calculations, the brunt of the swell was going to start around ten or eleven," said Clark. "So my partner, Jaws surfer Chuck Patterson, and me just kind of paced ourselves and waited for it to come."

Others did not. Mike Parsons and Keith Malloy (who filled in for a North Shore-bound Brad Gerlach) were the first tow team on it, whipping into 20-footers before first light. Eight other teams soon followed, and Mavs' first real tow session of the year was on.

The tow fun stopped at around eight with the arrival of the first paddle-in surfers, but most came prepared. While Malloy and Parsons packed it up and headed down to Todos Santos for another incredible tow session on Thanksgiving Day, Darryl "Flea" Virostko, Shawn "Barney" Barron, Josh Loya, Ken "Skindog" Collins, Matt Ambrose, and a handful of others gave it a go with their bare hands. Flea picked off a half-dozen huge ones, Ambrose pulled into a giant second bowl and was clipped on the way out, while Loya nabbed a set that some are calling one of the bigger Mavs waves ever paddled into. Right on schedule, the first 30-foot set arrived around 10:00 a.m.

"The second that monster came in," said Skindog, "we knew it was tow time. We'd all broken our paddle-in boards, and it was just getting out of hand. You couldn't even get near it paddling in."

Meanwhile, Clark and Patterson skipped the paddle session and towed at Blackhand Reef, a shallow slab a half-mile south of Mavericks. "It was like Teahupoo in reverse," said Clark. "I even had a two-wave hold-down on one—*with* a lifejacket. Chuck said, 'I came in to save you, but you just weren't there.'"

Unshaken by their Blackhand beatings, Clark and Patterson headed to Mavericks just as sets started breaking well beyond the bowl. Rain hammered down; winds howled from the south; boats were warned to head back to the harbor. Nevertheless, a handful of hellmen charged full throttle on the historic swell.

"I watched Alistair Craft going on pure adrenaline," said Skindog. "On one wave, he faded, and the whitewater came close. On the next one, he faded a little more, and it got even closer. On the third one, it just mowed him."

Surfers at Mavericks are now paddling into waves that were formerly considered "tow-in only."
PHOTO © ROBERT BROWN

Craft's partner, Vince Broglio, came in for the rescue, but by the time he got to him, Craft was far on the inside. Broglio ended up nailing a submerged rock and putting a pricey crack in the ski.

The building swell also caught up with Flea and Barney. After failing to emerge from a giant bowl, Barney was floating deep in the impact zone with a six-wave set bearing down. Skindog watched in horror from the channel in the moments that followed: "When Flea rushed in to pick him up, Barney tried to grab the sled. But the sled broke like kindling, and he ended up hanging onto the tow rope, which was basically like an anchor. When the first one hit 'em, I was like, 'That's it, Flea's history.' But he came flying out of the whitewater a couple of seconds later. And then another

Experiencing a big wave surfer's
worst case scenario: over the falls
on a single breath and a prayer

one came, and he somehow made it out of that, too. But Barney had to let go after that first wave, and he caught, like, six right on the head, went through the rocks, and just got beat."

The warriors were falling, but Skindog/Loya (who filled in for Peter Mel, who was also on the North Shore), Clark/Patterson, and Brazilians Carlos Burle/Eraldo Gueiros held their ground. Chuck Patterson survived a barrel for the ages. Burle and Gueiros were riding waves that seemed as far out as the Farallons, and Skindog and Loya used every last note from October's Billabong Odyssey training. "It was hands-down the biggest I've seen it out there," said Skindog. "We're talking waves 70, 80 feet on the face. And just nonstop."

And it got only bigger, so big, in fact, that Skindog figured they'd brushed against the unridden realm for tow-in surfing. "Brock Little said there are no limits to tow surfing," said Skindog. "But I'm not so sure now. On the biggest waves I rode, the ones that broke way beyond the bowl, I'd be going, like, 40 mph, the waves were moving way faster than they were at Cortes, and I was hitting these chops going sideways. I was feeling it in my legs halfway through the wave. Plus," continued Skindog, "we got to see what Mavericks does at that size. The big ones completely missed the bowl, which means, I guess, that it was too big."

But Skindog's last wave didn't miss the bowl. In fact, the humble 60-footer jacked up ahead of him, and the rest was his-tow-ry.

"I was on the way outside bowl," said Skindog, "and I thought, 'Cool, I'm way ahead of this thing.' But then it hit the double-up and just started jacking and throwing. I had no choice. I was, like, 'Oh my God, I'm going to have to do this.' I pulled in way high, started driving, but I couldn't see it bend. It looked like I was going to get swatted, but I kept angling down, down, down, and suddenly I was out. I was like, 'Okay, that's it. Quit. Stop. I never need to come back here again so long as I live.'"

"It was a buttery 30-foot barrel," said Clark. "There was only one of them that really stayed open like that, and Skinny was right there for it."

And while Clark agrees with Skinny that it was clearly the biggest day ever at Mavs, he's not at all convinced they exceeded the size limit. "It wasn't the size," said Clark, "it was the conditions that held us back. I was, like, 'Bring it on.'"

In fact, Mavericks did bring it on, in early afternoon, just as the last tow teams were counting their blessings in the harbor. According to psycho water rescuer Shawn Alladio, the mythical 100-foot set landed about a quarter-mile outside the Mavericks lineup at approximately 2:00 p.m.

"I rescued a few people who were swept off the jetty," said Alladio. "I headed back out 'cause I didn't want to miss seeing this amazing sight. I got more than I asked for—a rogue set of five waves all 100-plus feet on the face, closing out. I had 3-mile visibility, and this was a solid 3-mile-wide wall of water moving fast. My partner and I ran for our lives full throttle to get out of the impact zone. When we cleared the first wave, which I thought was all there was, there were four more stacked up, all much bigger and farther out. We had to blast on for the race of our life. It was terrifying. There were no safety zones. The speed was critical. I glanced down at my LCD display and saw the number 5. So we were racing in the open ocean straight into these waves at 50-plus mph in very rough conditions. The fall behind the wave was about 50 feet, straight down, then hit, bottom out, pull throttle, and do it again. An amazing experience."

Making history: Tony Moniz
pulls into the barrel at
Waimea during the ground-
breaking 1990 Quiksilver/
Eddie Aikau contest

AAMION GOODWIN'S CIRCLE PACIFIC

by Daniel Duane

The archetypal big wave riders had traditionally been easy to spot: rugged, stoic, hard men, their weathered faces and fighter pilot's eyes seasoned from years of staring into the abyss at spots like Waimea Bay. But no longer. Today's danger-wave surfer comes in all shapes, sizes, and sensibilities, the only common threads being transglobal mobility and commitment to a code of apparent fearlessness in any size surf, from 6 feet to 60. In 2007 Surfer's Journal *tapped Daniel Duane, the award-winning journalist and author (his 1997 book* Caught Inside *is still one of the best ever written about surfing), to profile one of the most fascinating of this new breed.*

Our rented Land Cruiser was bouncing over a bad dirt road on a cacao plantation, and we were all hoping to find a good point break. Aamion Goodwin was in the passenger seat, all 6-foot-6 of him. He's an island boy, and he's big on that island concept of "just cruising," like when you ask somebody what they're up to and they say, "Not much, just cruising." I like the way that phrase puts a positive, proactive spin on doing absolutely zero; watching television, for example, qualifies as "just cruising." Getting high in the Ehukai parking lot on a flat summer day definitely qualifies as "just cruising." But getting your cruise on is also a great way to grease through the rigors of international surf travel, and Aamion is such a pro that he cruised right through our New Jersey–to-Lisbon red-eye, a long day in Lisbon, and a second red-eye out to this mid-Atlantic speck of a jungled island. And now, during the inevitable jet-lagged dog days of searching for surf—driving up every ridiculous dirt road and bushwhacking out to views of the water, squinting into the equatorial sun, and shaking your head and speculating about what the right swell could probably do at the useless *bombora* you're pretending might actually be a surf break—Aamion wasn't just cruising. He was at home, as if he'd been born to the island low-ride, and he kept leaking these freaky little details suggesting the low-tide birth was a simple fact. Like coconuts.

The island's Saturday market was so third-world chaotic, in such a ruined, postapocalyptic concrete shell of a bombed-out building, that I wondered if I might rather go hungry than try to buy lunch. Aamion, on the other hand, with that self-contained curiosity common in people who've grown up traveling, waltzed into the market, did a little relaxed haggling, bought twenty pounds of coconuts, dumped them into the passenger seat foot-well, and, as we went off searching for surf, started hacking and drinking away.

Later, at the best right-hander we found—a zippy little point with fun bowl sections—a band of local boys hung out watching us, hooting whenever Aamion got air. He's not a big aerialist incidentally, although he can boost if he needs to. Aamion's a waves-of-consequence guy, a card-carrying member of both the Kauai Wolfpack and the serious Pipeline underground, the guy who comes into his own at Cloudbreak and Teahupoo, where his huge frame and Kauai childhood and preternatural calm place him in the freakiest pits.

Following our session the beach kids hacked open a coconut for me, and I had to ask them how to eat it properly. Back in the car, Aamion gave me a little clinic for next time, telling me that young coconuts are the drinking ones and that the older dead-fall coconuts are the ones with the thick meat and that you can strain the white meat through an old sock or even through coconut husk to get out the milk and boil it, and once you've boiled it you've got a good oil for your skin or for cooking—makes fish taste pretty good, especially if you're eating fish for breakfast, lunch, and dinner and getting pretty sick of it—and that says nothing of what you can do with the fronds, like weaving them into rope or making shelter via the technique that Aamion calmly, painstakingly explained from what was clearly personal experience.

Or bananas: Aamion Goodwin could not say a simple phrase like, "Yeah, I like bananas," because he didn't think of bananas monolithically. He thought of bananas in terms of cooking bananas, apple bananas, and about a dozen other banana varieties, some of which he liked, some of which he hated, and others he said you could use only in certain ways. And when I asked what he'd meant before about eating fish for breakfast, lunch, and dinner—"What's that all about?"—he said that was just how he'd grown up, and so I asked who was catching all that fish, and he said that he was, for the most part, and I asked how, and he said he usually threw spears off rocks on the beach, and then I asked why the hell there were always fish right at the surface waiting to get nailed, and he said, "Well, when I was a kid I used to walk along the beach on the island where I grew up and catch crabs and mash them up with rocks and toss them in the water, and by the time I'd walked all the way around the island there'd be big fish coming in for the chum so I could brain them with a spear."

"And how about Slurpees?," you want to ask. Were you into the jumbo size or the super jumbo? "Oh, yeah, and also, *What freaking planet are you from?*"

"Fiji and Kauai, mostly. And New Zealand. Hey, stop the car," Aamion said. "Seriously, stop the car. I want to get out."

Aamion unfolded his endless limbs and jogged into the cacao orchard and pulled down a few huge pods and jumped back into the car. Then he cut one open with a knife, dipped in a finger to scoop out this goopy white membrane, and started sucking the gelatinous shite off his finger. "Okay, you can keep driving," he said.

To place Aamion Goodwin in the surf world, picture a Kauai childhood contemporary with the Irons brothers, growing up in the shadow of Laird, and surfing down at Pine Trees with Andy, Bruce, Roy Powers, Jesse Merle-Jones, Danny Fuller, Dustin Barca, and Kamalei Alexander. Lots of heavy older guys, too: Kala Alexander, Clay Abubo. But, of course, it wasn't all Pine Trees; that's just the only Kauai surf spot that Kauai boys are allowed to say exists. That's why it seems like an entire generation of heavy-wave chargers came out of a lame little beachbreak perfect from grom contests. But anyway, Aamion tried the contest route—amateur events around Hawaii, a second place in the Hawaiian State Championships—and then he realized that three-to-the-beach would never be his strong suit. He landed a *Surfer* cover in 2000 in the tube at Teahupoo: "That kind of jump-started my photo-slut career," is how Aamion describes its effect on his life. Now he's with Hurley, Etnies, Wave Riding Vehicles, etc., but mostly he's all about Pipeline and about his friends at Pipeline. He started working his way into the lineup in '98, sat out there for hours at a time catching the odd closeout, finally started picking off occasional set waves.

"Now it's a great feeling to be out there with your friends and be the guys getting waves," he says. But then he catches himself and adds, "Not that I get a lot of waves, either, and I certainly don't get my pick."

Then he makes sure to tell me about the older guys who do get their pick—Derek Ho, a few others—and he also makes sure to say that those guys deserve it, they've earned it.

They're very primitive, very tribal, these Kauai guys: always thinking about their friends, always paying respect.

"Any memorable days at Pipe?" I ask, knowing it won't work. Naming a memorable day would require claiming size, and that's a flat-out no-no.

So he says, "Memorable waves, maybe."

"Tell me."

"Last year, I got one that feathered on second reef but didn't break, and then it shelfed."

So I ask what "shelfed" means, and suddenly we're off and running because we're talking specifics about the wave, with no risk of accidental boasting: "Pipeline breathes, right? When you're in the barrel on a big one it breathes, and it'll kind of pull you back toward the foam ball—it's this weird, weightless feeling, and it usually does that right before it spits its guts out, and there's so many ways you can fall right then, like you can get blinded by the spit, or you can catch a boil. See, if you're already extended when it breathes, you almost always fall. So you keep your body compressed so you can compensate for that weightless feeling. But, anyway, somehow I got lucky and did everything right and came out. That was a memorable wave."

So low key, right? It's what these guys are like right now: no hyperbole. Spend enough time with them, and you imagine some mysterious figure standing over them with a baseball bat, ready to flatten them if they misspeak or speak openly about the dangers and outrageousness of surfing big Pipe and beyond. Like, here's Aamion's friends commenting on his presence at Pipeline.

"He's definitely out there at Pipeline," says Danny Fuller. "He's definitely out there getting the bigger waves. He's good. Aamion's one of the boys, and he gets his fair share of waves, and he's a standout. He's out there whenever it's big, doing his thing."

"Shit, he's really pretty much come into his own, found his niche, and surfs fucking really good out there," said Kamalei Alexander. "He can surf all right everywhere else, but at Pipeline he's starting to be a force with his fucking 10-foot arms; real healthy person, positive, always stoked to see other people do good."

Daize, Aamion's wife, is a little more expressive, talking about how they were fifteen when they met, and she had a job at Aamion's father's health food store: "He was skinny and tall and lanky. He hadn't filled out yet, and he had braces and acne. He was really safe. I could hang out with him every day, and my boyfriend wouldn't care. He was this hippy kid who would do anything fun,

Brad Gerlach wins a 2006 Billabong XXL Global Big Wave award with this 68-foot leviathan at Todos Santos, Mexico.

like cover each other with mud or pick ticks off the dog. But I didn't see him for maybe five years there, and one day my boyfriend was like, 'Look at this,' and he was pointing at some guy on the cover of Italian *Vogue*. He said, 'It's that guy you used to hang out with, Aamion.' After that, when I'd see him on North Shore, I was so scared because he was this ugly duckling who turned into the most beautiful swan."

But what's behind the person you become? When we're talking about well-endorsed young pros getting showered with money and free clothes and not caring about too much beyond hanging with their friends, I bet a lot of us think we know: not a lot, right? Well, check out Aamion's nativity story, which emerged that night in the hot darkness of a kerosene-lit deck at a former slave plantation, rain hammering the tin roof and spraying off the railings. The four of us, on that surf trip to the jungled Atlantic island, were eating pork and rice and drinking Portuguese beer, and when I asked what exactly Aamion meant about growing up in Fiji, New Zealand, and Kauai, I got a start-with-the-beginning story about two American kids in Vero Beach, Florida, in the mid-1970s, much in love and caught up in all the hope and changing values of that era. Making love by firelight, on the beach, they got pregnant, set out for Mexico, birth the baby *au naturel* in a mud goat shed with no midwife. Soon after, Dad's mom and grandma show up unannounced and help the little family back to Virginia Beach.

Aaron and Marion split up, Aaron takes custody of their baby, Aamion, and lights out for the Pacific islands, looking to escape industrial civilization—lands in Fiji, living with locals on a riverbank in the upland jungles, with friendly Fijian mothers caring for Aamion while the young father makes his art. Visa problems lead them onward to New Zealand, a few months of migrant farm work and surfing and hitchhiking. "I would bundle Aamion up before light," Aaron recalls of those farm working days, "place him still sleeping under the cherry tree and have an hour or more of first light to pick by, until the little bundle popped his head up and monkey-climbed high into the cherry tree to help drop some cherries in my bucket between breakfast mouthfuls."

Then came a berth on a dubious French yacht headed back to Fiji. The yacht had no working motor, a hole above waterline, and a sketchy French crew with a mysterious past, and they did run into a violent storm just offshore. "My dad had to hand-pump the bilge all night, and I kept running up on deck screaming, 'Dad, where are you?' Waves were smashing over, and I remember he's like, 'Don't come up again! You stay down there!' I came up again, and he grabbed me by the ankle and dunked me overboard and said, 'That's what it's like! Stay down there!'" The wind died, too, after the storm, and it stayed dead for two weeks—a serious problem when you don't have a working engine. Aamion recalls being knee deep in flying fish on deck and watching the captain spear a big shark. But seventeen days later, they limped into Fiji's Suva Harbor.

Everybody has a story; some are just better than others. Aamion's grew deeper and stranger as our Atlantic surf trip wore on, and I grew more and more curious about the gulf between his calm, well-adjusted normalcy and the astounding dysfunction of his childhood. Back in Fiji, for example, he and his father were invited to join a Fijian village, so they lived in a lean-to for several months while Aamion played all day with the local kids, catching prawns and gathering wild yams. "At the tender age of three," Aaron writes, "Aamion was immersed in this culture so freely— every day foretold how Aamion's heart would always dwell with these people in a way I could never know." There's a Hawaii chapter, too, all about being homeless on Maui's Makena Beach, living in caves with other hippies and Aaron finally remarrying.

Back in Fiji, yet again, Aamion, Aaron, and Aaron's new wife, Ave, got invited to a small group of outer islands that turned out to be paradise—one with a tiny village, the other four uninhabited. So they simply stayed, moved in, joined the village. "At seven years old," Aaron says, "Aamion could make his own spears, dive deep into the lagoons, hunt and spear fish, use a hand line to pull in big fish, use a machete, and climb tall coconut trees for nuts to drink and leaves to plait, scour the islands for food, and help return with the bounty for the waiting hum of coconut scraping and expectant fire tenders to feed all."

"We'd go throw spear with the young Fijian guys," Aamion says, "and we were all learning, and the older guys would teach us how to stalk the fish and how to throw at the right angle." He also went trolling off small boats, catching mackerel and rigging them with double hooks as bait for bigger fish. Idle-trolling across a pinnacle once with five hundred-pound test, he saw a marlin nail his line. Aamion was just a kid at the time, with a couple Fijian friends. "Bam, we just see the thing jump, and we're freaking out. It was probably like 7 feet, 8 feet from tip of the bill to the tail, and it was too big for me to hand-line in, so I just tied the line to the seat, and we towed it to the beach, and it was jumping and thrashing, and you could see the fins of four other marlin swimming right next to it, and we ended up bringing it in close to the beach and throwing a spear into its head, and we spread the meat around the village.

"But realistically," Aamion told me, "breakfast, lunch, and dinner were fish. No joke. Sometimes you were eating the boiled fish from the night before for breakfast, and as a kid I remember dying to have something sweet, something that was different tasting, so I would be in the lime trees when they were in season like, 'Oh, limes!' If there was a stalk of bananas that was going to be ripe, the whole village would know about it, like 'There's bananas on the other side of the island, don't tell anyone!' And it would be gone. When the mango trees go off, they don't even wait for them to get ripe, they're just grinding them. There were a few papaya trees, which the birds would get to before you, guaranteed. You'd be eating the scraps, which was fine, just to have a different taste in your mouth from fish." To season the fish, apparently they rarely did more than boil it in seawater or, after cooking it over a fire, dip it in seawater. "What they really looked forward to," Aamion said, "is a different fish for dinner, or a different fish for lunch, and, of course, their favorite things are like the eyeballs and the slime off the head. I don't particularly like the eyeballs that much, but the head is really moist, and the taste is really nice."

All my life I've wished I could spearfish, so I asked Aamion to give me a lesson. We borrowed a spear gun and fins and masks from the resort and got a guy with a dugout canoe to run us out to an offshore rock pile. Dropping into the water, Aamion took the gun first and went searching while I followed. Water depth ran down to about 30 feet, among various blocks and alleys, and small schools drifted in and out of sight. The local islanders bring home dinner every night this way—amazing watermen—and Aamion, I could see, would have no trouble doing the same. I shot at three fish that day and missed them all, but everything about Aamion's water presence spoke of absolute comfort—and as I lay in bed that night, only a few hundred yards from a plaque marking the equator, I decided that comfort seemed the great take-away from Aamion's miraculous experience in Fiji. Comfort with himself, comfort with exotic places, comfort with the sea—but most of all, comfort with Fiji, a specific place he can always call home.

Aaron did move them along to Kauai again and also New Zealand, where they lived in the orchards. A strong, young Aamion helped with the picking, but they got back to Fiji as soon as they could afford the trip, and that circuit became the annual migration path of Aamion's entire childhood and youth, right up until he was a teenager. At some point, Aaron's and Aamion's Fiji trips started to become separate affairs: Aaron and Ave now go for a month or so each year, staying on an uninhabited outer island with a freshwater drip that provides five gallons a day. They get dropped off without a boat or a satellite phone. Aaron makes art; Ave makes jewelry. When I ask if it's a lovely place, Aamion says, "It's a platform on top, drops off 200 feet to the water; in order to get on to the top, you have to climb up the roots of a banyan tree. You sit up there and just look over the reef, and where it drops off into the deep blue you can watch schools of fish swim by all day, sharks. They bring brown rice, and they drink coconuts and tea and relax. I'm not exaggerating. My dad doesn't even fish. And there's a mango tree on top, so they have mangos right now."

Aamion eventually started taking his friend Mark Healey; they head first to that one little village on the outer islands, where males old and young wear cast-off clothes left behind by Aamion over the years. After a good, long visit, including hellos to various villagers who have been named after Aamion, his father, and Ave—who once helped birth a baby in the village—Aamion, Healey, and a few old Fijian buddies load a boat with fresh water and make a two-hour trip to an uninhabited island. Sometimes they stay two weeks. Sometimes they stay a month. Mostly they just dive all day long and maybe throw spear in the afternoons. Aamion admits that there are waves on these islands and that he surfs out on these trips, but he says that for years he never even thought about surfing there. "It was all about fishing and hanging out with Fijians, and time would pass quickly," he says. "You just fall into the experience of being there. It's easygoing and satisfying and constant."

Aamion never pretends his life has been any easier or better than anybody else's. After all, another way of looking at his past is that his mom and dad split up right after he was born and that his penniless father dragged him all over the planet in pursuit of art and meaning. Along the way, the baby boy spent a lot of time either genuinely homeless or living in marginal circumstances. He also grew up hardly knowing his biological mother, which isn't a picnic for anyone. That's probably why Aamion's tips on how to eat coconuts or cacao pods or how to build yourself a home with palm fronds or how to mash up rock crabs and toss them out for chum don't ever smack of boasting. In every life, a little rain must fall, but Aamion has seen his downpours. The home Aamion has made on the North Shore and among his childhood surf buddies—the Wolfpack, that is, filling up the pecking order at Pipe—reads in this light as a very natural commitment to the safe and the familiar. But Aamion seems to know that he's had his share of blessings, too, and that his father had an astonishing reservoir of courage, commitment, and love—how few fathers would really stand by a baby son all on their own? Most of all, Aamion seems to know that he's found something in Fiji that most people never find anywhere: a genuine home on earth.

"For certain people," he says, "there's a place where you're absolutely content with everything. That's what Fiji is for me."

GERRY LOPEZ: THE LAST SOUL SURFER

The Gerry Lopez–Pipeline union in the 1970s was another one of the sport's perfect matches, like Miki Dora at Malibu and Greg Noll at Waimea Bay. But he added a twist. Where everybody else used the wave as a platform upon which to perform, Lopez's idea was to literally disappear into the wave. In his best moments he didn't seem to be performing at all—or at least not in the way Dora, Noll, and the rest performed. Lopez stood quietly, hands and arms relaxed at his sides, knees just slightly bent, face calm. He wasn't the first less-is-more surfer. But he did it in the ionized center of Pipeline tubes that exploded around him like cannon fire, making the most difficult thing in the sport appear not just easy but meditative.

Nobody had better timing than Gerry Lopez. He was a gifted surfer who would have left a mark no matter when he came on the scene. Yet, every surf-world event, trend, and development seemed to go Lopez's way, beginning with Jock Sutherland's bewildering announcement in December 1969 that he'd voluntarily joined the U.S. Army and was shipping out forthwith, leaving the position for top Pipeline surfer wide open. Anticontest sentiment was peaking, too, which created a need for a new kind of surf hero. Lopez filled both roles, immediately and effortlessly. For six years, he was surfing's preeminent figure.

By shrewdly managing his image, Lopez was able to be different things to different people. He was never really an anticontest surfer, for example. He traveled to California, Peru, and Australia to compete and entered just about every pro event on the North Shore during the early and mid-seventies. Being involved didn't mean he was consumed, however. He took contests on his own terms—a trait first demonstrated in 1969 when Lopez, then twenty years old, showed up at Huntington

Pier for the U.S. Championships. He was small and slender (5 foot 8, 140 pounds), quiet and watchful, unknown outside of Hawaii, and he wowed the Huntington judges with his patented fin-drift maneuver.

He surfed through the prelims, into the finals, and took fifth. He made an equally strong impression on the beach, sitting next to the pilings just before the last heat of the contest, eyes closed, in perfect full lotus position. It looked as if he'd completely tuned out the entire whirligig beach scene—twenty thousand spectators, the PA announcer, the damp lime-green nylon competition vest he was wearing. Lopez was in his own world. By such means, he was able to surf in all the contests he wanted yet also remain the epitome of the soul surfer.

Modesty was part of Lopez's charm. All he ever really hoped to do at Pipeline, he once said, was "figure out how not to eat it." But he wasn't above the occasional quiet display of confidence. During a filmed interview in 1974, at the end of a detailed address on the mechanics of tube-riding at Pipeline, Lopez paused, gave a little shrug, and said, "It's a cakewalk." He knew better. A brief clip in *Pacific Vibrations* showed him catching an edge halfway down a smooth 12-footer at Pipeline and getting horribly pitched into the maul. In 1972, while surfing an oversized afternoon at Pipeline that the magazines would immortalize as "Huge Monday," Lopez went head-first into the bottom and walked off the beach with loose teeth and blood running down one side of his face.

The failures just underscored Lopez's mastery. He walked an impossibly fine line at Pipeline. The fact that Lopez had scars on his back, shoulders, and head from bouncing off the reef made it that much more incredible that he could ride with such poise. Everybody else grimaced or frowned as they came off the bottom and set a course through the tube section. Lopez usually rode with an expressionless tai chi gaze—except when he broke out into a little smile, at which point it really *did* look like a cakewalk.

Lopez defied expectations throughout his career, in ways both large and small. While fortifying himself on the path to enlightenment with a twice-daily yoga practice and endless servings of brown rice and steamed veggies, he also turned up in an ad wearing a hunter's vest, holding a shotgun. For a surf magazine portrait, he arranged to stand dutifully behind his mother—a small, fine-boned Japanese *okaasan* in a white ankle-length silk dress. He built a three-story dream house directly in front of Pipeline, then rented it and moved to a twenty-acre ranch on the foothills of Maui's Haleakala crater, then left Hawaii altogether for the Pacific Northwest. Finally, Lopez built up a towering surf-world commercial presence, which seemed to have no effect whatsoever on his reputation as "The Last Soul Surfer"—as *Surfer* magazine entitled its longest and best Lopez profile. He attached his name to a failed surfwear company called "Pipeline," played Arnold Schwarzenegger's sidekick in the iron-and-blood fantasy movie *Conan the Barbarian,* and played himself in Warner Brothers' overwrought surf drama *Big Wednesday.* These were the kind of career moves that typically got a surfer branded a sellout. Lopez walked away clean every time.

—From *The History of Surfing,* by Matt Warshaw

THE EYE OF THE STORM

as told by Mike Parsons and Greg Long

It is considered one of the greatest surfing exploits of all time. In the winter of 2008, during a massive North Pacific storm that ravaged the entire west coast of North America, while the rest of its more reasonable population cowered out of the rain and wind, an intrepid crew of big-water hunters spit into the eye of the hurricane, daring the tempest to do its worst. They were going surfing, come hell or . . . well, read on, and we're sure you'll agree that these guys should've either been committed or given a medal. We recommend the medal.

Mike Parsons: We were watching the storm develop for a few days. Of course, swell prediction is such a science these days you can get all these projections for about a week out—the size and frequency of the swell, what the wind's likely to do, cha cha cha. So I'm camped on the computer, studying swell models on all the various websites, figuring that it has to be rideable somewhere. But this storm gave every indication of being a total blowout, no surfable conditions anywhere. We're talking raging southwest winds along the whole western coastline, from Oregon to Baja. Mavericks would wash out; Oregon would be blown to bits; Todos Santos, a complete mess. Anyway, the whole time I'm talking with Greg Long—he's kind of my partner in crime so far as planning epic trips—and we kept asking each other, "Where are we gonna go?" All the figures pointed to one of the biggest swells in decades, but the conditions said we wouldn't be surfing, anywhere, and we'd have to like it. It was so frustrating.

So the swell is supposed to hit land the following day, and I'm reading the weather charts for the hundredth time. And 3:00 p.m.

I speed-dial Greg and say, "Are you lookin' at this?" And he says, "I can't believe you just called me. I'm looking at the exact same thing." The latest weather charts were predicting that the wind would lie down out at Cortes Banks for about three hours in the afternoon, during a brief lull between storm fronts.

Greg Long: As the day wore on, the weather charts were all over the place. Half were calling for a raging, windy nightmare out at Cortes, all day long, while the other half were saying the winds might die off for a few hours, meaning we might pull off a guerrilla-style trip out there. So what do we do? The logical side says, "There's a storm raging. Don't bother going outside today, and forget about bashing all the way out to Cortes Banks, 100 miles out to sea." Then the other half goes, "Okay, but what if?" You keep pacing around and checking the swell models and wondering what if? And you die in your mind like a hundred times because you know you're going to go.

MP: So we put out the call to Brad (Gerlach) and Twiggy (Grant Baker). They didn't even hesitate, even though Twiggy was sitting out the same storm up in northern California, and to make it here in time, he had to immediately gas it for San Clemente, an eight-hour drive. Our next call was to photographer and Cortes skipper Rob Brown, who was at a boat show down the road in San Diego. He answers his cell right there on the showroom floor, and I said, "Hey, R. B., it could be on tomorrow at Cortes." And he was, like, "Are you guys crazy or what? It's supposed to be a howling southern gale out there. For days." But he must've heard the fire in our voices because he considered for a moment and said, "Well, if you guys are serious enough to commit, then I'll drive up tonight and get the boat ready. If you're really serious." But he already knew the answer, and he never asked again.

Greg Long gives Mike Parsons some lineup beta during their crazy Cortes Bank mission.
<small>PHOTO © ROBERT BROWN</small>

GL: The whole mission was so last-minute that we had no time to prep our backup safety equipment—the backup boats, skis, and all the water safety rescue gear normally considered essential for an adventure this serious. We couldn't have organized a more bare-bones expedition to Cortes Bank and in the heaviest conditions ever seen out there.

MP: I called Matt Wybenga, who'd shot video with us for years, and told him to start packing his gear. He bursts out laughing, like, *"Tomorrow?* You're jokin', right?" By now it's just hammering rain, one of the heaviest winter storms in years to hit the California coastline. I told Matt, "Just be ready." By then we were so gung-ho I could barely stand still. But we could still back out if the predictions all changed. Then around midnight we started seeing the buoys light up in northern California, the biggest buoy readings we had ever seen. Greg and I both knew we had no choice. I think he said it first: "We have to try."

GL: Rob's boat is just insane. He pretty much custom designed it for Cortes runs. But we couldn't get all the gear onto just the one boat, so we'd have to drive one of the skis, tag teaming all the way out to the bank. We're talking 100 miles, and it's like *Victory at Sea* out there. So as we're loading up at Dana Point Harbor, I volunteered to go first. I pulled on my wetsuit, and over that I tugged on one of those Coast Guard survival suits—this big-ass orange thing that keeps you nice and warm in the heaviest conditions. But none of us was prepared for how heavy it would get. Soon as we cast off and start motoring out through Dana Point Harbor, I could see these massive swells smashing against the seawall, exploding up and over it. This rarely if ever happened and then only during a big northwest swell. But this swell was coming from due south. And soon as we carved around the corner we slammed straight into an 8- to 10-foot south wind swell chop. After half a mile I was barely hanging on.

MP: So we're pounding along at about 10 knots, and Greg's slamming along in the wake, just getting worked on the ski. And I looked at my watch and started doing the math. At the rate we wouldn't make Cortes until about 5:30 p.m. Right around dark. I yelled this to Rob, up front muscling the helm. "We can do one of two things," he yelled back. "Turn around. Or I can throw the hammer down. We'll average about 30 knots like that, but you guys are gonna have to hang on for your lives." We stopped and pulled Greg up, and I said, "Dude, this is gonna destroy you, but we pretty much have to go full bore. It's the only way we'll ever get to surf. But it's your call." He dove back in, dragged himself onto the ski, and yelled, "Hit it."

GL: I've never been on a rougher mission. Not even close. No break, just grinding up those swells and slamming down hard, like cratering off 10-foot moguls. We had to get out there by 1:00 p.m. at the latest to hit the window, and Rob's just powering through this mountain range of swells and wind and furious cross chop. I'm back there getting the crap knocked out of me. My shoulders are aching and super tight, and I figured any minute now we'd be past Catalina Island, about 22 miles out. Finally I pull along side the boat and scream, "Hey, guys. Someone else has gotta take over. I'm done." The only sound was the howling wind, and the guys on board start looking at each other, almost embarrassed. "Well, how far have we gone?" I finally yelled up, and they're like, "We've barely gone 14 miles, Greg." I shook my head and said, "Okay, let's go." And we pushed on out. I could see the guys on the boat were taking a serious beat-down as well, so I figured maybe the ski wasn't such a tough ride after all. At least I wouldn't get seasick. At least not for another half an hour, when Mike and Twiggy took their turns driving the ski.

MP: Everyone on board had experienced rough ocean crossings, hundreds of them, really, and none of us ever had problems. But 15 miles out, and we were into open ocean storm surf on a completely different level. After a couple hours all but Greg were violently ill. In all of my time on boats I'd never seen someone look so sick as Matt Ybenga, almost comatose. He must've thrown up ten times. I'm just staring at him, letting it fly over the gunwales, and I start wondering, "Can a person actually die of sea sickness?"

Cortes Bank whitewater
PHOTO © ROBERT BROWN

GL: I never get seasick. Ever. But after a few hours beating into that storm I was pretty close to losing it. I was also thinking we should turn around, but I didn't say anything. Then about 65 miles out, maybe 15 miles past San Clemente Island, everything went dead calm.

MP: The wind, the chop, everything started lying down, and the next thing we knew we're closing in on the bank. Around 1:00 p.m., when we were around 6 miles off, we started seeing the avalanches of whitewater in the distance, and we were just beside ourselves.

GL: The Cortes Banks aren't a true reef but the tip of an underwater seamount, some hundred miles offshore. But plowing out there on a day like that, in the rain and wind and giant swells, you don't see any land for 95 percent of the time, so it feels like you're a thousand miles out in the ocean. Then suddenly you pull up, and there's this gigantic wave breaking in the middle of nowhere at all. It's one of the most incredible things in one of the most out-there places I have experienced in my life. That such a wave exists at all is a miracle. That it's a quality, perhaps matchless, big wave, breaking 100 miles out, is a wonder of the world. And this time it was unbelievable, all these giant plumes of whitewater exploding. It didn't matter what we just went through, how beat up, exhausted, wet, freezing, and seasick we were. The moment we hove to, we were all reborn. Now it was time to surf.

MP: We all were pretty trashed. Just wasted. But we were crazy stoked to try and surf this place—plus we wanted to get the hell off of that boat. So we all scrambled into our gear and got the skis out and the gear sorted in record time.

GL: Straight away it was obvious the bank was just going off, that these were the biggest waves any of us had ever seen. We had to be right on our game, or else. During the next four or five hours, had any of us made a mistake, it immediately would put everybody in a life-threatening situation. We made it clear going out there that everyone was on point—no mess-ups. Not there. Not on that day.

MP: Rob was up against it, having to drive the boat and shoot photos at the same time. Because the waves were so gigantic, they were breaking in places we'd never seen before. Right before we went out, Rob says, "Just remember, anything happens to the boat, and we're all walking home."

GL: We started feeling our way into it, edging over into this massive A-frame widow's peak, breaking way out and way over from where we normally would line up. Of course, "line up" doesn't mean much in a place with no landmarks. But anyway we towed in as deep as we could so long as we could make the waves. Each set kept getting bigger and bigger, until about halfway through the session I towed Twiggy into an absolute bomb. The second wave in this set was bigger than I'd ever imagined. I powered over the back of this beast and glanced back at Mike and Brad, towing into the biggest wave I've seen in my entire life.

MP: In massive surf, the third or fourth wave of the set is often the huge one. So Greg towed Twiggy into the second one, and we went over it, and there's this massive, flawless wave standing up in front of us like a drive-in movie screen. Brad was driving, and he looked back at me, and I yelled, "No, go over this one." And he was giving me that look, as if to say, "You gotta be kidding me. You really think there's something better behind this? Or bigger?" He looked irritated that I didn't want it. So we motored over this macker, and right there rearing up in our faces is the fourth wave of the set, and I was like, "Oh my God, I'm going to have to try to ride this thing. Then Brad whipped around, and I was committed to the biggest wave of my life. The biggest wave I'd ever seen before or since.

GL: I could not believe the size of this animal. Twiggy's wave was huge, but Mike's wave was breaking so much farther out and farther over that Twiggy's could have been an inside break. Mike dropped the tow rope. I watched him drop in slow motion, looking like an ant on a mountain of dirt. And even with all his speed, he was barely going down at all.

MP: Brad put me right in the sweet spot, but about three-quarters of the way down the face, and my board started cavitating. Sometimes in giant surf your board gets going so fast that there's not enough space for the water to flow between the fins. The water loads up, and your board starts to drag in the water, which is what happened, like pulling an emergency brake. So I start getting pushed back up the giant face—the very last thing I needed on the hugest wave of my life, 100 miles out to sea.

GL: For a moment, Brad seemed glued in place, not making any headway down the wave. When you look at the photos it looks as though he's drawing *up* the face, like a video sequence run backward. And I'm going, "Go, Mike, go, Mike, don't fall, don't fall, whatever you do, *don't fall!*" Then the whitewater just exploded all around him.

MP: I was praying to God that I wouldn't fall off. Then I was covered by white water and couldn't see a thing, and I remember thinking, *Just point it and hold on, point it and hold on. Do not fall.* Then I come flying out of the spume, and I knew I was going to make it.

GL: I picked up Twiggy in the channel, and Mike was coming right up behind us. I looked at Mike, and he was trembling, completely speechless. Then Brad pulls up, and I told him that was the biggest wave ever ridden. I'm sure of it. Who knows how you could ever measure such a bomb, but it had to be well over 70 feet. The swell kept picking up through the rest of day, and later that afternoon we all rode waves approaching that size. I know that I caught the biggest wave I've ever ridden. Meanwhile Rob was dodging 60- to 80-foot sets and trying to shoot stills and video from over half a mile away, at the only place he could safely put his boat. Seasickness had so ruined videographer Matt Wybenga that he was semiconscious the whole time. So the session was poorly documented. But photos or no photos, video or no video, for the rest of my life, and with fear and gratitude, I'll always remember that afternoon

During a brief break in the storm, Mike Parsons drops the rope on the biggest wave ever ridden at Cortes Bank.

PHOTO © ROBERT BROWN

out at Cortes Bank. Hands down, the wildest adventure I've ever been a part of.

MP: Brad and I decided to drive the skis all the way home. The young guys, Greg and Twiggy, had pushed us all day, and we loved that, but it was our pleasure to say, "We'll take it from here." We battened down the gear and headed for land around dark. In pitch-black seas, Brad drove all the way to San Clemente Island, and I took it on home to Dana Point. It was a long, brutal day but well worth the struggles. And what a feeling to know we were scoring huge while Hawaii was junk and everyone else was sitting out the storm in northern California or hunkered at home watching *Pimp My Ride*.

Despite the dangerous conditions, our biggest concern was that someone else saw what we saw on the weather charts. We were all like, "*Please* don't let there be another boat there." I thought for sure we'd run into Garrett McNamara or some of the Santa Cruz crew. With all the wave technology available today and all the bold chargers, I never thought we'd have the bank all to ourselves. And when we beat it all the way out there and found the place empty, we kept screaming, in so many words, that it couldn't be real. There's no way, in 2008, that the waves of the century could be breaking out there just for us four. *It's just not possible.*

HIGH NOON AT BISHOP ROCK

by Chris Dixon

It is, quite simply, the most remarkable surf spot on the planet: Cortes Bank, a massive seamount whose submarine peak rises to within a few fathoms of the surface 100 miles off the coast of southern California. Giant North Pacific swells rolling over the bank create waves of almost unimaginable size—some of the biggest waves ever ridden, and these attempted only by jet-powered tow-in teams. But in 2010 New York Times *reporter and longtime surfer Chris Dixon signed aboard for a different offshore expedition, sailing over the horizon with a team of intrepid big wave riders bent on tackling Cortes barehanded.*

"When we were here the last time," Greg Long says, sweeping his arm toward the clanging bell buoy atop the Bishop Rock, "it was a whiteout the whole length of reef. And all the way up, I mean, you know how long the bank is, there were waves spotting and breaking all the way down right up to here in front of us. You could see waves breaking in slow motion, 5 miles away."

"As far as the eye could see, it was just a huge square of white-water," adds Grant Baker in his Durbanese dialect. "We had to sit way out past the buoy, and the waves were coming right through the buoy. This area in here was a nightmare, all the fucking white-water. If you lost your guy, he was gone. He would have just been lost in the expanse and you'd never find him. It was just so scary."

Baker and Long were recalling January 5, 2008. It was the day they teamed up with hellman boat captain and photographer Rob Brown, Mike Parsons, and Brad Gerlach and motored off into a tiny opening of calm air between the pinwheel arms of one of the deepest lows ever recorded in the North Pacific. On this Hail

Mary mission into surfing's greatest unknown, they returned with the rightful account of how they surfed the largest waves ever documented. I recounted the tale for the *New York Times*. The article, accompanied by Brown's famous photos of a diminutive Mike Parsons outrunning a cerulean avalanche, ended up being the week's most heavily trafficked sports story on the *Times'* website, even outranking the breaking news of Roger Clemens's steroid abuse. But for me, the story didn't end there.

Since that time, this 16-mile-long ridgeline, a sunken island that the first California settlers probably walked atop 10,000 years ago, has become an obsession for me. In fact, I imagine my mania for the place has come to somewhat resemble that of Long. But rather than surf the Cortes Bank, I'm writing a book about it. I ponder the fact I'm actually out here, and the company I'm with, and shake my head. With all the bizarre, terrifying, and fascinating stories I've heard over the last year, it's the strangest déjà vu: a homecoming to a place I've never visited.

This is Long and Baker's first visit to Cortes [together] since 2008. The fact that we can sit right off the Bishop Rock buoy, which serves as a small island for Cortes Bank's bickering troupe of sea lions, means that the waves are decidedly smaller than they were then. But this expedition is no less historic. Last summer Long, Sam George, Bill Sharp, and a young San Clemente hellman named George Hulse joined *Surfing* magazine's late, great photographer Larry "Flame" Moore on a successful, if unsung, paddle-surfing mission out here.

Long and a few of his closest colleagues have lately been rewriting the book on the kind of waves it is physically possible to paddle into. What better laboratory for this ongoing experiment in mortality, Greg reasoned, than the 12-foot-deep pinnacle of Bishop Rock? But he didn't just want to do the deed with Baker or Parsons (who was inexplicably absent from this trip); he wanted to include a cadre of the best big wave surfers in the world. Long brought up the idea to photographer Jason Murray, who has joined him on expeditions to spots only they will ever know. Long worked the surfer angle, inviting his brother Rusty, Peter Mel, Nathan Fletcher, Kelly Slater, Mark Healey, and Chilean hellman Ramon Navarro. Murray would work to sort out the transportation.

The last time Long and Baker visited these waters, they napped in surfboard bags in the open hull of Rob Brown's go-fast boat while trading frigid hours atop their second jet ski in a surplus navy survival suit. This time, Murray's well-placed calls yielded interest from Jerry Herbst, a billionaire with family interests in Vegas casinos, convenience stores, oil, and a racing team. He'd let them travel aboard his glittering 105-foot Westport, a yacht named *Mr. Terrible*, for the cost of fuel and crew.

A day before we boarded *Mr. Terrible*, Long and Baker had been in Hawaii, with no idea that they would soon be trekking out to Cortes Bank. The hardest-working duo in big wave surfing had spent the winter of '09–'10 jetting between the West Coast and Hawaii in a manic, epic quest to score El Nino's greatest bounty. With a healthy, long-period swell looming, there had been quiet chatter of a post-Christmas bank job, but the winds were looking particularly unfavorable. Thus, Christmas Day found Long and Baker enduring back-to-back, near-death experiences at Peahi (Jaws). Frustrated, and possibly nursing a slight concussion, Long needed rest. But then the call came from Murray. The winds were backing off.

By 11:00 p.m. on December 26, the dusty four-wheel-drive Econoline that doubles as Greg's mobile home rumbled to a stop in front of Terrible Herbst's waterfront Newport Harbor mansion and spilled out an overstuffed cargo of surfboards, surfers, and Long's and Baker's girlfriends, Kate Lovemore and Jess Spraker. Minutes later Bill Sharp rolled his video camera as a bleary-eyed Long greeted a team of the best big wave surfers on Earth.

For some reason, apparently unclear even to himself, Kelly Slater chose to simply say hello to everyone at the dock and then drive toward LAX on a quest to chase a big Atlantic swell through the Caribbean to Morocco. As *Mr. Terrible* passed the gilded palaces along Newport Harbor, Mark Healey's cell phone rang. Long laughs at the ensuing conversation: "Kelly says, 'I was just driving down the road, and I didn't really realize, did I just drive away from that whole production? That's a once-in-a-lifetime opportunity. I drove back. Can you guys come back and pick me up?'"

Long settled down alongside Pete Mel to a plate of tamales and took what appeared to be the first hard look around since LAX. "I almost drowned yesterday. Now look at this. I'm sitting on a yacht eating tamales."

It was a sense shared by everyone else on board. When the call came to me nine hours earlier that the mission was on, I was cruising down a hill on a skateboard with my four-year-old daughter in front of my mom's house. In Atlanta.

Through mouthfuls of tamales, Long told of his particular vexation at the punishment he and Baker had endured at Jaws, wondering whether to blame it on a bad set of fins, his board, or his surfing. "It's a pretty weird experience to think that you fucked up that bad," said Long. "It was everything you don't do. I did the Skindog. We were out there before the sun comes up and the first big wave. I haven't towed into something like that in I don't know how long."

"So, you got maybe a little overzealous, no?" Mel chided. "Slightly? Would that be the first mistake?"

"No, I mean, we sat there and watched a couple of sets go through, and it's a deceiving wave, because if you let go on the peak, then you're way too deep. You can't make forward momentum because all this water's drawing back. Let go at the shoulder, and then you're actually in the peak. I let go too early on my first wave, and it was massive. I got stuck behind it and took the west bowl on the head. The next wave I started going down the face and started to try to turn, but the board didn't want to. I was dealing with all the bumps, and as soon as I got to the bottom, it was like, bump, bump, bump, and I just fell straight on my face. Then I'm just like, skip, skip, skip, whoooosh. I'm upside down looking out of the tube getting the suplex. It was the most violent flogging I'd had in a long time."

The discussion turns to wipeouts, concussions, and near-death experiences. Slater and Baker recount hilarious and frightening stories of the amnesia they suffered after brutal wipeouts in Java and South Africa. Then someone asked Mark Healey about his recent excursion to ride on the backs of great white sharks off Guadalupe Island. It's an idea that for a world-champion spear fisherman–cum–hellman like Healey seems perfectly normal but that to everyone else seems perfectly insane.

When talk turns back to horrifying wipeouts, the subject of Mavericks reappears, in particular, a hellish hold-down endured by Neil Mathies ten or so years back.

"He played it off on film, but he buckled his back," says Pete. "I think he went back, but he never rode a wave. He was like, 'This isn't enjoyable anymore. I'm over it.' Which I think is way more admirable than trying to fake that you like it. It's like, 'I frickin' love this. I swear I do. Umm, I'm supposed to love this? Wait, I don't love this; I'm scared shitless!'"

"For me, it totally depends on the kind of mood I'm in," Slater says, strumming a vintage Kamaka ukulele. "Like the day before the Eddie, I was like, 'Fuck it.' I'm not even into it. But then I got there the morning of the contest, and I'm like, 'Let's go!' Then when I get out there, it's like, for me, I don't know that I'm going to go out there and push myself on a big wave. But then I get out there, and I'm like, 'My God, these things are perfect. If I wipeout, I'll just hold my breath for twenty seconds.' There's something to be said for putting yourself in a situation. Once you're in it, you're like, 'Well, I have to deal with it now.'"

Before we turn in, Nathan Fletcher, a guy I've never met before but come to like a lot, briefly recounts a tale related by his uncle

Phillip "Flippy" Hoffman of an experience off San Clemente Island, a spot we're due to pass in a couple of hours. "You don't know what to expect out here, really." Fletcher says. "It's at the edge of the continental shelf. Anything can happen. My uncle was out on a day, and it was 15- to 18-foot. All of a sudden, a 100-foot wave—a rogue wave—came, and they were motoring up it, and the boat went over the falls. He had to jump off and swim to San Clemente Island. He said it's still the biggest wave he's ever seen."

At dawn the next morning, the possibility of a rogue wave seems unlikely but not out of the realm of possibility. A quarter-mile off the bow looms a strange apparition. Solid lines of a new swell bump on the horizon in the middle of the ocean. The first rises glacier blue beneath diffuse morning sunlight, a majestic A-frame peak, perhaps 25 feet from trough to crest. Its concussion and the subsequent geyser of whitewater shatter the morning quiet like an artillery burst from the hills behind Trestles. Baker grins and then shouts below deck, "Healey, eeets a left!"

After motoring out on a scouting mission with Healey, Greg wants to be the first one in the water. But first he wants to give the comely Jess a chance to peer into his world from the back of his ski. In the distance, the WaveRunner makes a solo drop down a wave perhaps 20 feet from top to bottom. Greg expertly pilots right along the wave's massive flank. When they pull back up to the boat, Spraker is amped on adrenaline, and her eyes are like saucers.

"Nothing I've ever done comes close to that," she says. "And he said that wasn't even huge. I'm like, 'Oh my God, are you nuts?' Oh my God. That was so fun. The wave just exploded; we were getting sprayed by it. I was screaming. Oh my God. Kate and I always say Greg and Twiggy, they're drug addicts. Now I can see exactly why he does this."

Before long, it's my turn. One of the crewmen, a young fisherman named Nate Perez, has been ferrying surfers out to the lineup on a spare ski. He's not wearing a wetsuit, and so I figure I don't need mine either. Perhaps 50 yards from *Mr. Terrible*, I sense this is a mistake. My mind turns to a story I've been researching about a crew of crazy entrepreneurs who sought to create their own island nation atop Cortes Bank by sinking a massive concrete freighter on the exact pinnacle of rock that lies dead ahead. The leader of the operation went to sea with no life jacket, clad in fur après ski boots, a sweater, and cashmere pants. The mistake nearly cost him his life.

I peer down into the water, hoping for a glimpse at the wreckage of the ship. But all Perez and I can see is a forest of palm kelp, big, scary swirls of current, and an occasional tornado of what I can only imagine must be schooling sardine. Out at the peak, the surfers sit in a loose bunch, scattered in a circle at least 75 yards across. Every so often a sea lion surfaces and slings a yellowtail into the air. A seal carcass floats out at the edge of the lineup. Healey's jokes about sharks scare the bejeezus out of everyone.

The waves are shifty beasts. Some hit far up on the peak, capping over and rolling down the line like mutant runners off Old Man's. Others rise up into explosive cone-shaped wedges that Slater says remind him of Sebastian Inlet on steroids. Others shift a little farther to the east and jack up into steep, deep slabs that I can't imagine trying to paddle into. Ramon Navarro can, though. He strokes hard, and the wave drops out from under him. He slides down on his back like he's at a water slide, snaps his leash, and is pummeled on the inside. A few minutes later, Alfie Cater makes the same mistake. From a ringside seat, his freefall to hell is gut-wrenching.

We edge closer and watch Slater and Long stroke into a pair of bombs. There's the barest whisper of south wind. But it's enough to blow a cascade of spray off the wave's hulking back. The rainstorm shower is the only thing you hear until the tremor that's unleashed when the wave folds over. I've never heard or seen anything quite like it, not while sitting on boats at Todos Santos or

Mavericks and certainly not standing on the beach or the point at Waimea Bay. Silence punctuated by showers, hoots, and explosions.

Healey and Long slide down the face of a beautifully tapered right-hander. Fletcher sketches into a steep bomb atop a terribly skinny 11-footer. I never see Healey ride a left. For documentarians like Bill Sharp or Murray, or the surfers who casually call waves like these "20-footers," you can sense that it might be possible to eventually lose your sense of wonder at a scene like this. But because I have no desire to surf waves like these, just being out here is absolute sensory overload.

Perez idles around, trying to keep us away from impeller-choking strands of kelp, and we both just marvel at the whole damn thing. I've delved deeply into the geologic origins of this rock and have pieced together what I hope is the first coherent line of history on the horribly tragic details surrounding its discovery and first charting. I've listened to divers spin fantastic tales of the wonders that lie below. I've interviewed a man who traveled out here with legendary treasure hunter Mel Fisher on a hilariously ill-fated attempt to find the gold of a Spanish galleon. I recently located a man who surfed out here alone in 1961 and have interviewed another legendary big wave surfer whose boat sank out from under him in the middle of the night. That he is alive today is pure miracle.

I'm sitting on the ski pondering these imponderables and staring down into the depths when I finally get a view of the bottom, or the top if you think of the Cortes Bank as a 6,000-foot mountain. The water's as clear as an aquarium, and it's impossible to tell how deep it is, but you can clearly see dark rock interspersed with patches of very, very white sand. Golden fish, they must be garibaldi, weave through the forest. So complete is our distraction that Perez and I fail to notice a dark lump outside. When we do look up simultaneously, the view is, frankly, terrifying. A gray-blue wall the size of a house has erased the horizon and is bearing down. Perez fires the ski. Nothing. He hits the starter again, and the engine fires. I pray we've not sucked up any kelp as he guns it. We're nearly erased.

On the flight home to Charleston the next morning, I ask myself if the previous day really happened. Even though I've logged hours of interviews and unearthed rare photos and footage, the Cortes Bank has never actually seemed like a real place. Now that I've actually been out there, I'm not exactly sure if that feeling has changed.

Basque surfers in Spain and France have taken to the giant peaks of Biscay Bay with a passion. Benjamin Sanchis, on one of the first Billabong XXL Global Big Wave Awards entries set off the American continent

PHOTO © BONNHAME-AQUASHOT.FR/BILLABONGXXL.COM

THE HEART OF THE MATTER

as told by Vincent Lartizen

The Basque fishermen of the French and Spanish coast have a long history of seafaring, maintaining a centuries-deep respect for the giant Atlantic storm swells that sweep the Bay of Biscay. But in recent years a new generation of Basque watermen has been exploring the coast, discovering waves of a previously unimaginable size. In 2002 French surfer Vincent Lartizen was part of the first team to pioneer the bombora reef called Belharra, a previously unknown wave off the coast of the Côte Basque. Photos of that session—40- to 50-foot and glassy peaks—helped reconfigure the global big wave surfing maps. Yet Lartizen wondered what Belharra might be like on a really big swell. In the fall of 2008, he got his answer.

For at least two years, before we ever caught the first wave, I'd heard stories about Belharra from the local Basque people. They told us about this giant wave breaking way outside the port of St. Jean de Luz and how it was the fishermen's dread. They said that on the really big swells, the waves were so huge you could see them breaking all the way from shore. So, whenever the swell was up we sometimes would look out at Belharra and say, "Yeah, we should go out there someday." But from land, so very far away, it looked like just another big wave—nothing more than that. Then finally, during the huge swell that hit the Atlantic coast in 2002, we decided to go out there and have a close look. And it was a real shock.

The offshore reef at Belharra is located 3 kilometers out west from the breakwall of St. Jean de Luz. During our first exploration we could see it breaking, even from the water level, on the back of the ski. We just grabbed our boards, took aim on the break, and gunned it out there. And the closer we got, the bigger it grew. Breaking so far from shore, with nothing around it but water, the wave seemed to rise off the sea like a mountain. It's a very wide wave with a high peak, and it races across the reef with great speed—much different from other big waves we had surfed in France and even in Hawaii, where the waves slow down as they reach the shore. At Belharra, the swell does not slow down over the reef—at all. So in terms of size and speed, that first session was a shock, very intense.

Following our initial adventure we would check the charts and buoys, all winter long, watching for the swell to get big enough to make Belharra break once more. Over the next five years we had several good sessions out there but nothing close to that first day. It wasn't until 2008 that another huge swell was predicted. But the buoys showed that it was so westerly that it wouldn't be good for Belharra. Morning high tides would flood the place, which is also not good, so we decided instead to head for Spain and some better-known big wave breaks. Two days before the big swell hit, our preparations for Spain were nearly complete. On the next-to-last day in France, I thought, *I'll just check out Belharra in the morning, on our way over to Spain.* Then the morning comes, and the swell is huge, and we call a friend who lives right there at St. Jean de Luz—it was winter, so dawn was around 8:00 a.m.—and he says, "Yeah, it's breaking. Every five minutes there is a wave. And it doesn't look small."

Normally before a Belharra session we would prepare for three or four days, getting pumped up and gathering all the gear and the various teams. But this time we hadn't done any of that. No preparation at all. When I woke up that morning I was still planning on going to Spain and never thought I'd be surfing Belharra. An hour later we launched at St. Jean de Luz—four surfers with two skis. Despite our lack of planning, we were very mellow, very calm. A photographer showed up at the last moment and asked if he could tag along. I said there was no room, but my friend on the other ski said, "I'll take you." And so he did.

We motored the 3 kilometers out to the break, took one look at the wave, and knew immediately that we should have been there right at dawn because it was so giant and the tide was so high. As it was, only the biggest sets would break, and they were very bumpy. We started cautiously, way out on the shoulder, slowly putting ourselves deeper and deeper as we got used to such wild seas; it was not a perfect day.

Then this big set starts rolling toward us, and I told my partner to tow me deeper than before, right into the pit. This clearly was one of the biggest sets of the day, and in such difficult conditions, I couldn't lose focus. I knew this was a once-in-a-lifetime situation, and I wanted to be completely present, in the moment. As I shot across the ocean I entered a kind of emptiness. And within this emptiness there were no thoughts and no feelings. I started surrendering, letting myself be guided by the wave itself. I let go mentally—and let go of the rope.

I don't remember much of the experience. The ride was very tight, and I came around the lip at the very bottom of the wave. But I had little idea or appreciation for the actual size of this wave, not until later, when I saw the photographs. But you can't measure such an experience in feet or in meters alone. The truth and the feeling come at the end of the day, and they can last for weeks sometimes. And on this day my body was vibrating at a higher level, and I had a strange time adjusting to the new vibration. Once there, it took a day or two to come all the way back down. During that time I could only talk to my friends, the few who might understand, who had joined me out at Belharra. We experienced a great adventure and forged a bond, a rapport— born of shared and sacred moments—otherwise impossible with my very brother.

It is very intense, riding big Belharra, miles offshore, the mountains of Spain towering in the background, the mountains of water rising before us. And the terrible power of the sea. There is also the aura of the Basque country and the Basque people, the fishing people. These are very strong folk, full of nerve and vigor. Over the centuries, many have perished in their boats, wrecked on the distant reef. And so all of these elements make the Basque Belharra an uncanny and powerful place, a mystical place. When we first went out there to challenge the great waves, the fishermen thought we were crazy. But in another sense they were happy because a tradition of fear surrounds Belharra, and like so many before us, we passed straight through that into something beyond. When we returned to shore after that great day we visited the bar where the fishermen go. It was just us and the Basque fishermen sharing a moment, sharing our experiences, the old culture of fishing mixed with the new culture of surfing, now drawn together by the timeless sea itself. That conversation, that place, that day, that wave—here were the gifts of the sea that make a life.

SOURCES

Barilotti, Steve. "What the Hell Was That?" *Surfer* 42, no. 2 (2001).

Cook, James. *The Three Voyages of Captain Cook Round the World.* Vol. 7. London: Longene, Hurtst, Rees, Orne and Brown, 1821.

Davis, Mike. "Pat Curren Coffee Break." *Surfer's Journal* 19, no. 2 (2010): 10-15.

Dixon, Chris. "Beneath the Waves." Men's Journal (March 2008). Also appears in *Ghost Wave. The Discovery of Cortes Bank and the Biggest Wave on Earth.* New York: Chronicle, 2011.

Dixon, Chris. "High Noon at Bishop Rock." *Surfer's Journal* 19, no. 3 (Summer 2010). Also appears in Ghost Wave. *The Discovery of Cortes Bank and the Biggest Wave on Earth.* New York: Chronicle, 2011.

Doyle, Leonard. "How the Perfect Surfer's Wave was Conquered." *Independent,* http://www.independent.co.uk/news/world/europe/how -the-perfect-surfers-wave-was-conquered-472924.html. April 8, 2006.

Duane, Daniel. "Aamion Goodwin's Circle Pacific." *Surfer's Journal* 16, no. 3 (2007): 92–101.

George, Sam. "Beal's Stash." *Surfer's Journal* 18, no. 2 (2009): 14–18.

George, Sam. "Harsh Realm: Fifty Years on the North Shore." *Surfer* 44, no. 3 (March 2003).

Gugelyk, Ted. "Surviving December 1st, 1969." *Surfer's Path* 79 (2010).

Harrington, Tony. "Fisherman's Hunch: First Tracks at the Bosenquet Bombora." *Surfer's Journal* 18, no. 3 (2009): 40–51.

Howard, Jake. "To Hell and Back." http://espn.go.com. Accessed October 1, 2009.

Jenkins, Bruce. *North Shore Chronicles: Big Wave Surfing in Hawaii.* Berkeley, CA: North Atlantic Books, 1999.

Little, Brock. "Reflections on Waimea." Surfline. http/www. surfline.com, accessed December 2009.

Long, Rusty. "Dungeons Time." *Surfer's Journal* 13, no. 1 (2004).

Marcus, Benjamin. "Surf Like Jay: The Life and Death of James Michael Moriarty (1978–2001)." *Surfing* 37, no. 11 (2001).

Masters, Ryan. "Heroes and Ghosts: Pebble Beach Danger Wave Comes Alive." *Surfer,* http://www.surfermag.com/features/ghst trees/. July 22, 2010.

Melekian, Brad. "Road Agent: Greg Long's Life in Pursuit." *Surfer's Journal* 18, no.1 (2009): 70–75.

O'Connor, Maura R. "Big Wave Surfing: Tales from the 'Unridden Realm.'" *EnlightenNext* 33 (June–August 2006).

Paul, Taylor. "Dislocated: Maverick's and Me." *Surfer's Path* 79 (2010).

Slater, Evan. "Hammer Down." *Surfer* 42, no. 6 (2001).

Slater, Evan. "The 100-Foot Wave." *Surfing* 38, no. 3 (1997).

Taylor, Kimball. "A Searching and Fearless Moral Inventory." *Surfer* 50, no. 4 (2010). http://www.surfermag.com/features/surfer-profile -flea-darryl-virostko/. July 22, 2010.

Taylor, Kimball. "The Rush: A Profile of Garret McNamara." *Surfer* 50, no.1 (2010).

Warshaw, Matt. *History of Surfing.* New York: Chronicle, 2010.

ACKNOWLEDGMENTS

We would also like to acknowledge the following writers and surfers for their contributions: Shane Dorian, Mark Healey, Dave Wassell, Greg Noll, Maya Gabeira, Mike Parsons, Greg Long, and Vincent Lartizen.

Also thanks to editor Gregory Hyman. *Big Juice* took about fifty different forms according to what we could and could not get cleared, and Greg rolled smoothly with all the changes. If he ever cussed—and we gave him good reason to—it was entirely under his breath. Lastly, special thanks to Jessica Haberman, who essentially produced *Big Juice* and wrangled, month after month, everything from photo editing to tracking down permissions from writers holed up in Haiti and the jungles of Thailand. We have a hell of a book to show for her efforts.

ABOUT THE EDITORS

John Long's award-winning short stories have been widely anthologized and translated into many languages. His books—ranging from literary fiction to instructional manuals—have sold more than two-million copies. He has written big budget feature films and Emmy and Monitor (international) award-winning TV shows, but his first interest has always been books. His large format book, *The Stonemasters,* won the Grand Prize at the Banff Film and Book Festival, widely considered the most prestigious outdoor-oriented literary award in the world. Several of Long's large format books are in the Museum of Modern Art. He lives in Venice Beach, California.

Sam George is one of the world's leading authorities on the sport of surfing. A former professional competitor, world traveler, editor of *Surfer* and *Surfing* magazines, and author (*Surfing: A Way of Life, The Perfect Day, SURFER at 50*), Sam has also written and/or directed a number of award-winning documentaries, including *Riding Giants, The Lost Wave: An African Surf Story,* and *Hollywood Don't Surf.* He lives in Malibu, California.